RODIGAN

Rodigan

My Life in Reggae

David Rodigan

With Ian Burrell

Constable • London

CONSTABLE

First published in Great Britain in 2017 by Constable

3 5 7 9 10 8 6 4 2

Copyright © David Rodigan, 2017

The moral right of the author has been asserted.

A CIP catalogue record for this book
is available from the British Library.

ISBN: 978-1-47212-557-6 (hardback)
ISBN: 978-1-47212-558-3 (trade paperback)

Typeset in Bembo by SX Composing DTP, Rayleigh, Essex
Printed and bound in Great Britain by Clays Ltd, St Ives plc

Papers used by Constable are from well-managed forests
and other responsible sources.

MIX
Paper from
responsible sources
FSC® C104740

Constable
An imprint of
Little, Brown Book Group
Carmelite House
50 Victoria Embankment
London EC4Y 0DZ

An Hachette UK Company
www.hachette.co.uk

www.littlebrown.co.uk

To my mother, Selina Rodigan.

D. R.

Contents

Contents

1

Bob Marley

The music Bob Marley created was so magnificent it has transcended all styles and now lives in its own space. It's multigenerational. Young people know the songs because their parents and grandparents played them in their front room or car. When you hear them you don't think of them as Reggae or Ska records but simply as songs that have stood the test of time.

In Bob's lyrics — whether they're about love, broken hearts or social injustice — he had something to say to everyone. When people discover his work they become fans for life.

People assimilate those songs almost without knowing it because they have been part of the world's musical heritage for so long. If I have an audience of students and teenagers, I know I can play 'Is This Love', which was released more than thirty-five years ago, and I will only occasionally need to bring the fader up because they will sing along to every word.

Great clouds of smoke wafted from the doorway as if the entire shop was on fire. It was a warm night in May, one of those days that seem to go on forever, and as I walked down Fulham Palace Road in London, my ears were still ringing from the sounds of the greatest concert I'd ever heard and my head was light with exhilaration from what I'd witnessed.

On a night like that night, anything could happen. Now a shop was in flames.

Except that, as I peered into the alcove from where the white plume of smoke emerged, the air began to clear. And there he was, standing in the doorway, leaning on his guitar and clutching a big spliff. He was like an apparition.

Robert Nesta Marley, the King of Reggae, was right before me. The star of the music I'd been obsessed with since I was a schoolboy.

'It's him! It's him! What am I going to do?' I asked my girl-friend Sue. I could hardly think.

'Go and say hello,' she said.

For nearly a decade my life had been headed towards this point. Since I first heard the infectious 'My Boy Lollipop' in 1964 – when I was thirteen and the song's Jamaican singer Millie Small was only a few years my senior – Reggae had been my thing. Here I was now, studying to be an actor at drama college but with a love for Reggae that was greater than ever.

I'd really thought the shop was on fire because such a great cloud of smoke was belching out – a spliff is not like a ciga-rette when you exhale. Bob was standing there next to Wire Lindo, the keyboard player from The Wailers.

After a moment of hesitation, I took Sue's advice and walked over. Marley was not as tall as I'd thought but he exuded radiance.

'Bob, I'm such a big fan. I bought "Soul Rebel" and "Put it On",' I gushed, mentioning the group's early hits to let him know how dedicated I was. '*Catch a Fire* is a great album . . .

and I've waited for this day for so long . . . it was such an amazing concert . . . thank you so much.'

He stood there and just smiled at me. 'Yeah, mon,' he said. 'Everyt'ing cool!'

Wire Lindo didn't say anything – he just stood and nodded. And, with that, this car screeched to the kerb and Bob said, 'Mi affe go, y'know.'

He walked from the doorway and climbed into the car, followed by Wire Lindo.

Then, as the car pulled off – in a moment I shall never forget – he turned in the back window and waved to me. Talk about a fan's joy at seeing and meeting his hero in person! I'm standing in the Fulham Palace Road and Bob Marley is waving to me from the back of a car window. I think he must have seen in me, from the way I spoke to him, that I really was a diehard fan and I think he was slightly surprised.

From the moment I'd heard The Wailers were to perform at The Greyhound pub in Fulham I'd worked myself into a state. Ahead of the show, an article appeared in one of the broadsheet papers previewing the gig and saying this band called The Wailers had a profound musical message. Seeing that in print gave me a feeling of triumph. This music – *my* music – was finally being given serious recognition. I cut out the article and stuck it on the canteen noticeboard at Rose Bruford Training College of Speech and Drama in Sidcup. Next to it I pinned the tour schedule. I had to share this.

Shortly before the concert, The Wailers were booked on *The Old Grey Whistle Test*, the hallowed BBC music programme. I was home from college, with a holiday job pulling pints in The Dog in Kidlington, my home village in sleepy Oxfordshire. I begged the landlord, John Jackman, 'Please, please, please can

I sneak off and watch them?' He said, 'OK, I know you love this music.' I went upstairs and I watched The Wailers on the BBC in his front room over the pub. I was awestruck. It felt like everyone was finally being let in on my world. This sound – that for years had been mocked and stigmatized as music for skinheads – was finally being approved. The programme's presenter, 'Whispering' Bob Harris, was widely revered. Reggae was being given a stamp of authority by the cognoscenti.

On the day of The Wailers' gig, 20 May 1973, I arrived at The Greyhound very early with my girlfriend, Sue Rogerson, another student from my year at drama college. There were no tickets and you just paid at the door. It was still light outside when we went in because I was determined to secure a good position. As we walked through the foyer there was a poster for the album which Bob and his fellow Wailers were there to promote: *Catch a Fire*. He would appear to do just that in the doorway at the end of the night.

It's strange to think of a group of that stature playing in a pub, but The Greyhound was massive, with a high dome-like ceiling. The crowd was predominantly from London's West Indian community and there was a terrific sense of anticipation. The place filled up until there were even a couple of people hanging on to the rafters in the roof. The lights went down and I was straining to see through the mass of heads in front of me. You couldn't make anything out – you just heard a drum beat. Boom-boom, boom-boom, boom-boom. And then, out of the darkness, came the sound of The Wailers: 'I hear the voice of the Rastaman sing, Ba-by-lon your throne gone down . . .' The place erupted!

I finally caught a glimpse of them. The three Wailers, Bob Marley, Bunny Wailer and Peter Tosh, all sitting on the floor atop a tiny rostrum, beating on their Nyabinghi drums, singing the 'Rasta Man Chant'. They finished the song and stood up. Bunny had this red Fez on and Peter was wearing a woollen tam hat and dark glasses. Bob had on a red and black lumber-jack jacket, which he never took off for the entire performance.

During the whole show they hardly said a thing. It was one song into the next and into the next. I was stood in the thick of the crowd, about halfway back and slightly to Bob's left. The thing that blew me away was that it was like listening to their records, only better. This was sublime; the real music that I loved so dearly. Not only was I seeing one of the greatest bands in the flesh but their live harmonies were faultless. There was none of this modern Auto-Tune nonsense – The Wailers had been hard grafting for years down in Jamaica, rehearsing relentlessly before they had success. By 1973 they had been singing for ten years, since their earliest days together in the poor Trench Town neighbourhood of downtown Kingston where the great singer Joe Higgs gave them tuition in har-mony work so they could pass their audition to perform at the studios of Jamaica's most famous producer, Coxsone Dodd, in 1964. That's a long time in the music game. That's why that show at The Greyhound was amazing.

For a while I waited outside the pub, wondering if there might be a chance of seeing the group backstage. There was a side door to the pub but there were hundreds of people out-side and it was just chaos. So I thought, 'I've seen the band, I'm going home.' And that's when I saw Bob.

Almost seven years later, a similar thing happened. This time I was in St Peter's Square, again in west London, making a routine Friday-afternoon visit to the headquarters of Island Records, the iconic Reggae label.

By then my love of Reggae had determined my way of life and I was working as a DJ on Capital Radio, the biggest commercial station in the country and host network of my weekly show, *Roots Rockers*.

I loved to go to Island Records. As you entered St Peter's Square it was full of beautiful double-fronted stately houses and Island was at the far right-hand corner – you'd never have known it was a business premises. There was a slope down the side of the building with a gate and at the back they'd built a recording studio and canteen. I would head to the offices and PR department, where I spent most of my time selecting new releases for radio play.

I went there frequently because Island was so important. Its founder, Chris Blackwell, a white Jamaican entrepreneur who was educated in Britain, played a pivotal role in the global development of Jamaican music by releasing Ska and Rock Steady records in the sixties. I was always welcomed there. If I was going to be playing something on the biggest Pop station in London then that was important for the record company.

The open-plan ground-floor area where I'd hang out was overlooked by a gallery, which had a special listening room where you could hear the label's latest recordings. As I climbed the staircase to the gallery that Friday, I looked up to see a familiar face coming down the stairs towards me. It was Bob again.

Few people even knew he was in London. It was April 1980 and he had been to Zimbabwe to perform at the country's independence celebrations at the personal invitation of the new president, Robert Mugabe. Bob financed the trip himself to a large extent because he was so determined to perform at a momentous occasion in African history.

He was only in England on a stopover, breaking his journey back to Jamaica. When I looked up and saw him coming down the stairs I froze.

But this time I didn't need anyone to push me forwards and I seized the moment. 'Bob, Bob, I'm David Rodigan. It's a real honour to meet you. I do a Reggae show on Capital Radio,' I said, not presuming that he would have remembered the gushing student he met in a shop doorway after The Greyhound gig in 1973. 'Would you please come on my Reggae show tomorrow night?'

I'd jumped the gate on protocol – that's not the way you are supposed to approach Bob Marley. There were two or three people with him. He slowly turned to someone who was with him, a Rastaman. And the Rastaman nodded. So Bob said, 'Yeah, mon, mi do that.'

Then – and as with that wave from the back window of the car, this is something I will always remember – he said, 'Would you like to hear a new song I have just recorded?'

Would I like to? Oh, yes, I would! Aston 'Family Man' Barrett, who was now the bass player with The Wailers, was with him and we all went back up the stairs to the gallery and into the Island Records listening room. I was sitting on the sofa, struggling to believe that I had Bob Marley to my left and Family Man to my right. Bob took a cassette out of his jean jacket pocket, pushed it into the cassette player and pressed play. We sat there as the song ran for the full duration. It came to an end and he turned to me and said, 'So, what do you think of the mix? Do you think that would sound good on American FM radio or American AM radio?'

I remember staring at the carpet and thinking that no one will believe this. I'm in a room with Bob Marley and he is asking me my opinion of the mix of his new record. I told him I thought it was a good FM stereo mix because FM radio was relatively new in 1980. He was well aware of the subtleties of US radio.

Then Bob said, 'All right, tomorrow night you are going to get a world exclusive – I will bring in the master tape.'

Sure enough, the next night Bob Marley walked into the foyer at Capital Radio, a tall building we used to call 'The Rocking Tower', in Euston Road, central London. I came down Capital's sweeping Hollywood-style spiral staircase and he was down in reception in his jean jacket and jeans. I said, 'Gosh, Bob, you look really thin.' He said, 'Well, I've been on the road and working hard.'

We went upstairs and before we went into the studio I took him to one side. I said, 'I just want to talk about your music and play your records, is that cool?' He smiled and said, 'That's very cool.' Many of his previous interviews had been with people asking him about his political views and Rastafarian faith.

I was so nervous that in the interview you can hear my voice is higher than it normally would be. My heart was beating so fast it was affecting my breathing. I was actually shaking because I was in the presence of Bob Marley and I was going to do a live interview with him.

It was a huge deal for me to get time with a man who was not just the greatest Reggae star in the world but arguably the greatest musical star of any genre. He was at the height of his international fame. I tried not to sound too hysterical in my introduction. 'We have a slight change of plan from the advertised programme because Bob Marley has just flown in on his way back from Zimbabwe and he's my special guest tonight on *Roots Rockers*,' I told the listeners. A slight change of plan!

I began by playing some early material from his days with Bunny and Peter. 'What The Beatles did for Pop music these guys did for Reggae,' I reminded the audience. 'Revival time with The Wailers!'

And then I turned to my dreadlocked guest. 'He's here with me live in the studio tonight with hair that is somewhat longer than it was in those early days. Bob Marley, welcome . . .'

During the interview I don't sound as relaxed as I could be and I think the structure was too rigidly chronological. I asked him about his early times with The Wailers at Coxsone Dodd's Studio One records. The group was worked hard by Coxsone for minimal reward but Bob answered with the utmost discretion. 'It was good y'know, because [it was] my first experience within music, working with some good experience and trying to get the harmonies and t'ing. It was great.'

He confirmed that during this Studio One period – when he was living apart from his mother, Cedella, who raised him alone and later emigrated to the United States – he had been sleeping inside the studio building.

'I heard you actually lived in the studio?' I said.

'Haha, sometimes!'

'Coxsone made you a room out the back . . .'

'Aha, yes.'

We discussed the group's Upsetter period, working with the eccentric producer Lee 'Scratch' Perry, and then the founding of the band's own pioneering independent record label, Tuff Gong.

But I was desperate to play Bob's records as he sat alongside me. I lined them up, one after another. 'Killers every one of them,' I told the listeners at the end of a sequence of hits. '"Love Light", "Nice Time", "Bus Dem Shut" and "Hypocrites" – from Bob Marley and The Wailers.'

It was 1980, the time of a Ska revival in Britain when the 2-Tone record label in Coventry and bands such as The Specials and London group Madness were having hits inspired by Jamaican sounds of the sixties. I asked Bob what he made of it. 'I was surprised a little, still,' he said. 'Knowing that Reggae music gone through so much development [and] these people have just reached the Ska!'

I had to ask him about Bunny and Peter, from whom he had separated after the success of *Catch a Fire* and its successor album *Burnin'*, the two records that propelled the group to international fame. Now it was Bob Marley and The Wailers (comprised of Family Man, his drumming brother Carlton and other musicians, along with the superb female vocal trio of Rita Marley, Marcia Griffiths and Judy Mowatt: the I-Threes). Bunny and Peter were pursuing solo careers. 'Why is it that you parted company with Peter and Bunny?' I asked.

'The understanding is that every one of us have our work to do and sometime during life you have to start do it,' he said. 'Everybody get big, having children and having responsibilities and you can't just walk up and down, like, y'know. Sometime people have certain things to do and we can't be together all the while.'

'Do you miss them not being in the band any more?'

'Yeah, of course. Mi bredren mi really love, y'know what I mean?'

'I know this is an obvious question but people do ask it. Is there any chance of the band reforming with the original members?'

'Well, as long as we are doing the same work there's a possibility all the while.'

'But not in the near future?'

'Could be!'

But at the back of my mind I knew the real highlight of the interview was to come at the end. It was already cued up on the reel-to-reel by the engineer in the master control room. Just as I had been trying to rein myself in at the top of the show – talking of the slight change of plan – I tried not to go overboard as I told my listeners they were to hear the upcoming release from Bob Marley before any other audience on earth.

'Well,' I said. 'You've got a new single coming out in a few weeks' time called "Could You Be Loved" and we've got it here on tape. Everything's ready, we'll hear a bit of a sneaky preview . . .'

Then the unmistakable twang of the bassline came in. And that was the first time it had been played on air, that Saturday night.

'A *Rockers* preview for you there,' I said nonchalantly after letting the tape play all the way through. 'Coming out in a few weeks' time, the new single from Bob Marley and The Wailers, "Could You Be Loved". Good luck with the single, good luck with the new album when it comes out and thanks very much for coming on the show.'

Bob used one word to respond. 'Nice!'

The following year he died. The worryingly thin physique that I'd noticed in the foyer at Capital was not just the result of a punishing work schedule. When rumours began to circulate that he was seriously ill they were denied but eventually it was apparent he had cancer.

It was a tragic loss for everyone. I remember getting the phone call when he passed. It was in the evening and I jumped into the car and raced into Capital and spent the whole night preparing the tribute, editing together bits of the interview I had done with him. I went in on the breakfast show, presented by Mike Smith, and announced that there would be a full tribute to Bob on the network. His loss was catastrophic. We all felt so close to him because we connected personally with his wonderful songs.

My first real awareness of The Wailers had been in the mid-sixties when Island released the *Put It On It's Rock Steady* album which featured their song 'Put It On' and had two cartoon characters on the sleeve with their arms aloft. I thought The Wailers was a great name but only because I imagined someone at sea in a boat – I thought it was The Whalers, as in fishermen. The music wasn't so much Reggae as Rock Steady, a music form that evolved from Ska with a much cooler, slower beat. I remember the thrill of hearing the words of the title song – 'I'm gonna put it on . . .' – in my local music shop, Russell Acott's in Oxford High Street.

Acott's was a large traditional shop with a downstairs department where they sold classical music, sheet music, pianos and other musical instruments. On the first floor there was the record department selling everything from The Bachelors to Jim Reeves. Luckily for me, the assistants behind the counter, Margaret and Janet, were passionate about Jamaican Ska and Rock Steady. Island Records and other labels were releasing seven-inch singles and the two women bought them from the travelling record salesmen who would bring them to Oxford because of its small West Indian community. You could choose the songs you wanted to hear, and they would pile up your chosen records and you would be told to go into your private listening booth and stand there while they would play your selections. You then decided whether you wanted to purchase or not.

My nirvana moment with The Wailers was the *Soul Rebels* album, released in 1970. There was a girl on the cover photographed in the jungle, wearing a camouflage outfit and holding a machine gun. The Wailers weren't on the front but there was a picture of them superimposed on the back. I remember like yesterday the moment I went into the listening booth at Acott's. I heard: 'I'm a re-bel, soul rebel, I'm a cap-turer, soul ad-venturer, see the morning sun' – and these harmonies came in – 'on the hill-side . . .'

I couldn't believe the beauty and power of the words; the cadence of the singing, this bassline and these drums. The language was so raw and lean but set to the music it became incredibly soulful. I bought the album that day and played it and played it and played it. It was produced by Lee Perry and I guess you would say it was the first album by The Wailers – although previous to that there was one album made at Coxsone Dodd's Studio One which was accredited to The Wailing Wailers and featured the group wearing Beatles-style suits.

Soul Rebels was the cornerstone album for me. There were the three of them: Bob, Peter and Bunny – the three that we internationally agree to know and love as The Wailers.

Catch a Fire, the album which was essentially being performed at The Greyhound the night I saw Bob in the doorway, took the group to another dimension. The album had this magnificent sleeve, which was a work of art in itself. It was an album in the style of a Zippo lighter that you could lift the lid off. There was a picture of them all together on the Thames embankment in London coming down some steps. Bob had a mackintosh on, with the beginnings of dreadlocks. I thought they looked like rock stars. I bought it immediately and took it home. *Catch a Fire* had everything you wanted in terms of Reggaetivity. It was electric and full of soul but there were musical layers on top that were fascinating, like this electric slide guitar. There were critics who said there were too many overdubs and it was too rock-orientated but it didn't repel me. At that time I was listening to many other forms of music on the radio – I wasn't living in a cocoon. This was the band I loved and I thought *Catch a Fire* enhanced their music even more.

You had tracks such as 'Concrete Jungle' and 'Slave Driver'. The lyrics!

> *Every time I hear the crack of a whip,*
> *My blood runs cold.*
> *I remember on the slave ship,*
> *How they brutalized our very souls.*

I remember when I first heard those lines, the power and immediacy of the lyrics sent shivers down my spine.

But I also liked 'Baby We've Got a Date (Rock It Baby)', which was a love song with sweetness and sentimentality: 'I'll meet you at your house at a quarter to eight.' It reminded me of that feeling when you're fourteen or fifteen and going on a first date, you have the absolute hots for someone and everything is new and fresh. My favourite Wailers' albums are *Soul Rebels*, *Catch a Fire*, *Burnin'* and *Exodus*.

When Bob Marley died I attended the state funeral on 21 May 1981. If you were involved with Reggae you wanted to be there to pay respects. I was invited because of my radio work and flew out with Trevor Wyatt, who worked in A&R at Island.

I felt so privileged to be present. The world's press and television cameras descended on Jamaica. We stayed at the Sheraton Hotel in Kingston and you couldn't move for journalists and film crews. I had never experienced anything like that and it really showed me how big Bob had become.

On the morning of the day before the funeral I went to visit Coxsone Dodd at Studio One, where the young Bob once lived in a back room. Now Bob's body was lying in state in Jamaica's National Arena. I went into the studios and Lone Ranger was on the microphone toasting 'Tribute to Marley' on a vintage Studio One rhythm. I was standing outside in the yard listening and Coxsone called me inside. He was bouncing tracks onto a multi-track recorder for a Best of The Wailers compilation. He told me he was going to the Arena to see Bob's body. I later joined the queue for the lying in state but it was the slowest-moving line I've ever known. They said that a hundred thousand turned up to file past the body. I realized it was going to be impossible to get inside, and since I was going to the funeral the next day I returned to Studio One.

The night before the funeral I spoke to Neville Garrick, who did Bob's album artwork and was responsible for the way everything was laid out at the funeral, where the coffin was to be rested on a trestle table decorated with the national colours of Jamaica and Ethiopia.

The ceremony took place in searing heat. The National Arena was covered and there were six thousand in the congregation with a lot of people dressed in white. The ceremony was conducted by His Eminence Abuna Yesehaq, the minister from the Ethiopian Orthodox Church of the Holy Trinity, and it was deeply moving, especially when Bob's sons, Ziggy and Stephen, came on and started dancing and singing. In Ziggy, who had a little suit on and performed to one of Bob's songs, you could see the father right there.

Then the casket – containing Bob's embalmed body, his red Gibson Les Paul guitar, a Bible opened at Psalm 23 and a stalk of marijuana – was taken out and the journey began all the way back to Nine Mile, the country village in St Ann parish where he had been born only thirty-six years before. Huge crowds followed the cortège in various forms of transport. I did too.

It was so chaotic outside the National Arena that I can't even remember who I travelled with in the car. There were people everywhere. It was the same when we reached the hills of St Ann and the driver stopped the car and said we couldn't go any further. We carried on through the country-side on foot.

As I was walking on that long trek I heard a man remonstrat-ing with somebody over a motorbike that had broken down. The voice sounded familiar and when I turned the bend, there on the other side of this hedge was the Reggae artist I-Roy. He recognized me too because I'd interviewed him on Radio London and Capital Radio and he was signed to the Virgin Frontline label in England. He began to laud and applaud me. 'Do you know who this man is?' he kept asking the mourners. Given the sombre nature of the occasion I was embarrassed to be singled out but I-Roy was a larger-than-life character.

Eventually we got to the valley where the burial would take place. There were crowds on hillsides in every direction and I thought that's how it must have looked when Jesus gave the Sermon on the Mount. The internment took place on the highest hill in the village in a mausoleum decorated with the Rastafarian colours of red, green and gold.

There was a sense of loss: that Bob had gone way before his time. Although we knew his work was rich, powerful and deeply significant, I don't think anyone quite understood at that stage the gap that was going to be left. Only with the passage of time were we able to realize just how important he was.

2

The Birth of Sound System

Around the time I was born, in the summer of 1951, the very first sound systems were being created in Jamaica, founding a music tradition which has shaped my life. Initially consisting of little more than a single deck, an amp and speaker, they quickly evolved into thunderous music machines.

With names such as King Edwards the Giant, Count Nick the Champ, Tom the Great Sebastian and Lloyd the Matador, the early sound systems would 'string up' their towers of speaker boxes to play the latest Jazz and R&B tunes from America. Crowds would flock to fenced outdoor 'lawns' – including the famous Chocomo Lawn in downtown Kingston – where they would buy drinks, eat goat curry and dance to the record selections.

The biggest sounds employed an MC to take the microphone and entertain dancers with a new rhyming jive talk that, decades later in New York, would evolve into rap. The most famous was Count Matchuki, the first to inject his catchphrases over records. Another founding MC was King Stitt, who made an asset of his facial deformity to become a sound system celebrity. Jamaicans newly arriving in the UK, including Duke Vin and Count Suckle, set up their own sound systems to play for the growing community of Caribbean immigrants.

*By the end of the fifties, the Jamaican live music scene was dom-
inated by four men with suitably aristocratic titles: Duke Reid the
Trojan, Sir Coxsone Downbeat, King Edwards the Giant and Prince
Buster Voice of The People. They would pioneer a way of playing and
listening to music that is still thriving in the next century, having now
spread across the world and swept me along on its magnificent journey.*

*But at that time, I was making my own first tentative baby steps,
more than five thousand miles away.*

Few people know of my formative years in Africa. But my most
powerful childhood memories are of fierce heat and deadly
insects, exotic marketplaces and the sweet smell of jasmine.

When I say Africa, I'm not talking about the lands below
the Sahara, from where Reggae music draws its roots, but the
Arab world of the north coast. I was three years old when
I arrived in Libya and for the next four years of my life this
was home.

My father, Andrew, was a mechanical engineer attached to
the Royal Green Jackets regiment in the British Army, which
had been stationed in Derna, a port city in eastern Libya, close
to the border with Egypt. Although I didn't appreciate it as a
small boy exploring my sandy surroundings, I was living in
a place of critical strategic importance. The Egyptian mon-
arch King Farouk had been overthrown in a coup a couple
of years earlier and the new President, Gamal Abdel Nasser,
was flexing his military muscles. When the Rodigan family
arrived in neighbouring Libya, Egypt's Suez Canal, the vital
waterway linking Europe to Asia, was in danger of being lost
to Western powers.

None of that mattered to me as I played with my favourite Dinky toy, an open-backed Morris truck, in the dusty

garden outside our bungalow. There were other things to worry about: deadly scorpions.

When I was five years old I turned over a stone in the garden one day. I'd been repeatedly warned by my parents that you should kick away stones and never pick them up. A scorpion stung me and the pain was excruciating. My father rushed onto the scene and immediately recognized the potential gravity of the situation. He knew scorpions are often lethal.

Dad was a battle-hardened soldier with intimate knowledge of North Africa, where he served during the Second World War under Montgomery of Alamein, the British general who led his famous Desert Rats against German Field Marshal Erwin Rommel and the Afrika Korps. He was one of the original members of the Special Air Service (the elite 'SAS' regiment), having volunteered for this when it was formed, but he didn't talk about the war very much. His skills as a mechanical engineer, however, were very useful to the SAS in going behind enemy lines to blow up airfields. In his final mission, members of the regiment were stranded for days hiding in a wadi, a dried-up riverbed. When they were finally rescued he had been very badly scorched by the sun and had almost run out of water. That was effectively the end of the war for him.

When he saw I'd been stung by a scorpion he put me straight onto his shoulders and ran and ran. It felt like he would never stop. Eventually he came to the house of the regimental priest, who had a car. I was chucked into the vehicle and they drove flat-out to the infirmary.

I had been stung by a Deathstalker, or *Leiurus quinquestriatus*, the yellow desert scorpion. The Deathstalker's venom packs enough neurotoxins to be a deadly risk to young children – so Dad was right to be worried. But, though painful, its sting is rarely fatal. He was just relieved I'd not been the victim of a fat-tailed black *Androctonus*, which also hides under rocks and carries venom that can kill an adult in minutes.

Many people today think of Libya as a dangerous land of civil war and the deposed tyrant Colonel Muammar Gaddafi, but for me it was a place of trips to seaweed-strewn Mediterranean beaches and family meals on Sundays after church. My favourite dish was spaghetti Bolognese at a restaurant owned by one of Derna's many Italian families. We'd sit out on a veranda overlooking the busy main street and there was always that smell of jasmine in the air.

When it was Ramadan I used to get scared because the older boys of Derna would walk around the streets with masks on. I was a very trusting child, until the day I lost that favourite model Dinky truck. I was playing with it outside the bungalow when an Arab boy appeared at the garden gate and began pleading with me to let him have a go. I gave him the toy and he smiled and then turned and ran. My little world fell apart – I couldn't believe anyone would do that. I chased him frantically, then ran back to the house and my dad helped me to look. I couldn't bear to give up the search but we never found the boy.

My father would take me to get my hair cut in Derna's Souq Edlam, the 'Darkness Market', with its bustle and noise and smells. At the end of the haircut, the barber always gave me a stick of bubble gum.

Dad was a soldier but he was also a character. I remember going to see him in the army panto in Derna and he was playing one of the ugly sisters in *Cinderella*. They used an army boot for the slipper scene. I was sitting at the back of the theatre laughing at his performance; although he had no idea at the time, and neither did I, he was giving me a taste for the actor's life.

I have one sibling, my younger sister Mary, and the Libyan women would always want to touch her because they were fascinated by her blonde hair. Our family life in North Africa didn't make for an easy existence for my mother Selina. She washed our clothes in the bath and had to load a wood-burning fire to heat the water. A frequent hazard was the Ghibli, a searing hot, dry sandstorm that would suddenly blow up. Even with the doors and windows closed it was hard to keep the dust out of the bungalow.

Suddenly we moved from Derna, as my father was posted to the Libyan capital of Tripoli. I remember the adults talking of the Suez Crisis, which had broken out in the summer of 1956 when the Egyptian leader Nasser nationalized the canal. Months later, Egypt, which had ties with the Soviet Union, was invaded by forces from Britain, France and Israel, prompting fears of a new global conflict. British troops in Libya were on high alert and for a young boy it was all very exciting.

But after moving to Tripoli I developed other problems, which might not have troubled the United Nations but were a big deal in the Rodigan household: I was forever running away from school.

Time and again I would escape. My routine began with telling the teachers that I didn't feel well and needed to go to the toilet. That was all I needed to get out. I would sneak around the school corridors and out into the square of the army barracks where there was a parade ground. My biggest obstacle was the guardhouse but I would wait until the soldiers weren't looking before slipping through the gates. And then I'd run to the family flat in Tripoli.

When I'd performed this trick several times it was starting to become an embarrassment to the entire garrison. How – with the barracks supposedly on high alert – was one little boy able to breach security and get past the guards at the front gate?

Finally, my father came home unexpectedly one early afternoon. He wasn't pleased to find me sitting there with my mother having lunch. 'You must never do this again – ever!' He said this in such a tone of voice, and with such a look in his eye, that I could never forget the warning.

I never ran away from school again but I understand why I did it. One of the problems about being an army brat was that you are continually changing schools, and that's a difficult process for a young child.

We had some great days out from Tripoli – but there was trauma there too. Along with other army families we would climb into a ten-ton truck and go down to the beach. On one frightening occasion when I was paddling around in the sea I strayed out too far in an effort to reach a boat. Suddenly I was in trouble and swallowing water, which went straight into my lungs. For a moment, before I was helped to safety by my father, I was sure I was drowning and the shock left me with a lasting fear of open water.

The time came to leave North Africa and move to an entirely different part of the world. I flew over the patchwork of countryside on my first journey to England and asked the man next to me on the plane, 'What are those green squares?'

'Fields,' he replied.

I was seven years old and this was my first sight of Britain. I'd spent the previous four years in Libya, but had been born in Germany on 24 June 1951 at the British Military Hospital in Hanover, where my father had previously been stationed.

After my dad was rescued from the scorching heat of the wadi while serving with the SAS he was flown to Cape Town to recuperate before being brought back to Scotland and the Maryhill barracks in Glasgow. Maryhill is famous as the site where Adolf Hitler's deputy-Führer Rudolf Hess was held after being arrested following his solo 'peace flight' to Britain in 1941. But, more importantly for my father, it was where my mother lived and this was where they met. Soon after the war ended they moved with his regiment to Germany.

My earliest memory is of being in the sergeants' mess back in Hanover when I was three years old and my father got a call from the hospital where my mother was due to give birth to my sister. Pandemonium broke out in the mess room. My father had this look of absolute joy on his face as he grabbed me in his arms before running down the stairs and jumping into the car. He drove like the wind to the British Military Hospital. Because I was a child of three I wasn't allowed to go inside with him. I was locked in the car, crying and so upset that I wet myself because I couldn't see anything or get out to use the toilet. Then I remember that a window suddenly flew open, in an upper storey of the hospital, and there was my mother waving to me.

My mother was such a powerful force in my life. She was very loving but she didn't smother me. Most of all, she never doubted me. She was a devout Catholic and on Sunday mornings, whether in Libya or in England, she never missed Mass. Regardless of whether my father was away on exercise, we went to Sunday worship. I sometimes tried to wiggle away from her as she walked to church but she squeezed my hand and I couldn't get free. Her faith was like a rock and her patron saint was St Teresa. My sister and I had to say prayers every night before we went to bed.

Mum got up first every morning, and in the freezing cold of English winter, with no central heating, she would stand over a little electric fire and warm our clothes. As well as being the first to wake, she went to bed very late. She was always doing stuff: washing, ironing, cleaning, or making breakfast for the whole family. Breakfast was porridge with salt. I'd watch my father make the porridge spin with a spoon and then flick the salt on it and wink at me.

My mother, who was christened Selina but known to everyone as Teenie, was born in Ireland but grew up in Maryhill, where her father, Michael Roache, was posted as a soldier. We knew him by the nickname Gaga and he spoke with an Irish brogue even though he had fought in the Boer War for the British Army.

My father's family are from the town of Kirkcaldy on the east coast of Scotland, famous as the birthplace of the economist Adam Smith and the constituency of the former British Prime Minister Gordon Brown. It is part of what the locals call the 'Kingdom of Fife'.

After I moved to England, settling in Oxfordshire, I got to know Kirkcaldy well because my sister and I spent many summers there. My dad would drive us up in a Ford Anglia with plastic seats, leaving home early in the morning and arriving in Kirkcaldy late at night. That journey seemed to go on forever and my sister and I would wait to hear the words 'Scotch Corner', which meant we were close to the Scottish border.

The Scottish Rodigans lived in a tenement block on Overton Road, which was referred to as 'The Close' and was on a hill. You entered the tenement yard by walking through a dark narrow passageway that went into a back garden where the women did the washing in a laundry area. The block was around five storeys high and behind it was a big linoleum factory.

You could smell Kirkcaldy before you saw it because of the coal mining and the linoleum. The Rodigan family of six children – my father, sister Bunty, and brothers Mick, Willy, James and John – lived in three rooms. You climbed a circular staircase to gain access to the flat. There was a stove in the room as you came through the front door, to the left was the living room with a sink and fireplace and, finally, an all-purpose room known to everyone as 'Ben the Hoose'.

Kirkcaldy was a sing-along community where music was never far away. My father's father – Michael Rodigan – played a piano accordion in a band and taught my dad the instrument. I remember him putting me on his knee and playing it with great fervour. Dad had an audition for the army entertainment section, ENSA, while he was in Africa. But when he went to fetch his piano accordion from the tent it had melted in the sun. He used to say that was the closest he ever got to professional show business.

All the other Rodigan brothers worked at the coal pit. Dad was much younger – he said he was an afterthought – and his father would not allow him to become a miner. He was told to get an apprenticeship as a car mechanic, which he did. When war broke out he signed up. He never left the army but saw it through for the full twenty-two years' maximum service, which is why we ended up living in Libya and then in barracks accommodation in Headington, Oxford.

In those early years in England I also visited my mother's relatives in Ireland. The Roache family were from Cork and we would stay out in Cork Bay where they had a little summerhouse. You could stand on the cliff and if you shouted you could hear the echo across the bay. I had the chance to savour there the delicious taste of fresh milk drunk directly from a churn on the back of a cart.

Some Irish memories are not so fond. At around the age of eight I was taken on that famous rite of passage to kiss the Blarney Stone, which was a frightening experience. According to tradition, kissing the stone – high up in the medieval Blarney Castle just outside Cork – is supposed to guarantee you the 'gift of the gab' (always helpful to a future radio DJ). The trouble is that the stone is on the outside of a parapet and about ninety feet up.

With a sense of foreboding I climbed the castle steps and at the top was a man in a sailor-style striped shirt standing on a metal grill. The Blarney Stone was on the other side of a gaping hole above a massive drop and the man held on to your body as you bent over backwards in order to plant your kiss on the stone. As you throw your head back you are looking downwards and all I remember is seeing my mother way below, like a little dot. After I'd kissed the stone I went back down the steps with my head spinning, feeling sick with fear. I think that caused me to be afraid of heights and I suffer from vertigo to this day.

Both my parents were Catholics and when I arrived in Oxford I was sent to Our Lady's Convent School in Cowley. Coincidentally, it was the Oxford neighbourhood famous for the Morris motor company, makers of the lorry that inspired my favourite and much-missed Dinky toy. At Our Lady's Convent I had my first Holy Communion in 1960. The school's nuns were very strict and there was a Maths teacher who I lived in fear of. We studied by rote and it was all a bit Dickensian. I was taken for school swimming lessons, which terrified me as I hadn't lost my fear of drowning after getting out of my depth in Libya.

We moved yet again when my father left the army to take a job with the car manufacturer British Leyland. It was a big thing when he left the house for his interview wearing a suit instead of his military uniform. He was given a position as a lecturer in engineering and there was great joy in the Rodigan household that night.

My sister and I often imagined this mythical place called 'Civvy Street' that my father and mother used to talk of and where we believed we were going one day. I thought of Civvy Street as one long avenue where the rest of the world lived. The army families used to laugh and joke about these 'Civvy' people who, they said, would beat a path from their front doors to the office and back but would never see the world and never know the army life with its camaraderie, army dinners, army wives' club, tombola sessions and sports days.

When Dad got his new position at British Leyland my sister ran to Mum and said, 'Guess what, Dad's got a new job and it's called "work"!' It was no longer duty, it was work. What he actually had to do was travel around the country in a big touring bus, visiting garages and giving lectures to engineers and mechanics on the latest developments in motor engines. He had been an engineer from his earliest days as an apprentice in Scotland, and British Leyland later made him a head-hunter for graduate recruits.

I inherited my work ethic from my parents. My mother had been manageress of a shoe shop in Glasgow. My father had that army discipline and sense of timekeeping that came from being on duty. You couldn't lie in bed in my house – my father would just hammer on the door. To get a day off school I had to be very ill – and get clearance from my mother. Laziness and an untidy bedroom didn't exist in my childhood.

My father was quite a flamboyant man with a tremendous outgoing personality, and a lot of people loved him. 'Oh, Andy, he's such a character,' they'd say. He'd come home to our house in the barracks, throw open the door, take off his beret and fling it down the hallway. The beret would spin, spin, spin, and nine times out of ten it would land on the hook and he'd give a little twist of the head in delight.

The day we finally saw Civvy Street arrived as my parents went to buy their first house. The place they chose was Kidlington, just outside Oxford and known for being the largest village in England. We watched the house being built from scratch on a new estate called Gosford Hill. Our house was 51 Cromwell Way. The road backed on to a copse and beyond that was a meadow and a school playing field. It was all very green and a long way from the desert of Libya.

I moved to Kidlington Junior School and was immediately targeted by bullies. That's a danger when you're always going to new schools.

My dad, a warrant officer, had taught me about standing up for myself and not being intimidated. When I was still small he made me go up a couple of steps on the stairs at Cromwell Way and then jump. He caught me and told me to climb a couple more stairs and jump again. Once more he caught me. He ordered me up to the eighth step and this time when I jumped he stepped back and watched me fall on the floor. I was stunned and hurt and asked him why he would do that.

'Remember, son, never trust anyone.'

So, on my third day, I turned and gave it to the bully who was giving it to me in the lunch queue and really laid into him. There were shouts of 'Scrap! Scrap!' from the other boys and the teachers came and broke it up. Once I'd done that, the intimidation was over.

I understood why there was resentment towards me – I'd been put straight into the school football team after a trial and one of these guys lost his place. Football was very important to me as a boy. I really loved it and represented Kidlington on Saturday mornings, playing at right wing or inside right.

Football gave me my first experience of live music, at the age of eleven. It was the Kidlington Boys annual prize-giving at the village hall and because we'd won the cup, there was a presentation ceremony. I walked into the hall and a Skiffle group was playing. I was blown away by the sheer volume of sound. And there were girls there! I went home with a small trophy of a figure of a footballer kicking a ball but – more significantly – it was my first musical night out.

I was starting to become aware of the extraordinary Pop music taking hold in Britain in the early sixties. When I was twelve I went on a school Outward Bound trip to Holnicote House, a big estate in the Somerset countryside now owned by the National Trust. One of the teachers bought some music at a shop in the nearby town and to entertain us he would put on his two new records – 'Little Red Rooster' by the Rolling Stones and 'All Day and All of the Night' by The Kinks. During the evenings the teachers would read us passages from the West Country novel *Lorna Doone* as we drank cocoa and ate biscuits.

On the Saturday night there was a dance and I paired off with a girl called Lyn Vine. To my great embarrassment, one of the meddling teachers came up to me and lifted up my trousers because he thought I didn't have any socks on.

It was Lyn who gave me my first kiss when we went down into Minehead one afternoon and were allowed with the other kids onto the beach. The two of us slipped away and kissed each other by the seashore. We were only twelve years old and it was a sensational moment. It was extra special because Lyn's father was the local butcher in Kidlington and I was his butcher's boy. For that job I had to get up very early and go to the shop to collect my bicycle. The meat was cut and wrapped and put in my bicycle basket, and I was given a list of names and addresses for the deliveries. In the evenings I'd deliver the *Oxford Mail* for the newsagent and I had a Sunday paper round too. That was the work ethic I inherited from my parents.

3

Ska

The jerky rhythms of Ska were new and distinctly Jamaican, layering Caribbean music styles onto beat patterns inspired by the Jazz and R&B that Jamaicans picked up long distance from radio stations broadcasting from the southern United States. Its name is supposed to come from the ratchet-like sound of Jamaican guitarists, such as Ernest Ranglin and Jerome 'Jah Jerry' Hines.

Ska was different from the American music that the sound systems started off playing, and it was the competition between the great sound men that led to Jamaica developing a genre all of its own.

Ken Khouri was a pioneer and set up Federal Studios, where Prince Buster and his sound system rivals Coxsone Dodd, King Edwards and Duke Reid recorded some of their earliest songs. Coxsone, who built a childhood star in the shape of singer Delroy Wilson, founded what was to become a legendary recording operation, Studio One, at 13 Brentford Road, Kingston. Duke Reid set up his own studio, Treasure Isle.

Ska took the UK by storm and the Blue Beat label, on which Buster's recordings were released, soon became for me a source of obsession.

I was thirteen years old and sitting in front of our black and white television at home in Oxfordshire when I was first smitten. A young

Jamaican singer called Millie Small stood before me on the ITV music show Ready Steady Go! *and sang 'My Boy Lollipop', about a lad who made her 'heart go giddyup'.*

The rhythm was infectious and Millie's vocal was so bright and uplifting, effortless and pure. I was hooked. The song was an international hit, reaching number two in the UK charts in 1964. That was my introduction to Ska, the emerging new sound of young Jamaica.

My senior school in Kidlington – Gosford Hill – was one of the first comprehensives in Britain and I was in the first intake. Away from school, the highlight of the week was going to the village cinema every Friday night. You'd sit in the back row and smoke Capstan Full Strength cigarettes – or Player's Untipped (without a filter). I remember coming home and feeling a sickening nausea from the nicotine, with the whole room spinning around me. But in the cinema you tried to tough it out to show how big you were. It was the same on school trips, sitting at the back of the bus: 'I've got Capstan Full Strength.' That was supposed to translate as: 'I'm tougher than you.'

I still have the first record I ever bought: 'Telstar' by The Tornados. I climbed onto my bicycle and rode to Kidlington High Street where there was a shop that sold seven-inch vinyl records. I played it to death. One Saturday, my father purchased a radiogram from a music shop in Oxford. The gramophone allowed you to stack up records, which dropped down in turn, like a jukebox. My dad bought himself a Glenn Miller album and Mum had something from Vera Lynn. I was allowed to buy one record myself and I chose 'Dance On' by The Shadows. The radio part of the radiogram really fascinated me because there was short wave, medium wave and long wave, and I would endlessly twiddle the dial to hear voices from all over the world.

Television was my other introduction to music. You just didn't miss ITV's *Ready Steady Go!*, on which you would regularly see The Beatles and the Rolling Stones. It was introduced by Cathy McGowan and Keith Fordyce, with young people dancing in the audience and a spiral staircase in the studio. It was on that show that I first heard The Ronettes. That was where I first saw Millie. Suddenly there was Diana Ross and the Supremes from the United States and Little Millie from Jamaica.

I didn't know at that point that I would have this deep love affair with the music of Jamaica, because 'My Boy Lollipop' was just another Pop record of the time, sitting alongside the rest of my collection with songs from The Beatles and The Kinks.

But I was becoming more conscious of Jamaica, which was only two years into its independence from the UK. In the music shop where we bought the radiogram there was a poster of the singer Laurel Aitken, who was a figurehead for the Blue Beat sound that was taking hold in England and that would become a musical identity for me and many friends.

My teenage years were defined by the long summer school holidays. In 1966, as I turned fifteen, I was allowed to go away camping on the South Coast at Bournemouth. I went with my mates Pete Cripps, Bob Baldwin and Steve Hewett. Pete was a bit older and had a car which we used to get around. The highlight of that holiday, and the whole year, was the football World Cup final. England was hosting the tournament and reached the final against West Germany. We found ourselves on a campsite miles from home as England's most important match ever was about to take place. A girl called Angela Cubbidge came to our rescue. She was a Bournemouth girl who I'd met on the trip – and she said we could watch the match on her family's television set. There we were, in Angela Cubbidge's front room, witnessing football history as England won the World Cup for the only time, beating the Germans 4–2.

There were two worlds in Oxford, there always have been. There was the ancient university and all that came with it and there were the people who lived in Oxford. It's known as 'town and gown' and I was definitely town. I knew another world existed within the cloisters but I was never resentful of it.

The beautiful thing about the city was the architecture and the ambience. There were the college buildings, the punting on the River Cherwell, and the Hinksey open-air lido. We used to go swimming there in the summer when we were teenagers after cycling from Kidlington. That was a long, long ride and we would take peanut butter sandwiches and money from Mum to buy a shandy. There were several pools at Hinksey and when I think of the place, I hear the sound of the hits of 1965, 'Mr. Tambourine Man' by The Byrds and 'I Got You Babe' by Sonny & Cher, which would be blasting out of transistor radios.

As a family we used to love to go down to the Mayday morning celebrations at the Cherwell alongside Magdalen Bridge. We did that most years and would get up in the dark to drive down there and wait for the dawn to come up. Then it would be choristers singing and students jumping into the river. We were part of the city and felt we had every right to be there.

Although I was living in rural Oxfordshire I never felt out of touch with music, thanks to the growth of pirate radio. I had a twenty-four-hour wall of modern sound on medium wave coming in from floating broadcast ships in the North Sea, off the east coast of Britain. Pirate radio was everything. It fascinated me because it was dangerous and they were breaking the broadcasting laws. You would see the DJs sometimes on the television news, bouncing up and down in the ocean in these small boats as they tried to get out to the ship to do their shows.

Radio Caroline and Radio London were the two big pirate ships. Until then we had listened in our bedrooms to Radio Luxembourg, a commercial English-language station based in central Europe and with intermittent reception. Every night on Radio Caroline I listened to an amazing voice that just captured me – the sound of Johnnie Walker. His sign-on tune was 'Because They're Young' by Duane Eddy.

I was building up my own record collection and, in order to stop me continually playing the family gramophone, Dad bought me a little two-tone grey Dansette Viva open-box record player for my bedroom.

I worked hard in my holidays. On Saturdays and all through the summer I was employed in the despatch department at Webber's department store doing odd jobs, including crushing cardboard boxes. Another part-time job was at Milward's shoe shop. But all I lived for were morning coffee break, lunch break and afternoon tea break when I could head down the road to Acott's and see Janet and Margaret, the two girls who worked behind the record counter on the first floor. They became specialists in West Indian music and you'd go there hoping to hear a hot tune on labels such as Pyramid, Duke, Trojan and Island.

Acott's was where I first heard 'Monkey Man' by Toots and the Maytals and 'Red Red Wine' by Tony Tribe.

West Indians used to come there on Saturdays to buy records and I would look to see what they were buying. One day, I was sharing a record-listening booth with a much older Jamaican guy who'd had a couple of drinks. He was speaking in strong Jamaican patois and I was trying to pick up some of the language but found it very difficult to understand what he was saying. It was the same with the song lyrics – you listened hard but you didn't get all of it.

There were a gang of us in Kidlington who used to hang out: Stephen Peat, Bob Baldwin, Steve Hewett, Alan Raymer, Mike Slay, Pete Cripps and Keith 'Governor' Groves. Our spot was often the Brett's School of Dancing in George Street. Up on the top storey was a wooden dancefloor with four pillars holding up the ceiling. On Thursday nights they had a disco with a DJ who looked like Elvis and played with his back to the audience. He played records such as 'You Don't Have to Say You Love Me' by Dusty Springfield and 'The Sound of Silence' by Simon & Garfunkel. It was an early disco and it felt almost like sneaking out from school.

Brett's was where I went to see some of my first live music shows. Jimmy Cliff and his band played there in concert and he mashed it up. I shook his hand afterwards and said, 'Brilliant set!'

But the most memorable show for me was when the Joyce Bond Revue pitched up at Oxford Town Hall. Joyce Bond was a Jamaican singer who dressed as a cowgirl, complete with pistols and holsters. I had a ticket in the front row. Joyce's version of 'Ob-La-Di, Ob-La-Da' by The Beatles was on the first volume of the *Tighten Up* Reggae compilation series, which

was a must-have record for any British teenager with an obsession for the new sounds of Jamaica. Another of her songs was
called 'Do the Teasy', named after a new dance step.

There I was in the front row when suddenly Joyce was
about to do this tune, 'Do the Teasy', and beckoning me to
come up on the stage. She gave me a kiss – I don't think
I washed afterwards for a week – and held my hand to do
the Teasy.

Dancing was very important to us. Somebody would start
dancing in a circle and others would watch and some would
jump in. At Oxford Town Hall there was a guy called Colin
'Beastly' Looker and his mate Tim Inkpen. They came from
Witney, a small town outside Oxford, subsequently best known
for being the constituency of David Cameron, the British
Prime Minister from 2010 to 2016. Looker was the snazziest
dresser on the Oxford scene. His father owned a glove factory
in Witney High Street and he always had the best suits. He
was also ahead of the game in terms of the music he bought.
I went to his house and he had records by Curtis Mayfield
and the Impressions and James Brown before any of the rest
of us. I would be asking myself, 'How did he get this stuff?'
Not only did he have the best suits and the rarest records, but
Beastly was king of the dancefloor. No one could beat him.
If he started to do a turn in Oxford Town Hall people had to
step back and give him room.

In the mid-sixties we all wanted to look like Steve Marriott.
He was the singer from the Small Faces, the band with the
best suits and the best Mod haircuts. If you weren't suited
you just looked like trash. You would get your three-piece
suit handmade and customized at Burton's tailors. I remember getting my first bespoke suit in brown herringbone and

I wore a pair of brown Oxford brogues to go with it. Early on Saturday evenings, there would be a gathering of scooters in the centre of Oxford and there was also this Mod way of walking – a shake that we all used to do.

With my gang of mates I would venture out to see live R&B bands like Geno Washington and the Ram Jam Band or Jimmy James and the Vagabonds. The problem was you could never be certain who would come out on stage. On one occasion I thought I was going to witness The Skatalites, the most famous Ska band of them all, formed in the summer of 1964, around the time I first heard Millie. Many of the band's brilliant musicians were alumni of the Alpha school 'for wayward boys' in Kingston. But I was to be very disappointed.

The show had been advertised as taking place at a rural outpost called The Bridge Club – an unlikely venue. Instead of the cream of Jamaican musicianship that we had paid to see, we found ourselves 'entertained' by three imposters. One of them was white (so I knew he wasn't a Skatalite) and of the two black guys in the 'group', one was clearly wearing a wig. It was a complete rip-off.

4

Rock Steady

Quite suddenly, Jamaican music changed up again. Out went the jerky, up-tempo sound of Ska to be replaced by an easy-paced and laid-back cousin that went by the name of Rock Steady.

Wonderful singers came to the fore – Alton Ellis, Hopeton Lewis, Desmond Dekker, Ken Boothe – and basslines began to take precedence over the horn sections that had characterized Ska. Duke Reid's Treasure Isle was again in the vanguard, with Coxsone Dodd's Studio One, along with Derrick Harriott, Bunny Lee, Sonia Pottinger and Prince Buster also moving quickly to champion the new style.

But despite Rock Steady's smooth and elegant rhythms and the serenity of its vocals, its lyrics were often darker than the typically optimistic messages associated with Ska, which emerged in the wake of the proud moment of Jamaica's independence from Britain in 1962.

Reflecting harsh economic times, the new Rock Steady reached out to the Rude Boys, the ghetto youth who were taking control – by violent means if necessary – of the increasingly lawless streets in downtown Kingston.

Rock Steady reached its high point in 1967, just at the moment when my own teenage life was undergoing dramatic change.

The summer of 1967 is known as the Summer of Love and I spent mine with Annette Longshaw, my first serious girlfriend. Annette moved with an older set in Oxford and was a gorgeous Mod girl with real style.

Teenagers would assemble on Friday and Saturday nights in the garden under the Carfax – a twelfth-century stone clock tower at the crossroads in the centre of Oxford. I was sixteen. I'd often seen Annette at a distance and thought she was much older than me.

Then one Saturday night I was at a local house party opposite the village cinema in Kidlington with my mate Steve Hewett and the rest of our little crew when – my God! – in she walks. This was the girl I'd admired from a distance but never spoken to. Why would she be here in sleepy Kidlington?

I thought to myself, 'Do you know what, I'm going to try and get off with this girl', and to my surprise I did. I then needed to telephone my parents and tell them that I wanted to stay at the party all night. My father reacted like a typical parent.

'You're not staying all night at someone's house, I know what happens.'

'I'm not coming home. I'm staying here.'

It was the first time I'd really defied him.

'Son, I'm going to give you half an hour and then you'll see the Morris Oxford at the end of the driveway and I will flash the lights. You need to walk down and if you don't, I will come up to the front door of the house and ask you to come out. You've got a choice.'

I knew my dad and there was no room for argument. He was just trying to protect me from what he considered unacceptable behaviour for someone of sixteen in those days.

The boy who lived in the house had thrown the party because his parents had gone away. Inside, it was like the scene from the Mod film *Quadrophenia* where teenagers take over a house and are all snogging and grabbing hold of each other – that's what 16-year-olds are like.

After putting down the phone to Dad I knew my time was limited. I was able to kiss Annette in a slightly darkened room, and Steve got off with her friend Sharon. Too soon I had to tell Annette that my dad was outside. That was embarrassing. She'd done a deal with Sharon whereby each of them told their parents they were staying at a friend's house – they could go home when they wanted. But I had to go home.

Annette came outside with me and I kissed her good night. I asked her if I could meet her again – in those days, that's how it was – and she said yes. She didn't have a telephone in her house so we arranged to meet the next afternoon at Carfax. I'd seen my dad flash the car lights once and I knew I had to go. But going down the driveway to the car I was walking on air.

It turned out that Annette was not older but the same age as me. She was gorgeous. She had a Continental look with dark curly hair and olive skin. I went to Carfax and waited, thinking she would never turn up, but, lo and behold, I saw her walking up from the bus stop. I couldn't believe it.

I used to go to her house and she used to come to mine. I met her mum and dad, a big tall fireman. Because Annette didn't have a phone she had to go to a phone box to call my house. We went punting on the River Cherwell in Oxford, which was a lovely pastime.

By the summer of 1967, our gang was ready to go camping again. This time our destination moved eastwards from Bournemouth along the coast to Margate in Kent. It was just the boys – Annette and I were too young to go on holiday together. This was an altogether different adventure, and in Margate I had my introduction to Jamaicans and their culture. We travelled with nowhere to stay. The idea was that you took sleeping bags and spent the holiday 'crashing' on the beach. And that's exactly what we did.

As soon as we reached Margate I went straight down to the seafront and just stood there with the sun on my face. In California at that time it was the start of the hippie revolution and its message of peace and love had crossed the Atlantic. 'San Francisco (Be Sure to Wear Flowers in Your Hair)' by Scott McKenzie was a massive record that summer and 'All You Need is Love' by The Beatles was at number one. I looked out on this typically English seaside scene and some of the people on Margate Sands really did have flowers in their hair.

One moment on that trip really changed my world. There was a seafront coffee bar called The Grapes, which we used as our meeting spot. And beneath the coffee bar was another place, a little more mysterious, called Sloopy's. I dropped in there one afternoon to buy a cold drink. To my amazement, I was introduced to Jamaican music as Jamaicans themselves liked to hear it. I walked in and was spellbound.

It was the middle of the afternoon but inside Sloopy's it was dark. The place was owned and run by Jamaicans and you could buy beers and soft drinks from a small bar. Most importantly, there was a jukebox and it wasn't like any I'd seen before. I looked at it and recognized hardly any of the record titles. There was 'Guns of Navarone' by The Skatalites, 'Phoenix City' by Roland Alphonso and 'Sloop John B' by Al & The Vibrators, which was a Jamaican version of the Beach

Boys' hit and, presumably, the song that had given its name to the bar. There was '007' by Desmond Dekker, which was a Pop hit, so at least I knew that one.

I'd only gone in to buy a fizzy drink but I couldn't tear myself away. The beat was infectious. I went back with my friends and we realized that the place was open all day and into the night, so we went in the evening too, experiencing that vibe of dancing and hanging out late.

At weekends large numbers of Jamaicans would come to Margate from London and party. I noticed that one group had come on a traditional red London double-decker bus, which they'd hired for a trip to the seaside. These groups of Jamaican trippers would go to the beach but would also come in and out of Sloopy's throughout the day and into the night. That was my first encounter with Jamaican culture and I was absolutely smitten.

Our gang of mates were into American Soul music: Otis Redding, the Bar-Kays, Arthur Conley, Sam and Dave, Stax, Atlantic Records, and Motown. But this was something else. The Jamaicans didn't mind us being there – they just kept telling us to 'Feed the jukebox!' That was one way they earned the money to keep Sloopy's open.

After the holiday, one of my main missions on getting back to Kidlington was to identify the song which I most associated with Sloopy's. I'd heard the words as 'I'm Going to the Moon' and I was asking for it in all the record shops in Oxford without success. Finally, at a party, I heard the song again. Stephen Peat, one of the mates I moved with, was playing my tune. It was a track on an album called *Club Ska 67 Volume One*. I picked it up, with its bright pink sleeve and the names of the different songs emblazoned on it, turned it over, and there it was: 'Dancing Mood' by the great Delroy Wilson. I bought that album and lived with it for the rest of that year.

It was Tommy Vance, another of my early broadcasting heroes, who that summer gave me a nickname by which I'm still known. Vance had that combination of a great voice and a real love of music, and he played all the Soul and Ska records you could imagine. During that summer one of his favourite tunes was 'Ram Jam' by Jackie Mittoo. I loved it and played it so much that, henceforth, I was known to my friends as 'Ram Jam'.

In the September, the BBC launched Radio 1, a momentous occasion for young people in Britain. One of my favourite presenters was Austin Churton Fairman, or Mike Raven as he was known to listeners. He presented an R&B show and had a wonderful style: 'Now here's a rather interesting song on a West Indian label called Gas Records and the track is called "The Horse" by Eric Barnett.' I've never heard of Eric Barnett since but that record, with its wonderful organ instrumental and a label in green, purple and white, remains one of the most treasured singles in my collection.

For much of that long hot summer of 1967, Annette and I would go to dances at the Stage Club or Oxford Town Hall. As autumn arrived I finished with her. Why? I never really understood myself. I guess Annette must have wondered why as well. Maybe it was because she was my first girlfriend and I thought I was too young to get serious; the sort of thing Nat King Cole sung about in 'Too Young to Go Steady'. That was the end of the Summer of Love.

Annette soon started going out with somebody else. Of course I then started thinking, 'Maybe I could get back together with her?' But she was with a guy from the older set, so I was blown out of the water.

By 1967, the Mod look of sharp suits and loafers was competing with a new hippie influence of kaftans and beads. Bright colours were coming in.

Saturday was the big day of the week. White's Bar was the super-cool pub that everyone wanted to be in on Saturday lunchtimes – but you had to be old enough. Our gang finally managed to get in there for the first time in 1967 and the thing I noticed was the Soul and Reggae album covers mounted on the wall. The one that transfixed me was the cover of *Alton Ellis Sings Rock and Soul*, with the Jamaican singer's face in profile.

The place to go on a Saturday night was the members-only Stage Club next to the New Theatre. This was an actual discotheque – the new-fangled invention from America! You went to the top floor and there was a guy on a raised stage to the right who played records non-stop. It was always packed. There would be slow records at the end of the night and that's when you had to grab a girl to dance with, otherwise you had pretty slim chances of 'pulling a bird' – as the expression went back then.

Jamaicans from Oxford's small Caribbean community used to go there. One memorable night a guy said to the DJ, 'Play this – it's the biggest record in Jamaica.' The record had an anonymous white label. The DJ cued it up and the place went crazy to the sound of 'Liquidator' by the Harry J All Stars.

Pete Cripps had his Anglia car, which meant that on Friday or Saturday nights we could head further afield to the outskirts of London, to one of the Burton's Ballroom chain or to Aylesbury Town Hall, where I saw the Jimi Hendrix Experience.

These were the days of all-nighter clubs in London, but Burton's Ballroom in suburban Uxbridge was as close as we got. Of course I wanted to go to the Tiles club in London's Oxford Street where everyone cool went — but that was real London and an all-nighter meant I was going to have a problem with parents. I'd read about the magical Ram Jam Club, a Reggae venue in Brixton, and dreamt about the vast metropolis of London and all it had to offer. But it was a step too far. You were either in that world or you weren't, and I wasn't. I was in Oxfordshire.

London was less than fifty miles away but it was almost another planet. I went there on a school trip to visit the Tate art gallery. We had the whole day in the capital and the abiding memory had nothing to do with painting. We went into Soho Square and there we saw John Peel, star of the pirate radio airwaves and newly signed to the fledgling BBC Radio 1. He was wearing a white raincoat. All the way home we were saying, 'Oh my God, we actually saw John Peel!'

5

Reggae

At first no one seemed sure how to spell it. The genre that would come to define Jamaican music arrived in 1968 and appeared on early album covers as 'Regay' or 'Reggay'.

It was the description of a raw and richly creative sound that dispensed with the slow soulful smoothness of Rock Steady, and placed a new emphasis on the rhythm section of drum and bass.

Exciting new producers such as Lee 'Scratch' Perry, Bunny 'Striker' Lee and Joe Gibbs were in the Reggae front rank. Vocal groups including the Maytals and the Heptones, and instrumental bands such as Perry's the Upsetters, were among its stars.

Like Ska and Rock Steady before it, Reggae was instantly popular in Britain. Trojan Records had been created by Jamaican ex-pats Chris Blackwell and Lee Gopthal in London in July 1967 to supply the releases of Duke Reid and other leading producers, and its distinctive orange label became an icon.

As the sixties came to an end, Jamaican music was enjoying unprecedented commercial success.

Reggae was embraced by white working-class British youth, and most obviously by the young skinheads with their crew cuts and boots who were successors to the Mods. They championed artists including

Laurel Aitken and Derrick Morgan and helped make UK chart hits for Desmond Dekker, Bob and Marcia, and Dave (Barker) and Ansell Collins.

I was about to get a taste of how this music would shape my life and make my living.

It was Gosford Hill School's Art Club disco that gave me my first chance to play records to an audience.

It was 1968 and a group of my friends was studying GCE Art. We liked it so much that we had an after-school class called the Art Club on the top floor of the school but we needed more money for paint and materials.

Stephen Peat, the most passionate artist among us, had the idea of a disco at Thursday lunchtimes in the gym with an entrance fee of sixpence that would go to the Art Club. That's where I started DJing: with music from Soul singers like Otis Redding, the Isley Brothers and the Detroit Spinners, and Jamaican acts such as the Upsetters and Desmond Dekker.

This was the 'Year of Revolutions', when the Vietnam War prompted huge student protests in Paris and London. It was the era of counter-culture.

I'm not going to say I've never smoked marijuana. Most of my friends experimented with joints and to my great discomfort and the embarrassment of my parents I managed to get busted by the cops for possession of hashish in 1968 when I was seventeen. I only found out many years later just how we got caught.

There was me and my best mates, Bob Baldwin, Steve Hewett, Colin 'Beastly' Looker and Peter Cripps. Bob scored some hash in White's pub in Oxford that Saturday lunchtime and we were going to Burton's Ballroom in Uxbridge that night to see Jimmy James and the Vagabonds.

We were on the A40 heading to London for the show when suddenly a police motorbike pulled us over. There was a police car close behind with its lights and siren going. 'Get out the car,' we were told, before being subjected to a full search. They quickly found the spliffs we had built for later.

They took us down to the police station in Oxford and we were put in separate cells and asked, 'Where did you buy the drugs from?'

My dad had to come to Oxford and get me out. He was very quiet in the car as he sat outside the police station and waited for me to get in.

'Why did you do it?'

'It was just a joint, you know.'

It was a big shock for my parents and totally alien to the culture they knew. The next night was a Sunday and I was up in my room worrying.

'What have I done?' I was saying to myself. 'I've brought shame on the family and I'm going to get charged and get a criminal record.'

As I was trying to get to sleep, my parents came to my bedroom. It was dark but there was a light from the door and they both stood at the side of the bed before my dad started to talk.

'Look, son, don't worry, we're going to stand by you on this and it doesn't matter what happens, we are here for you.'

I will never forget that intense feeling of love from my parents over that incident – we all make mistakes, they were saying.

But there were still consequences to face. What happened was that all of us lads were called in individually to have an official caution from the chief constable of Oxford. That was how they dealt with things in those days. He had his hat on to give the moment an added air of formality and you had to go into his office and stand there while he spoke to you. My father was with me as the chief constable addressed me.

'We are not going to prosecute you and you will not have a criminal record but we are giving you an official caution, so you should never do it again. You are hereby officially warned by the Oxford Constabulary.'

It was a big deal for us at the time. We never knew how the police had caught us but I recently made contact again with Steve Hewett after many years. He had done some research into the matter.

At the start of our journey to Oxford we had gone to fill up in the petrol station in our village of Kidlington and the man running the petrol station had apparently seen us rolling something in the back of the car. He had phoned the cops and told them the registration number of the car and which direction we were heading in. That information went straight to a police hotline and they decided it was a big drugs deal and ordered the motorbikes to find us heading down the A40. There were no roadside cameras in those days but with the tip-off from the service station they soon found us. I felt sorry for Pete Cripps because he wasn't part of our joint-smoking gang and was completely innocent.

After that incident with the chief constable I didn't touch the herb for a long time; I was terrified of ending up in further trouble. But so many in my circle smoked pot – it *was* the sixties! You had Jimi Hendrix and Neil Young on the record player, so passing a joint round seemed only natural.

The most important things in my life at that age were girls, girls, girls. This was the year I got a big crush on a girl in the year below me at school. Her name was Alison Archer and she was hot (but she knew it) and I was reduced to trying to be Mr Cool, nonchalantly timing my emergence from the school cloakroom to coincide with her departure so that I could accidentally on purpose bump into her and strike up a conversation which would hopefully last all the way home, as we both lived at the same end of the village. It eventually paid off because we started going steady. On Saturday nights we would listen to Tamla Motown records in her front room with her mum and dad sitting in the back room watching television.

Whoever is with Alison now will have to cope with her absolute passion for horses. She had a horse called Jane, and she loved it more than any person. One day I went with her to the fields and tried horse riding. I took a tumble. I never rode Jane again and I wasn't going to the stables to change the hay.

But I really blew it with Alison by playing Mr Cool at a Thursday night session at Brett's club, when I asked another girl for a slow dance. Little did I know Alison was also in the club. Her payback was to start dating my buddy Steve Hewett – and that was me kicked to the kerb.

The year ended strangely. My DJ career hadn't exactly taken off but I knew a guy called Dave McArthur who had a mobile disco in a white van that he would hire out. Occasionally Tim Inkpen and I would accompany him to his gigs and help him set up. Being the actual DJ was still a long way off for me.

Dave got a booking to play in a village in Oxfordshire on New Year's Eve. The night was a complete flop and Tim and I tried to trek back to Witney in time for midnight to celebrate

New Year with our friends. As we walked through the countryside it felt like something out of a Thomas Hardy novel.
We walked and walked but no one would stop to pick us up.
From the top of a hill we could see Witney and hear the revel-
lers and bells ringing but we were not going to make it for the
midnight hour. We each had one miniature bottle of whisky
in our pockets, so we sipped on those and wished each other
a happy New Year.

Our school years were coming to an end. Some of my
friends were talented visual artists and at least three headed to
art college. I was mainly trying to do three-dimensional stuff,
painting and charcoal drawing. I had some talent but I wasn't
skilled enough in fine art and deep down I knew that. But I
did enjoy it.

How we passed our exams in technical drawing I'm still
not sure. Bob Baldwin's parents went away the night before
the exam and he decided to have everyone round for a party.
Sgt. Pepper's Lonely Hearts Club Band had come out. We were all
blown away by the album and stayed up listening to it all night
until the sun came up. Some people were smoking banana
skins, which were supposed to get you high. But somehow we
all passed the exam.

I stayed at school to do A-levels in English and Art and
was offered an interview for a place at the North London
Polytechnic doing Business Studies.

I went one morning in the car with my father for this
interview at the Camden Town building of the Poly. Tony
Blackburn's breakfast show was on the radio and he played
'California Dreaming' by Winston Francis as his record of the
week. It was on the Bamboo label and produced by Coxsone
Dodd, and I was blown away by such a lovely Reggae treatment

of the great song by The Mamas & the Papas. It seemed a good
omen and I was offered a place at the Poly.

Before taking it up, I went travelling. I saved money by
working in a dairy for twelve-hour shifts. Then I planned my
route. There was an amazing Reggae instrumental song at the
time called 'Leaving Rome' by Jo Jo Bennett. I kept humming it when I was thinking of a destination for my trip, so
I thought, 'I'm going to go to Rome' and bought a one-way
ticket. I stayed in a youth hostel for my first few days and then
hitchhiked to Florence. It wasn't easy going. I left early in
the morning and didn't get there until late at night but I saw
Michelangelo's statue of David and the Ponte Vecchio. Then I
thought I'd go to Greece.

There was a famous book read by all the 'Harry Hippie'
traveller types of the time called *Europe on a Dollar a Day* and
it seemed like every traveller was reading either that or J. R. R.
Tolkien's *Lord of the Rings*. If you had long hair and a beard and
a backpack, the chances were you had one of those books too.
I hitchhiked down the Adriatic Coast of Italy, spending one
night sleeping at the back of a petrol station, and took a ferry
to Corfu, where I lived for about a week on a beach, with my
rucksack, sleeping bag and travellers' cheques.

I got off the boat in the dark and began a conversation with
an American girl who was also travelling. As we passed an old
lady we asked her if there was somewhere we could stay and
she said we could sleep on her veranda. When I awoke it was
searing hot and the lady gave us Greek coffee, which I'd never
had before; sweet, thick and almost muddy in texture. She gave
us bread and marmalade and refused any money. That's how
Corfu was in those times.

I left for the mainland and took a bus into Athens, stayed

in a youth hostel, and went down to the port to decide where to go next. I settled on the Cyclades island of Ios, which was like paradise with a village on the top of the hill. I slept every night on the beach, and the tavern where you washed depended for business on us rough sleepers. At evening time you would join the other Harry Hippies and trail up to the town, where the streets were narrow, cobbled and white and the Greek ladies were dressed all in black. We ate inexpensively every night and drank ouzo before tumbling back down the hill to the beach.

That's where I met Brian Parry, who became a great friend. Brian was from Liverpool and studying to be a teacher. He had used an old Morris Oxford to get himself to Greece and had left it in Athens. When we headed home we picked up his car and – I don't know how – it got us all the way back to England. There were four of us on the journey, sharing petrol costs, and on the way we went to a beer festival in Munich and got completely hammered.

We went on to Amsterdam and I had my first and only LSD trip at the famous Milky Way club. It was the most amazing and frightening experience I have had with drugs and was never to be repeated.

The walls started wobbling and the trip lasted about eight hours. I was convinced I could have walked across the Amsterdam canals without having to swim and I suggested that idea to Brian. 'You won't be walking anywhere,' he said. He hadn't taken anything, thankfully.

The worst part of that experience was when we went to a late-night food joint and I watched a woman in front of me turn old before my eyes. She literally went from being a young smiling woman into an old hag, like a witch with a wrinkled-up face, as she turned and looked at me. That was the real horror and there was no way I was going to do LSD again. At the time I had long hair and it was a rite of passage.

I didn't have a care in the world that summer of 1970. Jimmy Cliff was high in the charts with 'Wild World', a song written by Cat Stevens. We got a ferry to Harwich and Brian headed back to Liverpool. He eventually married his girlfriend and emigrated to Australia. I returned to Oxford, having had my experience of 'travelling'. During my student days I would head to Scandinavia on a holiday work scheme backed by the National Union of Students. I stayed with the Finnish sculptor Mauno Hartman and his wife, helping their son with his English. Then I hitchhiked across Sweden to Norway.

I left home for the North London Polytechnic on a Sunday afternoon. I was given a lift by a neighbour who was going to London and I left my mother on the doorstep in tears. She didn't understand why I was going to London when I could have gone to the Oxford Polytechnic and done the same course.

She was a very strong woman, so to see her crying broke my heart. It wasn't an easy decision to leave but I had to spread my wings at nineteen and live independently of my mum and dad and sister. I was perfectly happy at home but I needed to break out and I wouldn't have got a grant to live in digs in Oxford.

In London I stayed in South Kensington in rooms allocated by the college with six people living in a room, dormitory style. You had your locker and your wardrobe next to your bed. Most of the hostel was occupied by civil servants who had moved to London and there were a few places reserved for students.

I came out of the digs that afternoon and walked up to Kensington Gardens, feeling a bit sorry for myself. It was the first time I'd left home and already I was missing it. I sat on a park bench and somebody had a transistor radio that was playing 'You Can Get It If You Really Want' by Desmond Dekker. It got to number two on the hit parade. It was just a fabulous song and it simply bounced out of the radio; I remember thinking it had to be a message, a watchword.

The next morning was my first day at college, and so began a year of abject misery. I had no real feeling for the subjects: Economics, Statistics and Marketing. I was told to do it to get a job in some form of business but it was so dull.

It's almost indescribable how unhappy I was.

Within a few weeks I managed to get new digs with other students from the Poly in North Finchley, north London. I was on a sandwich course with a work placement included and by the spring of the following year, 1971, I was sent to the Whitbread brewery offices in Chiswick, west London. I worked in every department, including going out on the road with the draymen, who started work very early because they had to deliver the beer into the pubs. It wasn't unheard of for them to have a quick half of beer at some of the pubs on the way round and their run was over by early afternoon. They were real characters but there were three of them in the truck and I was slightly in the way.

I also had to do dreary tasks in the accounts department. I remember sitting in a room with Max, an elderly gentleman heading towards retirement, and an Irish guy called Danny and all they talked about was what they were going to do when they stopped working. I literally felt caged. It was a torment that would only end when I determined on a totally different way of making a living – as an actor.

6

Toasting

This art form, where a vocalist would 'toast' jive talk over a beat rather than sing, would one day evolve into the billion-dollar industry called rap.

And it arrived in the early part of 1970 when the inimitable U Roy occupied the top three positions of the Jamaican charts for three months with the songs 'Wake the Town', 'Rule the Nation' and 'Wear You to the Ball'.

U Roy's success as a recording artist, delivering his infectious lyrics over the classic instrumental Rock Steady rhythms of Duke Reid, had been a long time coming. The origins of toasting – or 'Deejaying' as it is also known – were in the open-air Jamaican dances where U Roy and other Masters of Ceremonies, such as Count Matchuki and King Stitt, had been as much of a draw as the big sound systems. U Roy became a familiar figure, holding the mic at dances staged by King Tubby's Hometown Hi-Fi system, owned by the emerging Kingston recording engineer Osbourne 'King Tubby' Ruddock.

Although Jamaican radio stations were sniffy about the new style, other performers, including Big Youth, Dennis Alcapone, I-Roy and Prince Jazzbo also successfully made the transition from sound system to vinyl. Toasting was a music form that was here to stay.

But back in my world, as an obsessive Reggae fan, I felt out on my own.

It's at this point that I need to make a confession.

Reggae had become deeply unfashionable with the music cognoscenti and most of my friends, and – although it was still my great love – I found myself disowning it one regretful evening.

This is how it happened.

I was living with some great guys – Mick, Tony and Des – in Gunnersbury Avenue in Acton, west London, because I needed to be close to the brewery where I was doing my placement. There had been an advert in the rental columns in the London magazine *Time Out* and the other tenants had accepted me – but only after an interview to ensure we'd get along. Like most students of the time I had long hair and a beard – I looked like John Peel.

Close to my digs in Chiswick High Road there was a record shop where I'd purchased *Version Galore*, the classic 1970 album by U Roy. To tell you I was obsessed with it would be an understatement. 'Deejay' fever had hit Jamaica, a new style where a vocal artist would 'toast' lyrics over a well-known instrumental rhythm.

Version Galore changed everything. What U Roy had done was take older original rhythms built by Duke Reid, who owned the Treasure Isle label, and talk over the top of them. In the language of Reggae, he had 'versioned' them; that is, given them a new twist. It was revolutionary.

But all the guys who shared my house were into Rock music – for them it was all Pink Floyd and The Who. In our communal front room one of my housemates, a real hi-fi buff, had the most amazing sound system. I still had my little

Dansette Viva record player that my dad had bought me, with its open lid and speaker at the front of the box. That's what I used to play *Version Galore* and my other Reggae records, privately in my room.

Reggae wasn't considered cool. It was:'Oh, you like Reggae? They just do versions of Tamla Motown records, don't they?' It simply wasn't taken seriously by the Rock fraternity.

One evening my housemates said they were all going to the pub and I saw my chance: I could go downstairs and play *Version Galore* on that phenomenal hi-fi system; it was the whole horse and pony show with whistles and buttons.

I put on *Version Galore* at full volume and was dancing away to it in my own little world, imagining where each track had been recorded in Jamaica, staring at the album sleeve photo of U Roy holding a microphone and wearing his 'tam' Rasta bonnet.

When I turned around, the door into the front room was wide open and my flatmates were all standing there. 'What are you doing?' one said. They'd gone to the pub but someone had forgotten something and they'd come straight back and heard this music being belted out.

'What *is* this? This is Reggae!' they scoffed.

'Yeah, but it's not for me . . . I bought it for a friend.'

I'm embarrassed to say this. But that's how uncool Reggae was to the Rock intelligentsia because it was seen as music for shaven-headed thugs.

'You like skinhead music?' you would be asked. 'They're a bunch of racists! They beat up Pakistanis! How can you like their music?'

I had long hair and a beard like my flatmates – what was I doing with this stuff?

The Ska sound of the sixties had been hot and fresh, but by the end of the decade, as it morphed first into Rock Steady and then into Reggae, my close friends began to lose interest. 'You're not really sticking with this stuff, are you, Dave?' they'd ask.

Rock became dominant. Cream was the favourite band played at parties. I realized the world had changed and, musically, I was out on my own.

So much so that for a while I thought I must be the only white guy that liked this music. I couldn't find anyone who shared my obsession. Everyone I knew was listening to artists such as Neil Young and Free. I like them too – when it comes to music I've a very open mind.

As a student I was being driven mad with boredom by Business Studies. I was getting depressed and, to keep my spirits up, I joined a big arts educational establishment called the London Institute (now the University of the Arts London). You could go there in the evenings after work and I signed up for classes in acting, speech and movement. There were weekends away doing plays and practising the art of being an actor. I loved it. Those spring and summer evenings at the Institute were an inspiration to me and a total contrast to the mind-numbing existence I was enduring in my student placement.

It was during the weekend acting course with the London Institute that I met Sue Rogerson, who was also anxious to get into the theatre. I tried my best to get fresh with her but she wasn't remotely interested and shooed me away. But she was the girl I'd eventually take to The Wailers' gig at The Greyhound.

Deep down, I'd long wanted to be an actor. I'd done a couple of school plays and really enjoyed it. The head of the English department, Roy Bateman, gave me extraordinary support.

'You could do this professionally,' he told me. Those words of encouragement encapsulate the power of a good teacher.

Mr Bateman probably never realized it but he was a significant influence on my life. He was passionate about literature and filled us with enthusiasm for it. He directed me in Thornton Wilder's play *Our Town*, where I played the role of a small-time American stage manager, one of the key characters. The following year we performed *Oh! What a Lovely War* by the English theatre director Joan Littlewood, who instantly became someone I looked up to.

Acting in school was a new world. I didn't seem to have any difficulty learning lines and I looked forward to the classes immensely. What I enjoyed was this process of bringing the written word to life off the page and learning to figure out the characters. You would begin a play with a simple read-through and you would gradually see it take shape with costumes, lighting and a set. I realized it was something I felt for and it began to become my dream.

While Mr Bateman gave me confidence to go on the stage, everyone else I knew seemed to warn me against it. 'There's no security in it,' they told me. 'It's over-subscribed.'

Even so, the bug stayed with me and, when I was working in the brewery, I was going out every week to buy the theatre world's newspaper, *The Stage*. My heart was yearning and burning to throw it all in and study to be an actor. I started applying to drama schools and managed to get auditions for some of the best: the London Academy of Music and Dramatic Art (LAMDA), Webber Douglas Academy of Dramatic Art, the Rose Bruford College of Speech and Drama, and East 15, which was associated with Joan Littlewood, who had written *Oh! What a Lovely War*.

The place I really wanted to go to was Rose Bruford because it offered both a teaching and acting course; I thought it would be good to have educational qualifications as well.

The problem was that Rose Bruford had taken its annual allocation of drama students and wasn't offering more auditions. I refused to leave the college alone, however, and phoned relentlessly from the house where I was staying and from phone boxes all over London whenever I saw one. I kept pleading with this secretary: 'I know the auditions are over but could you please just see me?' After countless calls she finally gave in. 'We've decided we will see you,' she said. The audition at Rose Bruford, then, was just me on my own.

There was an auditioning board of four people in the Old Theatre in the college's main building in Lamorbey Park in Sidcup and I performed my audition speeches, one modern and one Shakespeare. They asked some questions and I went back to my digs hoping with all my heart that I'd done enough to win them over. I didn't have to wait long for the secretary to tell me I'd got a place.

In order to take up Rose Bruford's offer and continue to receive a student grant I had to persuade Oxfordshire County Council that it was a good use of public money for me to change courses after just a year. So I had to do another audition before them and yet another in front of a committee from Oxfordshire Education Council to persuade them I really wanted to be an actor and my training wouldn't be a waste of public funds. How I would have managed without a grant, I don't know. Fortunately the drama consultant seemed to be impressed and they allowed me to change courses.

Getting into drama school was the turning point in my life. Finally I was doing something I really wanted to do.

My father wasn't at all convinced that acting was a good idea but he realized how determined I was to do it. When I was still at school I didn't want to continue with education after my A-levels and had a blazing argument with him. I was on the stairs and he was down in the hallway. I said, 'I'm not going to stay on at school. I don't care.'

'You need to go and bloody well get a job and find out what you want to be.'

He was very angry with me.

'Well, I want to be an actor.'

'Don't be ridiculous, that's crazy.'

'I can and I will be.'

I'd been determined not to go back to do my A-levels but my mother had other ideas about that. She went to see the headmaster and within a day or two I was called into his office and sat down and given a talking to.

He said, 'You are not leaving, you have got talent and you can do A-level Art and History. Your mother has made it abundantly clear that she doesn't want you to leave and you need to stay on at school.'

I went home that lunchtime and my mother was singing at the sink – she always used to sing in the home. I walked in and closed the door and she carried on singing, then turned and looked and said, 'Did you see someone today?'

'Yes, I did.'

'And?'

'OK, Mum, I'm going to stay on.'

I think that was one of the happiest moments of her life.

My parents warned me of the pitfalls of acting; that I could possibly spend the rest of my life struggling to make ends meet. My dad's worst fears would resurface when I came home from college one holiday with long hair, a beard and a Che Guevara T-shirt. He refused to speak to me and when we met in Oxford High Street he passed me on the other side of the road.

But I would not be put off.

When I knew I was definitely not going to do Business Studies any more I got a summer holiday job as a deckchair attendant in Hyde Park. I had responsibility for all the adjoining London Royal Parks as well: Green Park, St James's Park and Kensington Gardens. And I worked seven days a week. You'd approach people with your ticket machine as they were sitting in a deckchair and – of course – as soon as they saw you they'd get up and walk away. You'd have to persuade them to stay there and pay for a ticket. The money wasn't great but I managed to get through the summer. I was a long way away from a life in Reggae.

7
Roots

The Jamaican vocal tradition that appeared in Ska and Rock Steady had its origins in American Doo-Wop. Pioneers such as The Wailers, the Paragons, the Heptones, Ken Boothe and Alton Ellis had a polished delivery which evoked the Impressions and other American soul groups.

But by the early to mid-1970s that sound had developed into something much more earthy and spiritual: Roots. The Abyssinians were crucial, recording three great Rastafarian anthems: 'Satta Massa Gana', 'Declaration of Rights' and 'Yim Mas Gan'.

Bob Marley and The Wailers, which had become so much more than a vocal harmony group, with its own rhythm section and female backing singers the I-Threes, released the Catch a Fire *album in 1973, immediately followed by* Burnin'.

Burning Spear brought out the colossal 'Marcus Garvey' in 1975. The Mighty Diamonds released their first LP, Right Time, *in 1976, another Rasta-inspired instant classic. The Wailing Souls recorded their eponymous Studio One debut album. Shortly afterwards, The Congos cut* Heart of the Congos *for eccentric genius producer Lee Perry, and Culture brought out* Two Sevens Clash; *both essential purchases.*

Reggae's Golden Age was truly upon us. The Rastafarian faith was at its heart and the Rasta colours of red, gold and green became its banner.

I had escaped from the dullness of Business Studies. Training to be an actor gave me the chance to be creative in my work. But all the time I was forced to live a double life to stay in touch with the music I loved.

The time came for me to start my drama course at Rose Bruford and I had to leave my old digs and move across London to Sidcup. I was allocated a shared room in a house with a student called Greg Hicks, who would go on to become a very successful classical actor, a member of the Royal Shakespeare Company for forty years. He has appeared in popular British TV shows such as *Midsomer Murders* and *Casualty* and was recently in the film *Snow White and the Huntsman* with the Hollywood stars Kristen Stewart and Charlize Theron.

There were three female students in the house. One was Barbara Kellerman, another successful actress who is best known for having played the White Witch in the BBC's adaptation of C. S. Lewis's *The Chronicles of Narnia*, and another was Vivienne Frankish. The third was Sue Rogerson, the girl I tried to hit on at the London Institute drama course. When I realized she was in my year at Rose Bruford I couldn't believe it.

Although she had given me the brush-off before, we were now housemates and eventually it became apparent that we really did have strong feelings for each other. After the first year, Sue and I and three others moved into a modern town house in a suburb with the unlikely-sounding name of Green Street Green. That's where we spent the rest of the three-year diploma course.

At Green Street Green Sue and I became a couple. She was a stunning-looking woman and very witty. She could fill a room with her presence and that made her an outstanding actress. We were soul mates and we fell in love, there's no two ways about it. Sue and I were strong together and the relationship continued through the rest of my time at Rose Bruford.

When I arrived at the college it was a culture shock. I had done a year of Business Studies and suddenly moved into this world of acting. We had to do ballet and movement classes in tights. I felt a little strange. I thought, 'What's this got to do with acting?'

My previous idea of dancing was doing Jamaican steps like the Rock Steady, the Ska or the Ride Your Donkey. And here we were doing classic Greek arm-lines in tights with a lady on the piano and an elderly ballet teacher. It's all to do with understanding your body and movement – and we also had sword-fighting lessons and voice classes.

I learned stagecraft from a great artistic director, Malcolm Morrison, the head of acting at the college. In our first class in what was called the Barn Theatre we had to do an improvisation, and at the end of it Malcolm said, 'You must never forget that no one is interested in OPP.'

The students sat there pretending to know what OPP was. It means Other People's Problems, he said, and when someone comes to a theatre performance, for which they have bought a ticket, they are not remotely interested in whether you've had a quarrel with your girlfriend, or your Auntie Ethel has died, or you can't pay your rent that week. So don't bring that onto the stage. He told us, 'I don't care what's happened in your private life; when you hit the wings as an actor you cannot bring your own misery and disappointment onto the stage because the audience has come to escape their own problems and they want to see the character.' I've never forgotten that advice when performing.

He had this particular way of talking because he was also the main lecturer in Phonetics. That's a science you had to study every week throughout the three years at drama college; you needed to be able to write down how every word sounded. Phonetics enables you to study an accent and replicate it, so that you're able to speak exactly like someone from East Yorkshire, say, or Dunfermline. The course enabled you to qualify as a teacher of speech and drama, and many students went on to become speech therapists.

Throughout my period in drama college, I was still relentlessly buying Reggae records at places such as Granville Arcade in Brixton. I would come home and play Prince Buster's *The Message Dubwise* album or *Chi Chi Run* by Big Youth on my little Dansette Viva. I did everything I could to introduce my flatmates to the music.

Robin Sampson, who lived with us in Green Street Green, was a classical pianist and later admitted to me that he'd been worried about moving into the house because he didn't know how he was 'going to cope' with my Reggae. 'But now I love it,' he told me a little later. 'I'm a fan.' The song he loved most was 'Pass It On' from The Wailers' *Burnin'* album.

Greg Hicks was fascinated by an instrumental called 'Now' by Lee Arab – an artist I'd never heard of before that record and haven't since in fifty years of following this music. Greg thought it was the most amazing piece. He'd say, 'Play that track by Lee Arab', and he would do this slightly theatrical dance, really getting into it. He'd become a Reggae convert. Everywhere I went I was always preaching: 'You've got to hear this!'

At drama school I indulged in hash cakes, which gave me the rampant giggles and munchies one Saturday afternoon. But my dope smoking was limited in comparison to other people. I didn't have a dealer and I didn't know where to go and buy it. It was mostly encountered at parties.

The big hippie expression of the time was 'Don't Bogart That Joint', meaning don't hang on to it too long – pass it on. The phrase came from the film *Easy Rider* and was a reference to Humphrey Bogart always leaving his cigarettes dangling in his mouth. The biggest high was when I was staying in Hampstead Heath in London. It was a technicolour experience. I was supposed to go out to see a concert that evening but I never got out of my dormitory. It was incredibly strong and, I'm pretty sure, hallucinogenic. That experience again put me off smoking for a long time. I was beginning to realize I wasn't cut out for this.

I took Sue to see The Wailers and we went to watch the Maytals too. That was at the Bouncing Ball club in Peckham, south London, and Sue loyally came with me because of my musical obsession. We turned up at 9 p.m., thinking the concert would start around then, but the place was still shut. There was a pub next door and we went in there and sat and waited and eventually the doors to the club opened and we went in and waited some more, and finally – by this time it was one or two in the morning – the Maytals came on. We had never known a concert take place so late and I had not experienced the West Indian time factor either. Not to that degree. We were shattered. But Toots came on stage and performed, and afterwards I shook his hand. It was nearly daylight as we got in the car and headed back to Green Street Green.

The music just wouldn't leave me. I used to buy my records from Muzik City in Lewisham Model Market in south London.

It was run by a very quiet and reserved Jamaican called Lee Laing and if it wasn't for him I probably wouldn't have got the break into the music industry that I got. Lee, who had been raised in London, was the manager of a chain of shops owned by Trojan Records and he later set up his own shops under the name Lee's Sound City.

I would go into that shop in Lewisham and usually be the only white man in there. That was where I bought my first ever Dub album, *African Dub All Mighty Chapter 1*, produced by Joe Gibbs. I would be staring and coveting Big Youth's *Screaming Target* album and wondering if I could ever save up the money to buy it. It's difficult now to imagine how I found £5 for an import album as an impecunious student, but I did. It was a hell of a lot of money.

Lee realized I was addicted to Reggae and would give me money off my purchases but never admit it. I would get the change back and it would always be too much, and I would look at him and he would just roll his eyes. After I became a regular customer, he never failed to give me a discount.

I've still got my records from those years and when I look at some of them I can see what an obsessive I was.

Reggae was such a marginal genre at the time that I would collect any articles I could find in the weekly music press and use them to cover my vinyl records, like I was wrapping up fish and chips.

King of the Road and Other Reggae Favourites was a compilation from 1972 on Sioux Records, including tracks from U Roy and the Harry J Allstars, Lloyd the Matador and Joe Higgs. I wrapped that up in an article headlined 'The Facts About Reggae'. It was a piece from *Melody Maker* which tried to pinpoint the essence of new Jamaican music. 'It was born in poverty and squalor as a necessary release from the over-bearing hardships of daytime existence,' reported Richard Williams. 'Indeed, the background of Reggae accentuates even more the racial discrimination, for it came out of the appalling ghettoes of Jamaica, the shanty towns which make even the Black districts of many North American cities look comparatively prosperous.'

Another of my albums I wrapped in an article headlined 'Suddenly Reggae is Hip . . . after being almost booted to death by the skins.' The story, which showed how dramat-ically Reggae had fallen in and out of fashion after being championed by skinheads, pictured Lorna Bennett, who had topped the charts with 'Breakfast in Bed'. It was part of a series at the start of 1973 by writer Danny Holloway called 'Reggae in Britain', described as a 'survey of West Indian Music'. The article reported how shops had refused to stock Reggae because they didn't want the skinheads to come in 'and give them trouble'. There was a quote from Lee Gopthal of the British-based Trojan record label who said, 'It was unfortunate that we got tagged as being skinhead music because it just gave us another battle to fight.'

I covered another record with a *New Musical Express* piece from 1973, which was a regular column by Henderson Dalrymple called 'Black and British'. The edition of 24 March 1973 was simply headlined 'Marley's gonna be big'.

Towards the end of my time at drama college I strongly considered turning away from acting in favour of becoming a schoolteacher. During my course at Rose Bruford I did teach-ing practice – TP as it was called – at primary school, junior school and secondary school levels. In my final year I was teaching at Orpington Boys' School on the edge of London and I loved it. And they seemed to like me because I was offered a job teaching English and Drama. That summer of 1974, I was twenty-three and seriously tempted to take up the school's offer because it would have given me job security in a profession I admired. In the end I decided against it – my heart was still beating hard for working on the stage.

What really swung it was that I had done a dramatization of the Russian poet Yevgeny Yevtushenko's *Zima Junction*, his long autobiographical poem about growing up in Russia. I loved this poem so much that I genuinely thought I could bring it to life on stage. I dramatized it as a one-man show and performed it at the Barn Theatre in Rose Bruford College, directed by Chris Baker, who became a very good friend. I finished that production on the Friday evening and by the following Monday managed to get a lunchtime slot at the Little Theatre in Garrick's Yard off St Martin's Lane in the West End of London. Lunchtime plays were popular with theatre-goers in those days. The theatre was up a little side alley and then up a creaky staircase on the first floor. But the play ran for two weeks and I didn't lose money because we had a pretty good audience every lunchtime.

In September 1974 I got an audition for Theatre North, an independent company that was a breakaway group from the famous Crucible Theatre in Sheffield. Theatre North had a strong lineage in the world of English drama. It was set up by James Tomlinson, along with the Scottish–Canadian actor Douglas Campbell and his wife Ann Casson, the daughter of the venerated actress Dame Sybil Thorndike. They created a traditional touring theatre company in the north of England.

The company gave me a job as an acting ASM (assistant stage manager), which didn't mean you were on trial for the job, it meant you were able to do 'acting' within the company as well as stage management. So you had to do props, costumes, set changes and set-ups, and organize rehearsal rooms. On top of that you were given small parts, but not necessarily in every production. That was enough to get you your provisional card for Equity, the trade union for actors, without which you couldn't work.

The job meant the end of my relationship with Sue Rogerson. It was a natural parting of the ways. I'd joined a theatre company in the north while Sue was going into the education side of theatre and moving to the South Coast. I was really saddened by the break-up but we were located so far apart that it was always going to be difficult to make it work.

I finished my run of *Zima Junction* in St Martin's Lane and immediately started work at Theatre North. We rehearsed outside Sheffield in a local village hall and after the first season we moved to a school close to the city's steel works. That was the start of a fantastic year and a half. We toured our productions across the north of England on a circuit that included venues such as Rotherham Civic Theatre, Mansfield Civic Theatre and Bradford Library Theatre.

I loved the discipline of theatre; the camaraderie and joy of being on the road, the rehearsing and long hours and watching other actors learn. I aspired to be like Alan Bates and Terence Stamp, who had great power on stage and in film. I'd admired them both in the film adaptation of *Far From the Madding Crowd*.

But my first part was an inauspicious one, playing a gorilla in a production of the Desert Island-based play *The Little Hut*. It was a typical light entertainment repertory play about two men marooned on an island, competing for the attentions of a woman who was stranded with them. A film version starred

Ava Gardner and Stewart Granger. But in this Theatre North production I was the acting assistant stage manager, a role so junior that I was the one who ended up in the gorilla's outfit.

My career took a step up when Theatre North moved on to Shakespeare and I was cast as the rebel Mortimer in *Henry IV Part 2*. I also had a second part as a messenger and had to run into a tent and shout the line: 'My Lord, My Lord, the King comes on apace'. I will never forget the lesson taught to me at that moment by Douglas Campbell, who was artistic director and really let me know I had to put everything into my acting, even if it was only a single line.

'You need to have left half a pound of flesh on the stage at the end of the performance,' he said. 'You have to realize you are in a privileged position as an entertainer.'

I still think of that advice. As a performer, you have always got to deliver.

Campbell taught me that you had to project yourself. During rehearsals of *Henry IV Part 2* he said to me more than once, 'You need to throw that line away.' At the final dress rehearsal at Mansfield Civic Centre he stopped everything – which is a big deal – and bellowed from the stalls, 'I've been telling you, dear boy, for the past four weeks of rehearsal that you need to throw it away. I don't normally do this but I shall . . .'

He marched onto the stage and went straight into the wings. I heard this step of a big man as he galloped back onto the stage and threw open the awning of the tent. He boomed, 'My Lord! My Lord! The King Comes on . . . A-pace!'

He turned to me and said, 'That's throwing it away!'

I tried to protest but he said, 'No buts, they need to hear you in the Gods! And if you don't do what I just did they won't hear you and there will be no sense of urgency. You are a messenger with a very important message. Deliver the message!'

His point was that you needed to be heard in the most distant seats, and if you could not be then you shouldn't be on stage at all. There were no microphone pick-ups to amplify your words – you had to use your ribs and diaphragmatic breathing to support your voice so that you didn't strain it. You're not supposed to shout, you're supposed to speak the lines clearly. You need to hear the soft consonants and the hard consonants – words have beginnings, middles and ends.

It was Douglas Campbell who taught me that subtle gestures on stage are lost. They can't be seen and voices can't be heard unless they are projected. It has to be larger than life or it's lost at the back of the stalls and it certainly would be lost at the back of the circle. These are important lessons I still remember now when I walk on stage to play Reggae music at live shows and sound clashes.

At Theatre North that season we performed Royce Ryton's play *Crown Matrimonial* – about the Royal abdication crisis that resulted from Edward VIII's relationship with the American socialite Wallis Simpson. I was a butler in that one. And we did *Close the Coalhouse Door*, a musical set in a mining community, written by the Hull playwright and television writer Alan Plater.

Working on stage was not an easy way to live and both my mother and father would ask, 'Do you really want to bother with this acting game?' There were occasions when I wasn't working when my dad would say, 'Why don't you get a proper job?' He had the concerns that any father would have had. Even so, he came with my mother to some of the Theatre

North plays, such as *Close the Coalhouse Door* at Mansfield Civic Theatre.

I was in awe of the experienced actors around me. I was a van driver for the company as well, so we would finish a two-week run at the smaller theatres and I would drive everyone back to base in Sheffield.

It was a fascinating period of my life, and Reggae was still a central part of it. I was living in a typical struggling actor's bedsit in the Nether Edge district of Sheffield with a damp carpet on the floor, very little furniture and going to Count Solomon's Friday-night Reggae dances whenever I wasn't on the road with the theatre company.

Count Solomon's sessions were in a basement and the Count himself would always play his record selection with his back to the crowd, wearing his trademark flat cap and car coat, which he never took off. I used to be fascinated by him.

Emboldened by a couple of beers I'd ask him if I could take the microphone. He would smile and give it to me. The sight of this white guy with the mic trying to toast like U Roy must have been absolutely hilarious. It's a bit embarrassing for me to look back on but that club gave me some treasured memories – it's where I first heard 'Rebel Music (3 O'Clock Roadblock)' by Bob Marley and the unforgettable introduction of its first few bars.

After Count Solomon's session I would invariably head off to Donkey Man's Blues, which was a popular after-hours drinking shebeen in Sheffield where I could continue to listen to Reggae until it was nearly dawn.

In The Wicker, a well-known street in Sheffield, there was a Reggae record shop called New Beat Records, run by a couple called Frank and Esmie. I almost lived in that shop – I used to go there on my way home after rehearsals because I had to change buses nearby. I was in there so often that in the summer of 1975 Frank and Esmie allowed me to work there part-time.

One morning the shop door opened and in walked Count Shelly, a well-known London sound system owner. He had arrived in his van, because he owned a record company called Third World and was selling his releases at Reggae shops around the country.

Count Shelly could sell fridges to Eskimos. But I was shocked by the sight of him that day – he had massive stitches across his nose and I found out later that he been brutally attacked with a knife by a Reggae singer with a bad-boy reputation. I said to him, 'Oh my God, what happened to you?' He wasn't letting on. He told me it was nothing, keeping to the ghetto code of never informing – no matter how badly you've been worked over. Nothing! The guy's nose was virtually hanging off and had needed to be stitched back on. With the state of his face and his abilities as a brilliant salesman I told him he had better wait for the owner, Frank. But in later years I got to know Count Shelly really well.

All the time I dreamt of owning a sound system of my own, so I commissioned a guy from the Jamaican community in Sheffield who I met in the record shop to make me a speaker box. I coveted a system with towering stacks of speakers but all I managed was this one big box. You can imagine the scene. I was living in a typical old Victorian house in an industrial city in Yorkshire, divided into bedsits with shared bathrooms. I was at the back of the house in a damp ground-floor room with a three-ring electric stove and a sink. It was an actor's garret. And there in the middle of the musty floor was a turntable and this single gigantic speaker.

I was so determined to get my own sound system that I decided to get a printing stamp to mark up all my records and show they belonged to me – which was what the owners and selectors of the big Jamaican systems did.

I wrote down on a square of paper the words 'Rodigan's Sound System', and took this to a rubber-stamp maker down on The Wicker. Instead of using the words to design an official-looking stamp, they copied my handwriting and made that the stamp. I've still got it. I would sit in my bedsit and obsessively stamp all my new records to make them look more authentic.

I spent Theatre North's summer recess of 1975 in London, and when my second season with the company came to an end, early in 1976, I moved back to the capital full time, with a speaker box and a pile of records but no one to play them to.

8

Rockers

The next genre to emerge under the umbrella of Reggae captured the increasingly militant attitude of a music that was always ready to protest on behalf of the ghetto poor.

Its signature was a new double-paced drumming pattern developed by Sly Dunbar, who would become one half of the famous 'Riddim Twins' rhythm section with bassist Robbie Shakespeare.

In the mid- to late 1970s Sly was establishing a reputation as the most innovative drummer in Jamaica while playing with the Revolutionaries, the in-house band at Channel One studios. He also recorded with the Professionals, the band used by producer Joe Gibbs. Sly's faster-paced 'Rockers' beat became increasingly ubiquitous between 1975 and 1978.

Another drummer, Leroy 'Horsemouth' Wallace, became a face for the new sound as he played a starring role in a feature film, Rockers, released in 1978 and showing the raw excitement of the Jamaican music scene at that time. There were also memorable appearances from Jacob Miller, singer with the band Inner Circle, Gregory Isaacs and Burning Spear.

Rockers was a name already adopted by one of Jamaica's great multi-instrumentalists, Horace Swaby, aka Augustus Pablo, as the title of

both his sound system and record label. His 1976 album, King Tubby
Meets Rockers Uptown, *was a work of extraordinary ingenuity.*

*Now totally obsessed with collecting Reggae records, I was torn
between making my musical hobby a way of life or forging a career as
an actor.*

I started Ram Jam's Record Shack in the red-hot scorching
summer of 1976 as I turned twenty-five. Each time I stocked
up on records I would pack them into a large 'grip' holdall
and carry that from Lee's shop to the bus station in Lewisham.

I would get the bus up to Victoria station and take a further coach to Oxford, where I would meet the local Reggae
sound system boys at Gloucester Green bus station. They
would meet me at the bus garage or in a little garden at the
Carfax clock tower on Friday nights. They would look at
the records and I would give them what they wanted on a
sale-or-return basis. Some evenings I would go and listen to
Black Harmony sound system in the Catacombs in Oxford
city centre, and records that I'd brought up from London
would be tested on the crowd.

I decided I wanted something more permanent and opened
a stall in the Sunday market on the Blackbird Leys estate in
the suburbs of Oxford. I didn't have my own car but Dad
used to get up at 5 a.m. to play golf and take me to Blackbird
Leys at the same time. I think his strong work ethic meant he
liked the entrepreneurial spirit of the stall, which we would
set up together. He went and bought an electric cable for the
record player and speakers, which he also helped to buy for
me. He would come back for me at 1 p.m. after he had played
his round of golf and put everything back in the car. His support was amazing.

From 7.30 a.m. I would trade until lunchtime. Word got around about my stall and a lot of Jamaican customers would come straight from having spent the whole night at 'Blues' parties in shebeens and private houses. Others would come along before or after church.

Ram Jam's Record Shack was a success and I opened another branch at Putney Saturday market in south-west London, near to my flat. Eventually I managed to scrape the money together to buy a Morris 1100 so I could put the records in the boot and drive up and down from London to Oxford – clap, bang, wallop until the wheels came off. I spent many months running those stalls until I landed a new acting job. Even then, Ram Jam's didn't shut down – I set up a mail-order business which I advertised in the back of the weekly *Black Echoes* music newspaper: 'Get your records from Ram Jam's Record Shop'.

I missed my actor's life in Sheffield although there were compensations: I could now go to see the great London sound systems – Sir Coxsone, Trojan and Duke Neville.

But I was often unemployed and most of the time I couldn't rub two shillings together. I was staying in a flat in Barnes with Peter Cripps – my old mate from Oxford – and his brother Dave Cripps. The digs were way out in the far south-west of the city, but the object of my working ambitions was all the way across town: namely a job with Lee Laing from Lee's Sound City record shop.

After working in Frank and Esmie's store in Sheffield I had some experience in Reggae retailing and I was ready to go it alone. So I went to Lee and said, 'Can I take records from your stock? I will sell them on the street and then whatever I sell, I will give you a commission.' And he said, 'Yes, you can.'

Of course, what I was doing – in drug dealer's parlance – was getting high on my own supply. By running this little business I could listen to all the latest releases, a wealth of music that I couldn't normally afford but which Lee was giving to me at wholesale prices.

Also in the summer of 1976 I decided to revive *Zima Junction* and toured the show in Edinburgh, Oxford and the crypt of St John's Church in Westminster, dressed in an old brown suit. I was really pleased with the reviews. 'David Rodigan performs the piece with great brio and versatility', said the *Financial Times*, while the actor's bible, *The Stage*, described the show as a 'tour de force'.

Before it opened at the Edinburgh Festival I went to check out the spec of the theatre, which I was sharing with another company. As I walked in I saw a girl at a piano singing 'Summertime, and the Livin' is Easy . . .' and I was absolutely knocked out. Her name was Pauline Siddle. She had a beautiful face, stood a petite five foot four inches, and I got the hots for her like crazy.

She was rehearsing 'Summertime', which she sang in the other play being staged at the theatre. I tried to talk to her on the staircase and she was very distant. I thought she looked like Elizabeth Taylor. She was going out with a theatre director but gave me her phone number and, although I didn't think she was very interested in me, I managed to get a date with her. It accelerated pretty fast and before long we were going out with each other back in London.

I made a film, *The Worp Reaction*, in which I played a mentally handicapped man who hoards scrap metal in his back garden until he has enough to build a flying machine. It won some awards, including Best Amateur Film of the Year, and I was featured on the cover of one film magazine suspended in a harness as if I were taking flight.

At the end of the year my agent, David Preston of David Preston Associates, landed me an audition for a season at the Victoria Theatre, Stoke-on-Trent. David was a theatrical agent – a *very* theatrical agent. He was based in New Bond Street above a Persian carpet shop.

Years later, when Reggae promoters would visit him in New Bond Street to book me as a DJ, he'd say, 'Some of these Jamaicans, when they come to put down deposits for your gigs, they smoke that stuff in my office. It's difficult for me to object because obviously I'm a chain smoker myself. But that stuff . . . it's marijuana, isn't it?' He was a wonderful character and I relied on him for work. I also had an entry in the acting directory *Spotlight*. You would get *Spotlight* photographs taken at drama school, and they were incredibly expensive, but in the acting world if you weren't in the directory you didn't exist.

I passed my audition in London before Peter Cheeseman of the Victoria Theatre company. He was one of England's great pioneering theatre directors and famous for developing 'in the round' productions. I joined the company in the autumn of 1976 for a year. The first play we did was *The Crucible*, and I played one of the prosecutors. Then, in Shakespeare's *The Tempest*, I was cast as the spirit Ariel. That was a real joy. The director had Ariel on stage for most of the production, just moving in slow motion, and it was actually quite tiring for me.

While I was in Staffordshire I took every chance to perform as a DJ, having honed my turntable skills at Ram Jam's Record Shack. After a Saturday-night theatre performance I would wipe off my make-up, jump into my Triumph Herald and head to the Stoke-on-Trent West Indian club to play my records.

The season finished and I moved back to London. Pauline, who had become my steady girlfriend, started working at the Albany Empire in Deptford, south London, where I later performed with the Combination Theatre Company and its artistic director, John Turner.

Since I was a teenager I'd wanted to go to Jamaica. I pictured in my mind these open-air dances with big sound systems, imagining what it would be like to hear them in the place where this culture started. When I dreamt of Jamaica I thought not of beaches and hotels but of the great recording studios – what did Studio One and Channel One look like?

But I never had enough money to get to the Caribbean.

I sometimes felt like an oddball with my Reggae fixation. I was a white man in a black man's world and for many years I had yet to meet anyone as fanatically obsessed with the music as I was – apart from Jamaican record collectors. I would spend long hours in Reggae shops absorbing the secret code of the other customers as they nodded and winked to the man behind the counter who was playing that week's consignment of freshly shipped pre-release seven-inch vinyl recordings. They would tap a finger on the counter each time they heard something they liked and the shop owner would drop a record onto the pile of purchases in front of them. When the customer was finished, the records would be counted up for payment. It was a ritual I quickly learned.

Buying the music wasn't enough for me – I needed to hear it played by Jamaicans in its rightful context. So I would go to West Indian clubs in the West End of London such as Cariba in Conduit Street or, most importantly, Columbo's in Carnaby

Street. I went there because the great London sound system Sir
Coxsone had a residency at the club, which reputedly took its
name from the raincoat-wearing American television detective Columbo, played by Peter Falk. The sound system was set
up by Lloyd Blackford – known to everyone in Reggae circles
as Lloydie Coxsone – and his long-standing colleague on the
microphone, Denzil. I remember going into Columbo's one
night and Coxsone were playing and I saw the great Jamaican
singer Alton Ellis just hanging out in the club. I was blown
away with the place.

People ask me what it was like, being a white guy going
to clubs where it was all black people. 'Didn't you feel intimidated?' The answer is yes, I got a few looks when I went to
some of these joints on my own, but I was so completely in
awe of Reggae that I had to go inside because I needed to
hear it in the way it was meant to be played. Quite often there
would be white women in the clubs with black boyfriends
but I hardly ever saw black girls with white boys; that wasn't
the way it was back in the seventies. I would just come in and
absorb the music; that's all I ever did. I wasn't trying to make
friends or meet people. I would stand close to the DJ, who at
Columbo's always played with his back to the audience, sitting at a turntable. Before I started broadcasting I didn't have
anyone to go with. The friends in my theatrical circle weren't
remotely interested so I had to go on my own. It sometimes
seemed like I was the only guy in town who was into this
scene apart from the Jamaicans themselves.

Slowly I came to understand there were others like me. I
was taking the bus down from my flat in Barnes to Shepherd's
Bush, a west London area with a big Jamaican community,
to buy records from George Price, who ran Peckings record

shop in Askew Road. One day in 1976 I walked in and there were these two white guys inside, Chris Lane and John MacGillivray, who turned out to be just as obsessive about Reggae as I was. I thought, 'I'm not alone any more.' They had a record stall in the Clapham Junction and Petticoat Lane markets in London called Dub Vendor, which became one of Britain's best-known Reggae retailers. They would also set up the influential Fashion Records label.

I religiously read specialist magazines such as *Black Echoes* and *Black Music* and I learned that another important record shop was Daddy Kool in Hanway Street near Tottenham Court Road. There was a hip young east London guy called Steve Barrow, who was the co-owner. He was also the Reggae singles reviewer for *Black Echoes*. He befriended me and I will always be grateful to him. Steve had a phenomenal music collection and I was in awe of his knowledge. He would later become a consultant and compiler to the famous Trojan record company and set up the excellent Blood and Fire label and sound system with financial backing from Mick Hucknall, the singer from the group Simply Red.

9

Lovers Rock

Britain's Caribbean community created an original sound in Lovers Rock, which took hold in the late 1970s. While it had Reggae at its core, it also embraced the lighter spirit of the latest American Soul.

Back in Jamaica it was a golden age for Reggae, but second-generation West Indians in Britain were equally as comfortable listening to the sounds of Motown and Philadelphia. Not all of them related to Rastafarian-influenced messages of suffering in the ghetto and, as its name suggests, Lovers Rock was rich in the language of romance.

Despite this it had its origins in London's unlicensed 'Blues' parties and clubs like the Four Aces in Dalston, where original Lovers Rock classic 'Caught You in a Lie' was sung by 14-year-old Louisa Marks at a talent contest in 1975.

Among the other stars of the scene was the female trio Brown Sugar, which included Caron Wheeler who later enjoyed success with Soul II Soul.

By 1978, Janet Kay was establishing herself as Lovers Rock's biggest star with a string of popular singles. It was at this point in the story of Jamaican music that I began my broadcasting career.

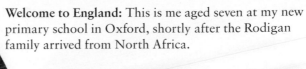

Welcome to England: This is me aged seven at my new primary school in Oxford, shortly after the Rodigan family arrived from North Africa.

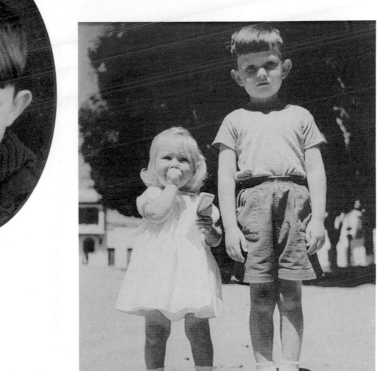

With my sister: Standing in a dusty street in Derna, Libya, with my younger sister Mary.

Mum & Dad: My mother Selina and my father Andrew (sitting either side of my cousin John Rodigan) at a family gathering in Oxfordshire.

Ram Jam: I loved this record so much as a teenager that it earned me my nickname – this copy was signed by Jackie Mittoo.

Long-haired student: This was taken when I was switching from Business Studies to Drama – I look like one of my DJ heroes John Peel.

ZIMA JUNCTION

by Yevgeny Yevtushenko

a solo dramatization performed by David Rodigan

Directed by Christopher Baker

Translated by Robin Milner-Gulland and Peter Levi S.J.

Zima Junction: I was very proud of this play, which I dramatized and performed myself. 'David Rodigan performs the piece with great brio and versatility', said the *Financial Times*.

Young actor: In an alleyway in Stoke-on-Trent, where I was working at the Victoria Theatre.

Theatre: Playing the character Tom in Ann Jellicoe's play *The Knack … and How to Get It*, at Mansfield Civic Theatre, alongside Graham Padden and Teresa Campbell.

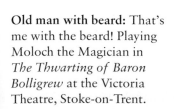

Old man with beard: That's me with the beard! Playing Moloch the Magician in *The Thwarting of Baron Bolligrew* at the Victoria Theatre, Stoke-on-Trent.

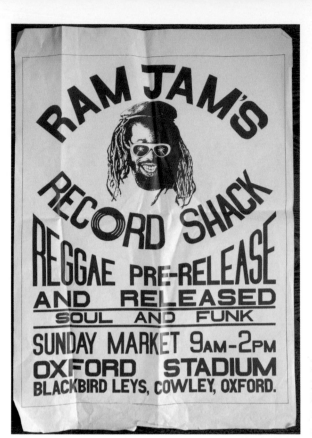

Ram Jam's Record Shack: The poster for my record stall at a Sunday market in Oxford, which my dad helped me to set up. I had another stall in London.

Radio: The start of my broadcasting career in 1978 – my publicity shot for BBC Radio London.

High Wycombe: Flyer for my ill-fated first live performance as a DJ, the bizarrely-named Tribal Hot 100. Note the misspelling of my name as David Rudigan.

Something New! Something New!
EVERY FRIDAY
AT THE
NEWLAND'S ROOTS CLUB,
HIGH WYCOMBE TOWN CENTRE,
IT'S A
★ TRIBAL HOT 100 ★
STARTING ON
FRIDAY 29th. JUNE 1979.
FEATURING
★ *DAVID RUDIGAN* ★
RADIO LONDON -- CAPITAL RADIO D.J.
(Reggae Rockers)

Every Friday it's a Different Selection, So Tune-in to the RUDIGAN Five Hour Show Case from 9 p.m. - 2 a.m.
First 10 People Free Entry, Plus Free Membership.

OUT NOW! NOW! NOW!
Two Brand New DISCO 45 on the TRIBAL LABEL.
"PEOPLE OF THE GHETO" & "SAME JAM"
By BERTHRAM SAUNDERS.
Promoter KINGSLEYMAN.

MOON SHOT CLUB
Lewisham Way S.E.13
OFFICIALLY
TOP NOTCH GIRLS TO MATCH
81 STYLE
IF NOT MAKE A SPRAT
on
Saturday 17th January
10 p.m. till dawn
 Raving To
JAH SHAKA
DAVID RODIGAN
AND
THE CONTROLLER
with CHARLESTON BLUE at the Microphone
REVOLUTIONARIES

Printed by B. & C. Printers 108 Balra Street, S.W.17. Tel.: 01-673 0413

Moon Shot Club: Playing at the Moon Shot Club in south London in 1981, alongside one of my great sound system heroes Jah Shaka.

HI FRIENDS! From 28th January 1981
Russell & King Enterprise
— PRESENT —
EVERY WEDNESDAY NIGHT
★ FROM 8.30 p.m. — 1.00 a.m. ★

Capital Radio's
DAVID RADIGAN'S
Reggae Show

— at —
THE BALI HAI
(STREATHAM COMMON, S.W.16)

FEATURING —
Also —
Neville King Sound

ADMISSION — £1.50
LICENSED BAR — BUFFET — REFRESHMENTS
★ Appearance must be acceptable for admittance ★

Coming Attraction
Wednesday 11th February 1981
Live on Stage
"ONE BLOOD"

Printed by 'Ka' PRINTING SERVICES, 200a Railton Road, Herne Hill, SE24. 01-274 1409

Bali Hai: Wednesday night session at the Bali Hai in Streatham, south London, the club where I joined up with my music soul brother Donald 'Papa Face' Facey.

King Tubby: With my hero outside his studio – it was actually Tubby who asked for the photo to be taken. I was blown away!

King Tubby's dub plate: Cut for me by the man himself at his Kingston studio, this was my signature tune track for the *Roots Rockers Show* on Capital Radio in 1979.

Phyllis Dillon: The Queen of Rock Steady. I found this picture at Treasure Isle studios and they gave it to me. She recorded one of my most valued dub plates.

DAVID RODIGAN
CAPITAL RADIO 194

Roots Rockers Show: Happy times at Capital Radio, the famous Rocking Tower in the heart of London.

Burning Spear: In the studio with Burning Spear – a much more successful interview than the one I'd previously done with him in Jamaica when I smoked his potent ganja.

At the decks: Playing live with Papa Face. I always had a cigarette on the go – and it nearly cost me everything.

'Mr Rodigan, I have been producing this show for some time and in fifteen minutes you have taught me more about Jamaican music than I ever knew. But I'm sorry, you're the wrong colour. We're looking for a black man.'

The words of David Carter, a white Canadian working as a producer at Radio London, very nearly ended my broadcasting career before it even started.

I wasn't angry. He seemed a nice man and I could see his point. It was 1978 – the year of the infamous Winter of Discontent – and economic conditions were making it extremely hard for black West Indians to find any kind of work in Britain. If the BBC's Radio London handed the only Jamaican music show on the airwaves to a white man it might be too much for the audience to bear.

'I perfectly understand,' I told Mr Carter, shook his hand and left the building. There were no hard feelings on my part.

A few days later I was playing Bob Marley's 'Is This Love?' on my Ram Jam's Record Shack stall in Putney market when I caught sight of my girlfriend Pauline, the girl I'd met in Edinburgh playing 'Summertime' on the piano. Since coming back from Scotland she had left her sister's place in Shepherd's Bush and moved into my shared flat in Barnes. As she came running through the rain, she had a big smile on her face and a letter in her hand. 'You've got it,' she screamed at me, 'you've passed the audition.'

Given the circumstances under which I'd left Radio London's studios in Marylebone High Street – having been told I was the wrong colour – I was surprised to say the least.

Going for the job in the first place was Pauline's idea. 'Steve Barnard's Reggae Time' was a show I used to listen to every Sunday lunchtime without fail. I used to record it on cassette tape so I could hear it all over again. One day they announced on air that Steve was leaving and they were looking for new presenters. Pauline, knowing my love for Reggae and displaying the innate confidence of an actress in wanting to audition for a dream part, immediately said, 'You should apply for that!'

I didn't agree.

'Don't be ridiculous. I'm not black – they won't give me a job.'

I knew Steve Barnard was black and I was quite sure the station would be looking for someone from the West Indian community as his replacement.

But Pauline wouldn't be dissuaded. She wrote a letter on my behalf without telling me. Her application got me the original audition and I went down to Radio London on a sunny morning and everyone in the basement was black, apart from me. I could see them thinking, 'Who is this guy?'

I was a nervous wreck. I approached the audition in the way an actor would approach a part. I scripted everything and made extensive notes because I wanted it to be absolutely correct. It was supposed to be a half-hour interview but they stopped me after fifteen minutes and turned everything off. That was when the producer David Carter emerged, shut the door behind him, and told me of the colour problem.

But after I left the building they must have had a change of heart. Instead of leaving the recording of my audition on the cutting-room floor they kept it and played it, along with some others, to a select group of people in the Reggae industry. And these listeners – I assume black Jamaicans – must have liked it because they picked out my tape on account of what I said in those fifteen minutes. I've no idea if they knew I was white.

Radio London made the decision to team me up with a Jamaican called Tony Williams, who was already working at the station on a Soul show. To hedge their bets they chose two more presenters as well and the rather odd idea was that all four of us would co-host together. We were given training by the BBC to be co-presenters.

I was still trying to run my little record-stall business. On the morning of the broadcast of my first ever Radio London show, in September 1978, I set up the Ram Jam stall at Hackney greyhound stadium in east London. The rain was torrential and unremitting. At the end of the morning, having sold virtually nothing, I packed my kit and caboodle into the back of my racing green clapped-out Morris 1100 car and drove home soaked to the skin.

As I went through the streets of the City of London that Sunday lunchtime, the financial district was inevitably quiet. Tuning to the intermittent medium-wave signal from Radio London, I listened to the show, which had been pre-recorded. I can't say I enjoyed the odd experience of hearing my own voice, but at least I was on the airwaves.

After a while Radio London dropped one and then another of the presenters and it was down to me and Tony Williams. We co-hosted the show for a while and then it was agreed we would present it individually on alternate weeks.

Recording the radio show made me a bag of nerves, even when there were four of us – in fact, the team approach made things worse. When I was alternating with Tony, they changed the name of the show from *Reggae Time* – as it had been called when Steve Barnard was presenting – to *The B&B Show*. To this day I've no idea who came up with that or even what it means. But in the West Indian community the show was widely known as 'Rice and Peas' because it was on when Caribbean families were having their traditional Sunday meal.

Radio London had a fine reputation because it was a station for the capital city and its people. The Sunday-lunchtime show had a massive audience and there were few West Indian households that weren't tuned in.

From very early on my approach to broadcasting was that you needed to be a companion to the listener. I felt that you were invited into someone's front room, their car or bedroom and you should behave accordingly. You would never patronize, shout or be demonstrative, because that would be an invasion of their space. You were a guest and you had to remember that.

I also understood that the music was paramount and it came ahead of the presenter, who was simply there to introduce the records, which themselves would do the talking. When you committed to the fader you had to continue with that movement – you couldn't bring the music back up.

It wasn't only West Indians listening to 'Rice and Peas'. Jamaican music had become well established. It hit the Pop charts in the late sixties and by the time I started broadcasting it was clearly recognized in Britain.

One of the problems I had with my early broadcasting was getting to sound more natural and less scripted. For years I continued writing it all down and making precise notes. It reflected not just my love for the music but also the fact that I was incredibly nervous.

I always felt a need to contextualize the records. I thought that was the responsibility of a broadcaster when dealing with a specialist subject. Jamaican music already had a great history and I wanted to secure for it all the credit I thought it deserved – and for that the audience needed all the information.

This enthusiasm for the music was one of the first things people commented on. It helped me to get known and because I didn't do any public appearances the listeners all thought that 'this guy Rodigan' was black.

But there was no hint of a Caribbean accent because I never tried to be Jamaican. I couldn't try and speak in patois because that would have been demeaning and insulting. My position was that I was a radio presenter so I spoke in standard English – just as I'd been taught at Rose Bruford drama school.

Coming from that acting background I was conscious of enunciating my words and needing to be clear and precise. When you first go on radio and start speaking it's not entirely natural. The idea is to make the sound of your voice more relaxed and informal, even if you're actually full of nerves. And of course you must avoid being patronizing and boring. I soon realized I needed to be able to laugh at myself and be less serious while imparting what I considered to be vital information about this all-important music.

Another lesson I learned very early on was that when you play a record you never 'crash the vocal' by continuing to talk over the start of a song. We were trained at the BBC to work with a stopwatch. You timed the song from the very beginning to the start of the vocal and you knew exactly when there was a bridge and how and when the record ended. With that information there was never an excuse for talking over the singer.

'Rice and Peas' went out at Sunday lunchtime but it was pre-recorded on Saturday morning. It was too complicated a show for it to be made live because we presenters were still raw.

My arrival in radio coincided with an explosion of British Reggae. Pioneers ranged from Birmingham's Steel Pulse, who arrived with 'Ku Klux Klan' for Island in 1978, to London groups such as Aswad, Anthony Brightly's band Black Slate who had the hit 'Amigo' in 1980, and Dennis Bovell's group Matumbi. This was the cream of British Roots Reggae.

The Lovers Rock movement – love songs which combined musical elements of Soul and Reggae – had taken off in south London in the late seventies and made stars of people such as Janet Kay, Carroll Thompson and Louisa Mark. There was an explosion of musical creativity in the country's Caribbean communities, especially among the black youth that had grown up in the UK.

In fact, we were approaching a high point for Reggae in London. Richard Branson had just gone to Jamaica and signed numerous artists for his new record label Virgin Frontline. He had great acts such as The Abyssinians, the Mighty Diamonds and U Roy. Chris Blackwell's Island Records, which had big offices in London, had signed Burning Spear and the Wailing Souls. Bob Marley and The Wailers had played their two great concerts at the Lyceum in 1975. It was an amazing time.

From the time I was on Radio London in 1978 I was a writer for *Black Echoes* music paper. I reviewed Reggae releases and had to get my copy in every week. Those deadlines used to drive me up the wall.

Black Echoes had offices near Islington market in north London and if I didn't finish the reviews in time to send them in the post I had to drive up there to hand the copy in person-ally. The publication is now called *Echoes* and I'm good friends with its esteemed Reggae writer, John Masouri, who is deeply knowledgeable and has a very similar sense of humour to me. I wrote for *Black Echoes* under the name of Sky Juice – the Jamaican syrup and ice drink – in order to protect my real identity. But I couldn't keep the secret forever.

Castro Brown was one of the most important figures in British Reggae and had an office and shop in Battersea, south London, as well as running a record label with the great singer Dennis Brown called DEB Music (the initials of Dennis Emmanuel Brown). Castro was a great character; a promoter and entrepreneur who had the most amazing luck as a gambler and was famous for putting everything on a racehorse and winning.

In his office he had a big desk – like an executive from Tamla Motown – and I remember him reading *Black Echoes* one day and exclaiming, 'If I ever find this raas-claaat Sky Juice . . .! Him disrespect mi music!'

I sheepishly looked at him and said I'd got a confession to make. 'Look, I'm sorry, it's me, I'm Sky Juice.'

'Ah-you?' he asked me. 'But David, how could you write about my music like this and disrespec' it?'

'It's just my opinion . . .'

Not long after that I stopped writing the column because it was too much. I realized I exerted a lot of influence. If I was giving a record a bad review and also not playing it on the radio then it was like the record didn't exist.

I was getting pressure from producers. 'Bwoy, Rodigan nah play mi tune on di radio. Him seh mi tune nah good! An' him nah write it up. It nah work! Y'affe support di music!'

I learned early on that a lot of record producers and artists couldn't take criticism. I was supposed to like everything. It reminded me of an old actor's joke about the two most useless things in the world: the Pope's balls and a good review in *The Stage* – the paper bought by everyone in the theatre world. There was never a bad review of any play in *The Stage* because it was usually written by an out-of-work actor who didn't want to insult anyone he might later work with. Reggae producers expected a similarly easy ride.

But I wrote honest reviews in *Black Echoes* because I thought it was the only way to conduct oneself. There's a saying: 'The truth is an offence but not a sin'.

I also came under unwanted pressure from various individuals to play records. In one very difficult situation an experienced Reggae producer and former artist tried to get me to accept 'payola' by passing me a brown envelope of cash in a pub opposite the radio station. When I refused to accept the bribe he appeared bemused and asked why.

'Because then I will always be your boy,' I answered, 'and have to play everything you want.'

10

Dub

One of the most distinctive sounds in the whole Reggae spectrum, Dub is typically a rich instrumental soundscape in which multiple effects are layered onto the drum and bass of a song after the vocal and melody have been removed.

It began in 1972 when the great Osbourne 'King Tubby' Ruddock began to experiment mixing records in four-track at his home studio in west Kingston. Tubby was an electronics whizz kid and musical pioneer. He used sound effects, delay, reverb, echo and other techniques to transform tracks and in doing so created a brand-new genre of Reggae: Dub.

His 'Dub versions', or instrumental B-sides, became in great demand and Blackboard Jungle, the 1973 album he made as one of numerous collaborations with Lee 'Scratch' Perry, became one of my most prized records. Tubby also worked prolifically with Bunny Lee, while other engineers such as his disciple Lloyd 'King Jammy' James, Philip Smart and Errol 'Errol T' Thompson also became revered Dub producers.

By the time I finally reached Jamaica at the start of 1979, Dub was at its height and King Tubby was one of my idols.

Snow was on the ground when we took off from Heathrow Airport and that was no preparation for the wall of heat that hit me as I crossed the tarmac to the terminus on arrival in Jamaica.

It was January 1979 and I was still very short of money. My broadcasting job at Radio London paid £12.50 a week – £25 split between me and co-presenter Tony Williams. My Jamaican adventure was essentially a business trip.

I'd built up this network of Reggae friends, and Chris Lane and John MacGillivray introduced me to Dave Hendley, another collector and a professional photographer, and Mo Claridge, who had a music distribution business called Mojo. It was Mo who came up with the idea that I should accompany him and Dave on my first pilgrimage to the hallowed 'Land of Wood and Water' that I had dreamt about for so long.

Mo had just founded a record label called Ballistic and was signing up key Reggae artists, including Prince Lincoln Thompson and the Royal Rasses. As a contribution towards the cost of my trip I wrote some sleeve notes for two albums that Mo was making, one for the Royals vocal group and a Dub album produced by the brothers Jo Jo and Ernest Hookim, who ran Channel One studios.

That first night in Jamaica we stayed at the house of a friend of Mo's at Edgewater, a housing estate outside of Kingston. During that evening the Jolly Brothers turned up at the house. They had just recorded a beautiful song, 'Conscious Man', for the eccentric genius producer Lee 'Scratch' Perry. Mo had licensed it and the track was getting a lot of radio airplay in England.

Jamaicans have long had a fixation with the British shoe brand Clarks and the first thing the Jolly Brothers said to Mo

was, 'Did you bring any Clarks booties for us?' They specifically requested them and when you visited Jamaica in those
days you were expected to bring stuff with you, especially
Clarks.

I found it very difficult to sleep that night because I was
so excited. And the local mosquitoes ate me for dinner. I was
woken by the heat and the sound of a cock crowing. I looked
outside at what appeared to me an estate of bungalows. There
was a bus parked up and I realized from the queue of people
it was a mobile shop, so I wandered over and bought breakfast – some juice and the traditional Jamaican fare of bun and
processed cheese.

We weren't tourists, we were on the island to do music
business – and there was no time to lose. Jo Jo Hookim sent
a minibus for us and we headed straight to the Channel One
studios in Maxfield Avenue, west Kingston. En route, Dave
Hendley – who'd been to Jamaica the year before with Lane
and MacGillivray – spotted the roots singer Earl Zero, who
is best known for writing the song 'None Shall Escape the
Judgement'. We got out of the minibus and I was introduced
to him.

Shortly afterwards I found myself standing in the blazing sun outside Channel One. I was spellbound and felt I'd
finally arrived. The studio had a big imposing frontage and
a black sign with 'Channel One' painted on it in white. It
was very busy. We went through a gate into a yard and the
keyboard player Winston Wright was playing dominoes with
other musicians. There were a lot of people milling around. I
had brought a tape recorder to gather material for my Radio
London show and did an interview with Ernest Hookim, asking him about the early history of Channel One. He explained

that the Hookims ran jukeboxes around the island, for which they would provide the records. Ernest became fascinated by the sound of Reggae and decided to build his own studio.

On the corner of Maxfield Avenue was a juice vendor selling delicious papaya. There weren't many cars about but lots of lads on bicycles and people riding motorbikes without helmets. And there were handcart men, pushing incredibly sturdy vehicles that were mobile shops, selling bun and cheese, crackers, juice, beers, chewing gum. One song seemed to be playing continuously everywhere on the street – 'Kingston 12 Tuffy', an anthem on ghetto life by The Morwells.

It was a whirlwind first full day in Kingston. We hired a Japanese car from a rental service on Up Park Camp Road and – after the savaging we'd had from the mosquitoes in Edgewater – checked into a guesthouse with air conditioning on Halfway Tree Road called the Green Gables Hotel. Then we jumped into the car and headed straight to the mecca: King Tubby's studio at 18 Dromilly Avenue.

Dromilly Avenue, which was in a rough part of west Kingston, wasn't a recording studio so much as an electronics shop. Tubby repaired all types of electronic goods: hairdryers, radios – if it was an electronic piece of equipment you could be sure he could fix it.

He had his own sound system, King Tubby's Hometown Hi-Fi, which used to play in that western Kingston neighbourhood and was hugely popular. But the police broke up his dances on more than one occasion so that in the end he stopped playing.

I have a clear memory of the first time I saw the name King Tubby. It was 1974. I had been down to Lee's Sound City record shop and bought a song by Larry Marshall called

'I Admire You', which is on a label called Black and White. I turned it over, played the other side and couldn't believe what I heard. It was a track called 'Watergate Rock' and on the label it said 'King Tubby'. It was actually the same song as 'I Admire You' – an instrumental Dub version of it – but with such sound effects that you could hardly recognize it. I ended up playing 'Watergate Rock' more than 'I Admire You', even though I love the original song too. That was an Osbourne Ruddock creation and that was what he did – Dub.

We drove out in the late afternoon and it quickly became dark. The sun in Jamaica goes down just like that – whoosh! Tubby's house was a bungalow with a side gate. As you went through into the backyard there was a wooden shed, like a summerhouse, where a number of musicians were gathered.

We were ushered into the studio, past a lathe where someone was working, and through a creaking door. I had arrived in the inner sanctum. There was a voice-recording booth the size of a broom cupboard filled with egg boxes and foam, and that's where the artists would go to sing.

We were welcomed by King Tubby's recording engineer, Lloyd 'Prince Jammy' James. Prince Jammy was just starting to venture into record production – a year later, at Mo Claridge's home in London, I would meet up with him and his good friend Ken 'Fatman' Gordon, one of the leading figures in the UK sound system world.

As Jammy greeted me in Kingston, he took me into the studio. There was a man standing there, quietly staring. Jammy said, 'Tubby, I'd like you to meet David Rodigan. He is a radio DJ from London and he's supporting our music.'

Tubby gave me a long look. He extended his hand. I asked if I could record an interview with him and he said, 'Not now.'

He was very quiet and reserved. The studio was immaculate, the floor shone and there was no smoking allowed whatsoever. Everything was of its place and to its place.

My reason for going to Tubby's was that I wanted to cut some exclusive recordings, or 'dub plates'. So there we were – Tubby, Jammy and me – and Tubby said, 'What do you want to cut?' There was a sign on the wall saying how much each plate cost and I asked to hear some music.

He played a song and I listened and then he looked at me for my decision and I said, 'It's OK, I don't want to cut that.' Then he played another and again I said, 'No.' He played a third song and I rejected that too.

I was feeling embarrassed because they were playing me these tracks and I didn't want to cut them. But it was my money and I wasn't going to waste it. I was on a budget and carefully counting dollars.

The idea of cutting a dub plate was that you would have something that was unique and that no one else would be able to play. In the formal world of sound recording a dub is a copy, a reference disc. It's made from acetate – soft wax – and can be cut and then immediately played on a gramophone player. The Jamaican sound systems were the first to realize that this was an opportunity to obtain an advance copy of a record that wasn't yet in the shops. They could bypass the usual distribution process and be the first to play the tune. A dub plate could be mixed there and then for you in the studio from a four-track recording. You would have both a vocal mix and a dub instrumental mix.

Artists and producers encouraged this process because they saw it as a way to promote a record in advance. Tubby didn't have his own label at that time but big producers like Bunny

Lee and Vivian 'Yabby You' Jackson would come to him with tracks they'd made. They would leave the tapes there and encourage Tubby to cut dubs from them for the sound system men.

This was how 'Dub music' developed, because the buyers were so desperate to have stuff that was unique that engineers in the studios were encouraged to come up with ways of making completely different dub instrumental mixes of these songs – and Tubby became the master of the craft.

After I refused the third song Tubby offered, he smiled slightly at Jammy and took some keys from his pocket. He passed them to a youth and told him to open a special cupboard, which contained a fat reel of four-track tape. They strung it up into the tape machine and pressed play. I heard the now unmistakable opening bars to a Reggae classic and the opening lyrics: 'I&I go mash down Rome in pieces . . .'

I looked at Tubby and said, 'I want that cut now.'

I asked, 'Who's this?' and they said, 'It's a young singer called Michael Prophet and he's been discovered by Yabby You.' I didn't know the track, 'Love and Unity', and had never heard of the artist. But I cut two songs by him with the dub instrumentals and I got these two precious discs from King Tubby. He put them in printed Tubby's record sleeves with the logo 'King Tubby's the dub inventor' and the artwork of an eight-pointed star in gold and black. I walked out of his studio as happy as a little boy on Christmas morning.

I had been taking a risk by saying no to the earlier tracks and possibly wounding the great man's pride. Subsequently I have wondered whether he was testing me out and I like to think I passed an audition and he and Jammy played these other songs to see if I knew what I was doing.

Tubby's studio was a magnet for artists. We later returned during the daytime and Dave Hendley instantly spotted the great singer Sugar Minott, who was wearing a red weatherman hat, which was then the last word in stylish headwear among Jamaican musicians. It was so cool that the artist Trinity even toasted its attributes in the song 'Weatherman Cap', devoted to the 'weatherman cap with the buckle ah di back and di zip upon di top'. Little John, a young boy who would go on to become a leading artist, was also in Tubby's yard.

It seems extraordinary to me now but my first day in Jamaica had begun with some bun and cheese and ended up with me clutching these dub plates cut for me by King Tubby himself. In between I met the Hookim brothers, Earl Zero and Prince Jammy to name just a few. We headed back to the Green Gables Hotel, which was a home from home for the rest of the trip. It was run by an elderly Jamaican lady who had lived in Putney in London, where I had run my record stall. She spoke with an English accent. It was a quaint place and at night the bar became like a pub where members of the Jamaican Defence Force would come and drink and talk in their uptown Jamaican drawl – a rather rich accent. They were captains and senior ranks, and being surrounded by so many military types was a bit like being back in the sergeant's mess in Germany with my dad.

The next morning I accepted the offer of a cup of tea from the lady hotel owner. The concoction she brought was so sweet I could barely drink it. I asked her what she had put in it and she went into the kitchen and brought back a tin of Carnation evaporated milk. 'If you wanted cow's milk you should have asked for it,' she told me. That was another Jamaican lesson.

Outside on the streets I did feel vulnerable. An advantage was that we were befriended by the great music producer Bunny Lee, who I remember rolling into the Green Gables one morning after breakfast. Bunny – recognized everywhere by his sailor's cap – has been responsible for some of the greatest Jamaican recordings ever made. With him around we were safe. But he wasn't the only music person to seek us out. It soon got out that there was an English record company executive in town – Mo Claridge – and artists started showing up outside the Green Gables with product they wanted him to release. What's more, Dave Hendley was then the consultant A&R for Trojan Records and he was responsible for signing artists as well.

I even had offers myself. One day I headed down to Skateland at Halfway Tree, the famous Reggae venue where so many shows I'd heard about back in London had taken place. I took photographs with Glen Brown, a musician and brilliant eccentric producer, standing outside Skateland next to a sign saying 'No Ganja Smoking'. At the Kingston waterfront the singer Freddie McKay gave me a cassette and said, 'Why don't you release my album?' I had become swept up in the whole business and I remember going back to England thinking I would love to release this amazing record. I decided not to because I thought it was important to maintain a neutral position as a broadcaster, with no allegiances to particular artists.

I had no interest in doing the usual things tourists do in Jamaica. Instead I went down to Treasure Isle studios, where Duke Reid built his recording empire, and met Marcia Griffiths – one of the great Jamaican voices and a member of the I-Threes, the famous harmony singers for Bob Marley and The Wailers.

I went there with Errol Thompson, who was a Jamaican radio DJ and Marcia's partner, and as I climbed the rickety staircase at Treasure Isle, there she was, wearing a long blue dress. I had my picture taken with her on the roof of the studios overlooking the city of Kingston. All the time we were up there I could hear this voice from downstairs: 'This one will inform, educate and inspire . . .' It was Mikey Dread voicing the track 'Rootsman Revival', his cut of the 'Stepping out of Babylon' rhythm.

'Mikey Dread' Campbell was a radio engineer for the Jamaica Broadcasting Corporation (JBC) in the days when engineers were allowed to play records back to back late at night because the stations wanted non-stop music. The Mikey Dread show was called *Dread at the Controls* and developed a cult following, with people recording it and selling it on cassette.

The show was successful because Mikey played Roots Reggae. He would broadcast instrumental dubs that he would mix at King Tubby's studio and he would put his signature jingles into the mix, using sound effects from specialist BBC albums that he found in the music library at JBC. He made other jingles that featured local Jamaican artists, such as Big Youth. The key thing was that Mikey never spoke during his show but just sequenced records one after another. It revolutionized radio because there hadn't been anything like it before. You could even buy the cassettes in England.

At that time, Mikey was suspended from work over a dispute and I met his programme controller at JBC and asked him why. He said it would resolve itself. Mikey came over to the Green Gables Hotel and we spent a lot of time talking. We discussed radio broadcasting and what was happening to him at the station. He voiced a couple of jingles for me to use on my show.

Mikey Dread was so popular he seemed unstoppable. The year after our trip, Dave Hendley released an album in the style of his show, called *African Anthem*. When Mikey came to England to promote it he stayed in my flat in Barnes. On his first Saturday night in London, we climbed into my orange Volkswagen Beetle and I took him around the West End and showed him Buckingham Palace. We went to Columbo's, the West Indian club in Carnaby Street. The record made his name and he was championed by The Clash, the English punk rock band.

Later in life Mikey became very unpleasant to me and others. He would call me on the phone in the middle of the night to berate me. He made bizarre claims that I owed my career to him and that he had produced my radio show, which he never did. I had an inkling of that dark side to his character when he stayed with me in Barnes and a brick came through my window with a note attached to it addressed to Mikey. It was from an aggrieved girlfriend. Years later a woman approached me at a show in America to say she had thrown that brick. She apologized for breaking my window but felt she'd had no option at the time because she was young and he had treated her so badly.

During that first trip to Jamaica I also visited Harry Johnson's (aka Harry J's) studio on Roosevelt Avenue, where I spotted Bunny Wailer getting into his jeep. I approached him with Dave Hendley to ask for a photo and interview. It was too short notice and he told us no, quite curtly, although I interviewed him later in downtown Orange Street. I was impressed with Harry J's studio, with its big mixing desk.

I met Harry himself and Sylvan Morris, who was the recording engineer at Coxsone Dodd's Studio One before he left to join Harry J.

I went downtown to the famous Randy's Records in North Parade to buy music. As a white man from Europe I really stood out.

One guy at the counter started hustling me and demanding money.

'Bwoy, yuh come from Inglan, you could give me somet'ing, eh?'

I turned and found myself fronting him in my version of Jamaican patois.

'Give me a break, mon, mi jus' a record collector . . .'

He just collapsed in hysterics. He went out and when I came out of the shop sometime later he was still laughing on the boardwalk outside.

The man behind the counter told me that if I'd realized who I was talking to I might have thought twice.

'Bad man y'know? If you knew, you would not say dat. You lucky dat man find it funny.'

Spending so much time in downtown Kingston I couldn't escape from the sight of social deprivation. In the Waterhouse neighbourhood, near King Tubby's studio, I saw burnt-out buildings and people living in very difficult circumstances. One of the biggest shocks was going to Hunt's Bay, alongside Kingston harbour, in search of Prince Lincoln Thompson. He lived in a shanty town on the edge of the water where he farmed a small plot, growing callaloo and other greens. As the car arrived, children swarmed around us strangers. We were directed to Prince Lincoln Thompson's dwelling, a one-room shack built above the ground with steps leading up to it. I was introduced to his partner Binta and two or three of their beautiful children with dreadlocks.

The shanty was disturbing. But inside, the house was immaculate, considering there was a dustbowl outside with no surfaced roads. The floor of the house was shiny and clean. As someone fortunate enough to have grown up in an Oxfordshire village with running water I was humbled and embarrassed to be there and didn't know where to look or what to say. Prince Lincoln Thompson's own magnificent song 'Kingston 11' came to mind, with its moving refrain 'the ghetto is our heaven', where he describes what this life is like. He was an amazing talent as a songwriter and as a singer.

Binta sent for him and, as we looked outside, I saw this man walking towards us with the dust blowing around him. Dave took a photograph. Prince Lincoln was wearing his Rastafarian tam hat and didn't have a top on because he had been working in the field. He was lean like a fighter and looked like he had lived his life in the gym, although he'd probably never been near one. I was introduced to him and he became a dear friend – a soulful, kind and loving man, softly spoken and very philosophical.

That first weekend of our trip he rode with us as we drove to Ocho Rios on the touristic north coast of Jamaica, where we stayed in a guesthouse. One evening he picked up his guitar and sang a song – 'There Ain't Nobody Here But Me' – and I recorded it on my tape recorder and interviewed him. Mo signed him and when that song was released I was very happy to play the exclusive acoustic guitar version on my radio show.

I went to Ocho Rios to see the great Burning Spear at his youth centre. The intention was to do an interview with him but my plans went awry after he began building a marijuana spliff and invited me to share some ganja. I wasn't a pothead but neither was cannabis unknown to me. As it seemed impolite to refuse, I built a spliff too.

I turned on my tape recorder and started asking my questions, but as we moved outside the youth centre to continue the interview in a nearby field, the weed was going straight to my head. After about fifteen minutes, I realized the great Burning Spear could see that my eyes had turned red and that my interviewing was rapidly becoming incoherent because I was so stoned I couldn't make sense of the questions I was trying to ask him. I was beginning to talk gobbledygook and he started laughing and I started laughing, and I just had to sit down on the ground to get my head together.

I was annoyed afterwards. I'd had the opportunity to do a great interview with one of the biggest stars in Jamaican music and I'd literally blown it. I couldn't handle the ganja. But it was difficult to say no.

It seems extraordinary to me now how much we crammed in during that first trip to Jamaica. One of the great highlights was visiting the Black Ark studio, home of one of the most brilliant and eccentric producers of them all, Lee 'Scratch' Perry.

I remember approaching the building in Cardiff Crescent in the Washington Gardens district of Kingston. I was with Mo and Dave, and as we got closer to the Black Ark itself we heard this strange rustling coming from the garden. It was Lee Perry, pottering around among his plants. Mo – who'd licensed a track that Scratch had produced, 'Conscious Man' by the Jolly Brothers – called out to him: 'Lee Perry?'

'My name is not Lee Perry,' came the reply. 'It's Pipecock Jackson.'

Scratch's behaviour had always been unusual, but at that stage of his career it was simply bizarre. Part of that was changing his name to Pipecock Jackson.

As a long-time fan of his music I was concerned, but I also found it slightly amusing. I wasn't quite sure how much of it was a slightly wacky mind game that he was playing with us and others and how much was an escape route.

One story I heard was that he was becoming frustrated with the pressure he was getting from artists and gangsters who wanted to use him to further their own ends. It meant he was not able to get on and produce the records he wanted to make, which, for an artist of his undoubted genius, must have put him under a lot of stress. So he cultivated this façade of being slightly mad, even wearing ballet tights and cloaks, so that nobody wanted to have anything to do with him. That theory would make a lot of sense – but the only person who knows the real truth is Lee Perry himself.

That day in January 1979 he was in a jovial mood and after we talked to him in the garden we went inside the hallowed Black Ark itself. For me it was a big moment – only I was shocked to discover that the keyboards and other instruments had been daubed with paint and were no longer functional. Everywhere was this heavy gloss paint, a lot of it in the Rasta colours of red, gold and green. There were lots of X's drawn on the walls and Scratch had scrawled numerous statements and clever wordplays around the place. It was altogether extraordinary but the Black Ark was no longer functioning as a practical recording studio.

I was blown away just to be in his presence. He was such an innovator and personally responsible for creating a unique sound. Perry has been a great pioneer in Jamaican music – the first album of his productions, *The Upsetter*, came out in 1969 – and at the Black Ark's peak he was making wonderful records such as Max Romeo's *War Ina Babylon* and *Heart of the Congos* by The Congos. He also made the first Dub album, *Blackboard Jungle*, which was mixed by King Tubby and is a phenomenal creation rhythmically. That record is a work of art; I think they only pressed 500 copies of it.

What surprised everyone about 'Scratch' was that he achieved these extraordinary sounds by using just two Teac reel-to-reel tape recorders. How did he do it? It was by a repeated process of overdubbing additional vocals and instrumentation onto one of the four tracks on the tape, and dumping each overdub onto the original recording on a separate track, thus creating a unique and densely layered sound.

There we were, standing in the Black Ark on the engineer's side of the studios, talking to the great alchemist in the very space where he created his magic. A year later Scratch burned the place down.

11

Dub Plates

These special acetate discs, including the ones I ordered from King Tubby on my first trip to Jamaica, are the most precious commodity of my trade as a Reggae DJ.

The original purpose of a dub plate was as a promotional tool. They were recorded prior to the release of a vinyl record and distributed by producers to sound systems to get a track listened to. The 'sound boys' saw a way to get tunes ahead of the competition. They are sometimes called 'soft wax', because of the delicate texture of the acetate, which is usually layered over a ten-inch metal disc.

Dub plates became even more exclusive as the practice grew of artists quoting the name of the sound system – or in my case radio DJ – in a unique recording of a track, called a 'special'.

My dub plate specials are the most treasured possessions in my record box.

But at this early stage of my career as a live performer I was struggling to overcome some major confidence problems as I started to appear on stage.

One of the most important locations in British Reggae was as unlikely as you could imagine. Behind the net curtains of

Nassau Road in suburban Barnes, close to where I rented my room in a shared flat, there lived a couple called John and Felicity Hassell. John Hassell was an elderly white man who we referred to as 'Mr Magoo', after the short-sighted cartoon character, on account of his thick spectacles.

And Nassau Road, or Mr Magoo's, was where everyone in London would go to cut dub plates – it was Britain's nearest equivalent of King Tubby's studios at 18 Dromilly Avenue in Kingston, Jamaica.

You would knock on the door and Felicity would answer. She smoked cigarettes and John smoked cigars. It was a lovely big old house. You came into the hallway and turned left, and the front room had a German cutting lathe on which the dub plates would be made.

There was always a distinctive fragrance at Nassau Road from the wonderful smell of acetate, on which dub plates are cut. The finished disc is heavier than a vinyl record and often referred to by sound systems as 'Black Steel'.

John was a distinguished sound engineer with a remarkable ear for music and frequency. He worked with the pioneering Australian engineer Graeme Goodall on building Federal Studios near Kingston, the first professional Jamaican recording studio, where the idea of cutting dub plates as tools for promoting records began.

In London, John had a small mobile rig which he would take out to record all sorts of entertainers, including the television comedian Jasper Carrott. The Reggae fraternity heard that he had a dub cutter and word got around. He was soon making a good living, as people knocked at his door at all hours with tapes that they wanted transferred and mastered.

The earlier in the morning you arrived at Mr Magoo's the better, because you would join the line. But the chances were that when you went there, Jah Shaka, the great and veteran London sound system man, was already in front of you in the queue, having coming straight from a long night in the studio. Shaka's prolific cutting of dub plates is legendary. He must have at least ten different versions of the Johnny Clarke song, 'Death in the Arena'.

There are certain people I owe a debt of gratitude to for the position I've been able to hold in the Reggae world. One of them is Jah Shaka, who I've always worshipped as a pioneer of the art of sound system. I was enthralled by everything he did and by his unbridled enthusiasm in playing this music in the most devout way. He has great faith in Rastafarianism and deep knowledge of the cultural aspects of Rastafari. Not many people know about his charity work in Africa.

When I first met Shaka in the late seventies I was running a record shack. It was before I was on Radio London but he always greeted me with a smile and was very friendly. Shaka and John Hassell really got on. Although he is a serious man when it comes to his music, Shaka has a very dry sense of humour. He can go from a London Cockney accent straight to Jamaican, and he knows all the big Reggae artists personally; they all respect and love him.

You would walk into Nassau Road and Gregory Isaacs might be there giving different mixes and advanced copies to Shaka, so he could make them into dubs. I saw so many artists in that house; the Twinkle Brothers, Jah Woosh, Pat Kelly, Al Campbell.

One day I went to Mr Magoo's and Barrington Levy was asleep outside in a car. He was sixteen years old at the time and joined me that day on my radio show, speaking on air in this teenager's voice. He had signed to Greensleeves and there was a big buzz about him.

On another occasion when I was at the house, the doorbell rang and it was Dennis Bovell, one of the figureheads of British Reggae. It was only 8 a.m. but I was ahead of him in the queue. Dennis said, 'David, I know it's your cutting time but I've just come from the studio and do you mind if I cut this dub? I've got a hit record here – I know it's going to go to number one.'

I agreed to let him go first and he strung up his tape recording and cut the dub with John Hassell. It was Janet Kay's 'Silly Games'. I stood there watching Dennis bouncing up and down with excitement and I knew immediately that it was indeed going to be a hit record.

Soon afterwards Janet Kay was the featured artist at what was my first radio outside broadcast for Radio London, in Brockwell Park, Brixton, south London. There was speculation in the crowd that 'Silly Games', which Janet performed to great excitement, would match Dennis's prediction and reach number one in the national Pop charts. In fact it peaked at number two.

I did another live broadcast from the Earl's Court Ideal Home Exhibition in London, where the great Dennis Brown sang 'Money in My Pocket', which was another Pop hit. As a result of that show I got to meet many important Reggae artists and interviewed on air two of The Abyssinians – Bernard Collins and Donald Manning – as well as the 'Cool Ruler' himself, Gregory Isaacs.

For me to get this close to these stars was almost indescribable.

My contact with the artists increased after I started to be invited to go to record company offices and meet people like Gaylene Martin, who did the PR for Richard Branson's Virgin Records.

One day a Rastaman by the name of 'Kingsleyman' turned up at Capital Radio, looking to make me a proposition. He was a live music promoter based in High Wycombe, a town in Buckinghamshire, just outside the capital. 'I want to give you your first show,' he said. I was flattered and agreed to my debut public performance.

'Something New! Something New!' was the headline at the top of the flyer. The dance was – quite bizarrely – called 'It's a Tribal Hot 100' and was planned as a weekly event on Friday nights at 'Newland's Roots Club' in High Wycombe town centre.

They managed to spell my name 'David Rudigan' and potential customers were promised: 'Every Friday it's a Different Selection, So Tune-in to the RUDIGAN Five Hour Show Case from 9pm-2am.' The first ten people through the door got in without charge and were granted free membership of the club.

It was 29 June 1979. The audience was mostly from the West Indian community in High Wycombe and – to be fair to the job that Kingsleyman had done – the place was absolutely heaving.

I turned up on my own and – just as I had been when I went to do my first radio audition – I was a bundle of nerves.

Did I learn a lesson that night!

Totally misjudging the audience, I'd gone to a studio and made lots of exclusive dub plate recordings especially for the gig. I was trying to impress the crowd with my upfront Reggae knowledge and hard-to-get selections. But I was going way too deep for them and playing stuff they didn't know. In fact I was playing music that no one knew apart from me because I'd cut these dub plates personally. To the crowd, who just wanted to hear the hits, this was utterly baffling, and after fifteen minutes they must have been thinking, 'Who is this guy?' If you imagine a whirlpool in the sink, then I was in it, circling the plughole.

It was my first lesson about the difference between being a radio DJ and being a club DJ. As a radio DJ you can play new music because you want people to be aware of it – but if you do that as a club DJ you can have people walking out the door, which no doubt was the case that sorry night.

The B&B Show on Radio London was only a Sunday job. To supplement it I was doing acting at the Deptford Albany theatre in south London and still working for Lee Laing during the rest of the week at Lee's Sound City record shop. Its latest incarnation was a hole-in-the-wall store inside the Peckham Rye railway station in south London. I was making the journey to work there by driving all the way across London from Barnes in a beaten-up old Volkswagen.

Everything changed for me one Friday evening when I had a phone call from Tim Blackmore, the head of music at Capital Radio. He wanted to meet. He came down to Peckham Rye dressed in a pinstriped suit, with a very distinctive beard and balding pate. Being a Friday evening, the place was packed with Reggae punters buying their seven-inch singles.

It was a bizarre situation. Tim was terribly well spoken and didn't look remotely like anyone in the radio industry, let alone the Reggae scene.

He told me years later that his father had told him, 'If you are going to do something, do it well and always be different.'

In the broadcasting world he was certainly that. He would become the producer for the famous *BBC Radio 1 Roadshow* but at that time he had just left the BBC to join Capital, a fledgling station set up by Richard Attenborough, who was a broadcaster before he became one of Britain's finest actors. Attenborough decided that London needed a commercial radio station and Capital became the hottest thing on the airwaves.

The man in the pinstriped suit walked into the Reggae shop in Peckham, shook my hand and said, 'Hello, I'm Tim.' Given that he'd come all that way to see me, I knew it was an important moment and I said to everyone in the shop that I had to close down early. We went to a pub round the corner and Tim made me an offer I couldn't refuse: 'I'd like you to leave Radio London and come and join us full-time at Capital Radio with your own show on a Saturday night.'

I felt I couldn't refuse.

Capital was where I really managed to gain recognition. This time I was producing the show myself. It was such a joy. I could play whatever I wanted and I was confident that I knew what was hot. I was allowed to put my mark on the show by giving it its own jingles that I'd made myself. The one that became the best known, and which I played from day one, was 'Roddy! You a Dubwize S'm'ody!'

For the first few weeks people just couldn't believe it: there was this guy playing real proper Reggae for one solid hour on Saturday nights. They'd had a Reggae radio show on Capital once before but late at night – *TV on Reggae* presented by Tommy Vance in the mid-seventies. But this was something else.

I got that show in September 1979. I had already trialled on Capital with a little guest slot, even though I was working at

Radio London on Sundays. I was asked if I would like to present a little Reggae 'News Desk' slot on Nicky Horne's Rock show *Your Mother Wouldn't Like It*. It began as a five-minute Reggae report, and then it was seven minutes, then ten and then fifteen.

Capital realized they needed a Reggae show because it had become such an important part of the music scene in the London metropolis. Punk kicked in towards the end of the seventies, and groups like the Sex Pistols, The Clash and The Slits embraced Reggae. By 1979, when I started at Capital, it was super-cool.

I called it the *Roots Rockers Show*. Originally it was 8 p.m. through to 9 p.m. after a Soul show presented by Greg Edwards, *Soul Spectrum*. Quickly they extended it until 10 p.m. and at one stage it was running for three hours, which even I had to admit was too much. Years later it found a 10 p.m. to midnight slot.

Roots Rockers became so popular that club owners complained that their venues were empty until the show finished. They would stand there twiddling their thumbs while their customers were in their cars listening to the show through to the final tune at midnight. They complained to Capital bitterly: 'Why can't you put the show on earlier, man? Yuh mash up the business!'

After my disastrous gig in High Wycombe, I recovered enough confidence to do my first live performance in London itself. This was even more traumatic. Aside from a couple of small outside broadcasts, I'd never performed in the capital in public. I could walk the streets in complete anonymity, knowing my audience had absolutely no idea what I looked like.

So when I decided to take a booking to play at the Apollo club in Willesden, north-west London, which was then one of Britain's most popular black music venues, it was a big gamble. I got the booking because I was on the radio, and for no other reason. I headed down there with my box of Reggae records.

I'd carefully worked out what I was going to play in advance, but one thing I hadn't considered was the fact that I'd have to cross the stage to get to the DJ box. So I was unprepared when the Master of Ceremonies took the microphone and told the packed venue: 'Ladies and gentlemen, for the first time in London, the man you've been listening to on Radio London and Capital Radio . . . Mister David Rodigan!'

There was lots of cheering and then, as I started to walk out across the stage, a deafening hush descended upon the London Apollo club.

Hundreds of black people took one look at me and said, 'What! I didn't know he was a white man!'

I took the microphone and started to speak and I could see that some people were holding their hands over their eyes as they listened to the voice they knew from the radio, trying to decide whether it was really me. I was struggling for words and the MC was starting to panic.

'David, if yuh nah play a record, dem a go fling t'ings pon yuh!'

I walked to the DJ box with feet so heavy my shoes could have been filled with lead. I was shaking so much I couldn't cue up the record without my trembling hand knocking away the stylus. Finally, I got the needle in place and the club's speakers burst into life with the sound of the introduction to my Capital Radio show, a dub plate cut by the greatest Jamaican producer of all, King Tubby.

'Nan-a nan-a na ...'

The fantastic crowd response came as an almighty relief.

For a while the gig went really well – then I got myself into trouble again.

'You need to play some Soul records,' I was told.

'But I'm a Reggae DJ – I don't have any Soul records.'

'You've got to play some Soul records and you've got to play them now! That's how it is in black clubs. You have to mix it up!'

This was something I hadn't really understood. I'd grown up listening to Soul music but I was so immersed in Reggae that I'd become blinkered. The saving grace was that, in those days, clubs always kept a 'Resident's Selection' of records for the regular DJs, so that they didn't have to bring in their own music. I was handed a Michael Jackson album and advised to play the title track from *Off the Wall*. I learned a lesson that night as Jacko saved my bacon.

My next gig came when the inimitable promoter Admiral Ken offered me my first residency, on Friday nights at his Bouncing Ball club in Peckham, south London. Admiral Ken was one of the great characters of the London club scene. He always dressed in a cravat and blazer as if he were running a casino in Monte Carlo. Everything he wore was immaculate. He'd have on patent leather shoes, his hair in a jerry curl and you could cut your fingers on the crease of his trousers.

I owe a great deal to Ken and his wife Vicky. He was a charming host who would waltz around the dancefloor with the ladies in the Bouncing Ball – not to get off with them but because he was a gentleman. You'd see him at weekends and he always had handfuls of promotional flyers. He never seemed to stop working and he put on some of the greatest live Reggae shows seen in Britain.

On my second night at the Bouncing Ball, Ken – in his utterly charming way – taught me another lesson on top of those I'd learned in High Wycombe and at the Apollo. Taking off his blazer, he came up on stage and gently said, 'David, you have to mix it up. Di people dem wan' get some different tune.'

He knew what he was talking about because he was a DJ himself with his own sound system. Once more, the 'Resident's Selection' box came into play. 'Hol' on a minute,' he said, and took out a stack of American import twelve-inch singles, 'Jus' watch me now . . .'

I watched my Reggae record come to an unlamented finish on one turntable, and then Ken played his American record and the whole club erupted. That was another lesson: always read your crowd and try to anticipate when a gear change is required.

'Yuh see, David, yu' affe change it up, man.'

Those fraught experiences of my early public performances as a DJ set me in good stead for what would eventually become my Saturday-night residency in Gossips club in Dean Street, in the heart of London's Soho.

Steve Walsh, a big Soul DJ in London and a larger-than-life entertainer, asked me if I would come down and play some Reggae alongside him at the club, which was owned by Vince Howard, then the only black man with a venue in Soho. It was just before Christmas 1979 and I had only been on Capital a few months when I got my first booking there. It was snowing outside and there were no more than thirty people in the club.

Soon afterwards, Steve left Gossips and Vince offered me a residency. Vince Howard was a flamboyant character who would often arrive at the club in a rented Rolls-Royce. He had a big Afro hairstyle and wore fancy handmade suits and big ruffled shirts. He worked out a lot at the gym and liked to show off that fact. He was also not slow to remind the patrons who it was who ran the club. Several times he slammed on the houselights, grabbed the microphone in the DJ box and asked the crowd, 'Do you know who owns this fucking club? I own this fucking club! And if I catch you smoking ganja, I will throw you out!' Vince had a very memorable accent – a strange mixture of Jamaican and the posh Kensington English he picked up hanging out in ritzy company.

But within three months we had Gossips at full capacity and the queue used to go round the street. It felt perfect – it was on Saturday night after the finish of my Capital show and I would jump in the car and head straight down there.

Next to me in the DJ box was Donald 'Papa Face' Facey and together we would run that residency for the next twenty years. It became one of London's best-known club nights. I'd been introduced to Papa Face by John MacGillivray of Dub Vendor when I'd told him I needed someone on the microphone at my live gigs. He told me, 'There's a guy that works on my stall called Donald Facey; they call him Papa Face. I'll send him round to meet you.'

Since the student days when I first played U Roy's *Version Galore* I'd always appreciated a good Reggae MC, the vocalists who would deejay or 'toast' lyrics over a record in a style that later gave birth to rap.

At MacGillivray's suggestion, Papa Face – who worked on the microphone for a London sound system called Mafia Black – came down to see me at the Bali Hai club in Streatham, south London, the scene of one of my early gigs. After that we teamed up and he has become a life-long dear friend and soul brother.

Mick Collins was the manager at Gossips and the main doorman was a huge guy called Bigga. One day Vince sent Bigga to pursue me along Dean Street in Soho after I quit the club following an argument over my low pay. I told him I wasn't going to return but Bigga knew he couldn't go back to Gossips without me. 'No,' he said. 'Boss say you affe come back!'

I went back and told Vince he was giving me 'praise but no raise' and we eventually came to an agreement and he persuaded me to stay.

The glass collector at Gossips when we started was Tim Westwood, who later became a long-running rap show presenter on Capital Radio and BBC Radio 1. He had a moustache and spectacles then and was a very quiet, polite, reserved man who repeatedly asked us if he could be our warm-up DJ. We already had a resident DJ guy called Mario who was doing the warm-up. But Tim was so insistent and keen we said he could have a go. Unfortunately he loved to turn the music up. He put all the lights on the mixing desk into the red danger zone. And on the last occasion he worked there he turned it up so much that he blew the entire system. Mick Collins, the manager, was furious and told Tim to leave the premises and not return. And he didn't.

Papa Face and I weren't that upset because we'd noticed after a few months of Tim warming up that when we played our big hit tunes we weren't really getting the usual response. One Saturday we came down a good hour and a half early without letting anyone know. As we suspected, he had gone out and bought the Reggae singles that were getting the biggest crowd responses in our gigs, and was playing them all before we arrived to play our set.

That night we came in the side door and when he turned round and saw us he nearly jumped out of his skin. He realized he'd been busted! 'This is not warm-up, Tim,' we told him. 'Warm-up DJs do not play the big hits!'

I didn't hold a grudge against Tim; it was a sign of his hunger to succeed and he has had a long and successful career as one of the best-known DJs in Hip Hop.

Gossips was in the heart of Saturday-night Soho and these were fantastically exciting times. The club became a multiracial hotspot for all lovers of Reggae music and you would have people from all walks of life coming down.

It was the era when people would send music tapes to their friends, and many people in the club had heard the Capital show via cassettes. People felt relaxed at Gossips. We played all forms of Reggae music, interspersed with some Soul because – as I had learned from Admiral Ken – you had to 'mix and blend'. The doors opened at 10 p.m. and we finished at 3.30 p.m. It was a real melting pot. There was black and white together. There were foreign tourists from Japan, New York and Los Angeles, Africa and Germany.

Away from Gossips and Capital Radio, I had some other business sidelines.

After my first trips to Jamaica I started to sell dub plates myself, after doing a deal with Jo Jo Hookim at Channel One studio. It was a bona fide business. I said to Jo Jo, 'You give me the tapes and we will cut these onto dub plates and sell them to sound systems in London, Birmingham and Manchester.'

Only one sound system in each city would get a dub plate, in order to maintain a sense of exclusivity. I would tell them,

'You can have this track but you can't have that.' I kept a book and it was all very organized and business-like.

Then one day I walked into Mr Magoo's, and Gregory Isaacs was there. He had a big fedora hat on and he was looking out of the window with his back to me as I walked in. I said, 'Hi Gregory', because I had interviewed him on the radio and knew him a little. He didn't respond. There was just silence.

He slowly turned around and stared at me, then said, 'You are making money off my music.' He was referring to my deal with Jo Jo Hookim.

'That's right. I've got a book and each track is listed, saying who's bought it.'

'They're my tracks.'

'But Gregory, I didn't know that. I did a deal with Jo Jo. Everyone knew how much everyone was paying.'

'But they're my tracks,' he insisted again.

His stern voice left me feeling nervous and uncomfortable.

Finally, he smiled and said, 'I hope you ate some food from it.'

I breathed a sigh of relief because the one guy you didn't want to get on the wrong side of was Gregory Isaacs.

He had recorded those songs but he'd used Jo Jo's studio. Jo Jo presumed that because they were recorded at his place he could do what he wanted with them. For my part, I wasn't hiding anything.

But Gregory had a reputation as being someone you didn't mess with. When I visited Channel One in 1979 I saw him pull up outside in his flashy Ford Capri. 'Oh my God, it's Gregory,' I thought, as he ambled towards the gate of the studio. He had this unmistakable walk, the trademark big hat, the 'ganzie' string vest with the shirt open – all in all, an incredible aura and style.

I turned to a juice vendor nearby and said, 'Oh, Gregory has left his car window open, do you think I should go and tell him?'

'No one a-go touch Gregory cyaarr! A-Gregory Isaacs's cyaar, y'know!'

That was the vendor telling me no one would even dare go near that vehicle.

Gregory was referred to as the Cool Ruler, which says it all.

As I began to get established on radio, quite a few of the big Reggae stars were coming to visit me in my little flat in Barnes, most notably Lee 'Scratch' Perry, who dropped by a couple of years after I'd seen him at the Black Ark studio on that first trip to Jamaica.

I did an interview with him on Capital and invited him to where I lived. He came to Barnes and it was even more bizarre than the encounter at the Black Ark. More than anything I was looking forward to him signing some of my treasured Lee Perry albums, given that he is one of my great musical heroes.

I handed him my copy of his *Roast Fish Collie Weed & Corn Bread* album but instead of simply signing his name, he took the pen and scrawled: 'TO DAVID RODIGAN FROM PIPECOCK JACK STONE JA LION LEE PERRY BLACK STARLING KING SOLOMON WILLIAM SHEK SPEAR EMPEROR HAILE SELASSIE'. Above the album's portrait drawing of himself he wrote 'YA GAA' and on the forehead of his likeness 'JO X HIGGS', a reference to Joe Higgs, the great Reggae pioneer who schooled The Wailers. I was somewhat bemused.

Then he set his sights on a print drawing by the Rastafarian artist Ras Daniel Heartman, which I had put up in my bedroom. I only had this one room because I shared the flat with two other guys. The room consisted of my record collection and this one picture which I'd framed but which didn't have a glass front.

Scratch went up to it with a pen and put a big 'X' across it. He had this complete obsession with putting X's on things – I had noticed them all over the Black Ark. I must confess I wasn't entirely happy about it. I'd invited him to my flat and he had promptly marked up my only picture on the wall. 'What are you doing? That's a work of art,' I told him.

But that's Lee Perry.

There is simply no one like him and he has gone through so many transitions. In his early years he was an associate at Coxsone Dodd's studio. He even voiced a couple of tunes referencing old Calypsonian risqué themes, with lyrics such as 'My name is Doctor Dick, I'm an injection specialist'.

Later he worked with Joe Gibbs and 'I am The Upsetter' was one of the biggest hits on Joe's Amalgamated label but Scratch was unhappy with that relationship. He made the single 'People Funny Boy' as an insult to Gibbs over the way he had been treated. Then he formed the Upsetter label as a platform for his unique production style, assembling musicians and getting from them sounds which others didn't seem to be able to get. He made the most stunning instrumentals such as 'Man from M.I.5', 'Night Doctor' and 'Return of Django', which put him in the British Pop charts in 1969. He definitely knew how to fire up musicians. The quality of the rhythms on *Soul Rebels* by The Wailers makes it one of the greatest Reggae albums ever made. At the height of his creative powers he was truly inspirational and a prolific producer.

The thing with Lee is that you ask him something and the chances of getting a direct answer to that question are remote. He will say something like, 'I am a fusion of air and water.' He has this amazing way of using words that sounds nonsensical but somehow later makes sense. You listen to his audio gymnastics and they're almost mystical. He is eighty years old but – even now – engaging him in conversation is to take a lesson in semantics.

12

MCs

At the start of the eighties change was afoot in British Reggae, where a new energy in the dancehalls emerged alongside the sweet sound of Lovers Rock.

The toasting style of Jamaican pioneers such as U Roy and Big Youth was transformed into something more obviously rooted in London, as a wave of young 'MCs' found their collective voice.

Switching easily between Cockney accents and Jamaican patois, artists such as Smiley Culture, Asher Senator, Papa Levi and Tippa Irie rode the rhythm at a frantic pace that ensured the style would be known as 'fast chat'. For a while it was so popular that it was exported back to Jamaica.

But the urgency in the British Reggae scene was also reflecting what was happening on the streets, where Caribbean communities were under pressure from racial discrimination and oppressive policing.

The riots that swept British inner cities in 1981 were no surprise.

In every Caribbean community there was a place known as the Frontline, a social spot where you could hang out and enjoy the street life. And on the Frontline they'd had enough.

In Brixton and Stoke Newington in London, in Handsworth in Birmingham and Toxteth in Liverpool, the story was the same: people just wanted to be left to live their lives.

'Sus laws' were used by the police to harass black people. My black friends told me many times, 'David, you will never know what it's like to be black. We are sick and tired of being stopped and searched and intimidated by the police – sick to death of it!'

I remember playing Linton Kwesi Johnson's 'Sonny's Lettah (Anti-Sus Poem)', which came out in 1979 on his *Forces of Victory* album and encapsulated the anger in the black community over the police's violent abuse of 'Sus' to stop and search so-called 'suspected' persons.

> Mama, mek I tell you wa dem do to Jim?
> Mek I tell you wa dem do to 'im?
> Dem thump him in him belly and it turn to jelly
> Dem lick 'im pon 'im back and 'im rib get pop.

LKJ's Jim gets beaten to death, which was not unusual in those times. Using authentic street language, that poem, set to music, is one of the most powerful and poignant pieces of writing I've ever heard. If you don't shed a tear at the end then you don't have a soul. LKJ is known as the Dub poet, and what a man he is!

Brutal policing and other long-standing sources of discrimination sparked an outpouring of anger as Brixton and then many other areas with large Caribbean populations exploded.

I was on air the night it began and we were getting details coming through on the news wires as the show went out: 'Riots in Brixton'.

The station bosses at Capital Radio told me, 'This is very sensitive' and I put on 'Cool Down Your Temper' by Linval Thompson.

But alongside the anger in the community at that time there was brilliant creative output. The decade was the most incredibly productive period for Reggae in Britain and I was in a very privileged position to be able to cover it on my *Roots Rockers* show on Capital.

One of the best examples of the new 'fast chat' style was 'Cockney Translation' by Smiley Culture, whose nimble lyrics switched effortlessly between the Jamaican and London slang.

> *Cockney have mates while we have spar,*
> *Cockney live in a drum while we live in a yard,*
> *We get nyam, while Cockney get capture,*
> *Cockney say Guv'nor, we say Big-bout-ya!*

During 1984 Smiley had big Reggae hits with 'Cockney Translation' and his follow-up, 'Police Officer', which made the Pop charts and cleverly used humour to expose the kind of harassment that provoked the riots.

> *As mi come out of the car, mi a think and mi a wonder*
> *What police officers could want with Smiley Culture*

The lyrics end with the officers recognizing the Pop star and asking for his autograph.

When Smiley appeared on the BBC television show *Top of the Pops* I was very proud because I knew that if this music was given daytime airplay it would be successful as long as programme controllers had the courage to back it. Capital Radio did – that's why his records became hits.

I took the new British music with me to Jamaica. 'Cockney Translation' was very popular because the Jamaican audience loved the mix of patois and London Cockney. I played Philip 'Papa' Levi's 'Mi God Mi King' on Jamaican radio. It became the first Reggae record from a British-based recording artist to be number one on the Jamaican charts, and Papa Levi became signed to Island Records.

This 'fast chat' style was pioneered in the dancehalls of south London by the Saxon sound system, another phenomenal success story in British Reggae.

Saxon was founded by Lloyd 'Musclehead' Francis, and run with his brother 'Mini Muscle' and other key members: Trevor Sax, Dennis Rowe, Henry Prento and Mikey Boops. They had an unrivalled line-up of MCs who could speed-rap in the 'fast chat' style. There was Papa Levi, Colonel, Rusty, Sandy, Asher Senator and Tippa Irie, who had chart success with 'Hello Darling' in 1986.

Saxon were from London and proud to be. Their music was saying 'We're here and we've got something to say', and it worked because they filled dancehalls.

Although my radio show opened doors for me, it also caused problems. After I had been on air for a while there was a bit of anger in the street towards me from the Reggae sound systems because I was playing new records before they managed to get hold of them. In those days, pre-release pressings came in from Jamaica every week. Because I was hot on the latest music I was hearing these songs as soon as they arrived and playing them on air the next weekend. Such fresh tunes had never been played before on radio and the sound boys thought I was stealing their thunder. 'Bwoy Rodigan,' they'd say. 'A sound man is supposed to play dem tune!'

If I didn't like someone's Reggae record they could take it personally. One London-based artist held me up against the wall in the 100 Club in Oxford Street saying I had a grudge against his group's music. I had to explain that I simply thought the group's vocal harmonies weren't good enough. When I gave him the reason he seemed to accept my position.

The most serious incident took place outside Capital Radio when Larry Lawrence turned up at the station – as record producers often did when I arrived at work – to give me music to play. He was waiting for me and asked me why I hadn't played a record he had previously given me. I told him bluntly that it was because it was no good and I didn't like it. With that he became really furious. 'Wha' the raasclaat you think you is?'

It turned into a vicious argument because Larry was a very tough Jamaican record producer with a shop in Brixton called Ethnic Fight. There were two sides to him: he could be incredibly charming but also a very militant hard guy. There was one young British Reggae band that went to complain to him about their record deal and he gave them a good hiding. That's how the business was at that time; it could be very rough.

Things came to a head one night as I was being pressured by various people about not playing certain records and I lost my temper live on air. I'd just had another big argument outside the Capital building and when I got behind the microphone I simply let go. It went something like this:

> Ladies and Gentlemen, I've got something to say. Do you ever wonder why I play certain records and you think to yourself, 'Why is he playing this garbage?' Well, I'm going to tell you why I play garbage on the show; it's because I get threatened and intimidated by certain people in the business who will not

accept the fact that I'm not playing their records. Sometimes I play them just to get them off my back.

But as of tonight you will never hear me play any garbage again. This is it. I'm laying down the law. I'm not being intimidated any more. I will play what I consider to be good Reggae and if you don't like it, tough.

The national press picked up on the story. It was big news because I had spoken out live on air.

A lot of people were supportive of me and from then on, if I didn't like a record, I just chucked it in the bin and I didn't care how much pressure the producer gave me. But that night when I played as usual at Gossips in Soho, virtually all the cars parked outside the venue had their tyres slashed. That was the comeback I got for speaking out in public.

Later, things turned even more sinister. I became the target of a vicious racist group calling itself the Black Music Protection Squad. They made images of me with a noose around my neck: 'Wanted for the rape of black music, David Rodigan'. One night, there was a big Reggae concert at the Hammersmith Palais in west London. I had introduced the show and been Master of Ceremonies, and when the audience came out at the end of the night all the cars had been stickered with a picture of me in a prison-block cell with a rope around my neck.

They pursued me for years. They would stay silent for a long time then re-emerge. Much later, after I had been on the air for more than a decade, they threatened my life. I was presenting a daytime show of many music genres. They phoned me up at the studios and said, 'If you don't play a Reggae record today you are fucking dead.' The police were called.

They issued a list of other people they wanted to take out. Tony Blackburn was on the hit list for all the years he spent playing Soul music. Chris Blackwell, the white Jamaican and founder of Island Records, was another target.

The victimization of me caused outrage among the black community because people didn't think it was fair. That meant a lot to me – black people don't take that kind of racist bullshit from anyone.

My Gossips residency night with Papa Face continued to grow. There were never fights at Gossips – it was unheard of. But on a couple of occasions people let off stink bombs inside the club and we suspected that the Black Music Protection Squad was responsible. The Gossips crowd were fine about it – they just reassembled when the smell cleared and we played on.

Word about Gossips spread. One night we were playing our records and looked out to see Mick Jagger and David Bowie together on the dance floor. There were a couple of women on the floor, which was the size of a postage stamp, and those two superstars were dancing, with no one paying them any attention. They were left alone because that's how respectful the crowd was at Gossips.

I couldn't believe it when Bowie came up to the DJ box and said, 'I recognize you! You used to play at the Ram Jam Club in Brixton!' That was a club I'd always wanted to go to when I was a boy in Oxfordshire but I hadn't ever played there. I smiled, though, and said nothing, because I was extremely flattered and couldn't believe David Bowie had actually spoken to me.

Another special night was when Prince Buster turned up. He was promptly stopped at the door by Bigga, our legendary bouncer, who told Buster he couldn't come in the club with a hat on. Buster was not the kind of man meekly to take his hat off, so there was a big altercation. We had to get special clearance to allow him to be the one exception who could enter the premises with his head covered.

Later that evening, he was standing behind the DJ decks – still with his hat on – with me and Papa Face playing records. That was a great feeling. Many Jamaican artists came to Gossips. I-Roy performed live on the mic inside the club. Then Brigadier Jerry came down and did the same.

To finish the night at the 3.30 a.m. curfew time, I always played Tab Smith & his Orchestra's 'My Mother's Eyes', a slow, saxophone-led Blues song that cleared the floor. All the lights went on and it was the signal to go home. But I absolutely loved that song and my father loved it too and used to sing it. Another reason I chose it was that the great Jamaican producer Duke Reid, founder of the Treasure Isle record label, used it for the signature tune of his radio show in Jamaica, *Treasure Isle Time*.

After Gossips finished for the night we would often head to the Candy Box, an exclusive members-only drinking club designed for people who worked in the West End and wanted somewhere to go after work. It was just off the famous Carnaby Street and you had to give a secret knock on the door. Everything inside was red and pink, with mirrors everywhere. Or we would go on to Count Suckle's Q Club in Paddington, west London, which went on even later.

I was also playing Reggae to the troops, via the British Forces Broadcasting Service (BFBS). There were a lot of West Indians serving in the British military, including

Jamaicans who had enlisted in the Caribbean. One day the BFBS presenter Adrian Love invited me on his show as a special guest and I was asked to do a broadcast of my own. As a result of that one-off, Dave Raven, head of music at BFBS, gave me a Thursday-night two-hour show. I made so many great friends among the BFBS managers and broadcasters, people such as Charles Foster, Richard Astbury, Mark Tilley, Tommy Vance and Bob Harris.

BFBS was broadcast mainly in Germany, where there was a big British Army presence, but it was also listened to in Cyprus and the Falkland Islands in the South Atlantic, where there was a bigger British military presence after the 1982 war with Argentina. It wasn't just soldiers listening. Cassettes of the show were even dropped off to Royal Navy ships so that sailors could listen to Reggae when they were out at sea.

Thanks to the BFBS broadcasts I was invited to perform at the Summer Show of the British Army on the Rhine. After I had played there in the afternoon, I went out and did a couple of gigs at local discotheques near the main British Army headquarters. I had Papa Face with me, my sparring partner from our Saturday-night residency at Gossips, and it was a new experience for us.

As a result of that I was booked for a string of shows in clubs all over Germany, and the cassettes of these events began to circulate among young German Reggae fans. One place we played every few months was Neons discotheque in Steinhagen, near Bielefeld, close to the British Army HQ. The club was run by a guy called Dougie and among the other DJs was Calvin Francis, who was in the British Army and became a successful broadcaster on the Choice FM network in London.

In the crowd it was mostly British soldiers but young Germans were there too.

Most importantly, I was going back to Jamaica year after year. On my trip in 1983 I went to record two special shows for Capital Radio. They were made with the Jamaica Broadcasting Corporation's JBC Radio and I used the station's facilities to record interviews with a host of Reggae stars including Derrick Harriott and Leroy Smart. Word got around and the car park filled up with artists who had found out the time I was recording and were anxious to get international exposure. JBC said they'd never seen so many Reggae artists at the station.

The number one radio deejay in Jamaica at that time was Barry Gordon – aka 'Barry G, the Boogie Man'. I invited him to join me and record a news segment for London listeners describing what was hot on the Jamaican chart and telling stories about the island music scene.

Barry agreed and reciprocated by making an invitation of his own. He said, 'Why don't you come on my Saturday show and be my guest?'

That offer was to have a profound effect on my entire career.

I arrived in the studio at 8 p.m. as the news was being read and, just as we were about to go live on air, Barry suddenly turned to me and said, 'Let's do a clash! You've got a radio show in England and you play Reggae – let's clash!'

He was challenging me to a contest where we would take turns to play our best records – the classic model of competition for Jamaican sound systems. It was a game-changing moment for both of us. Until then, no radio DJs had ever done a clash, only sound systems.

Barry and I had unique chemistry. We were both passionate about broadcasting and the joy of sharing music and talking to audiences. We were trained in radio and knew what we were doing in the studio. We knew what the traditional rules of radio were but we were now breaking them by putting sound system culture on the airwaves.

We started clashing at 8 p.m. and didn't finish until 2 a.m.

I'd only brought records with me for the Capital Radio show I was recording and I had to rely on those.

I didn't realize the extraordinary power of Jamaican radio, which was a bigger medium than television on the island. Not everyone had a TV but virtually everyone had a radio set and deep in the countryside radio ruled.

Our clash idea had such an amazing response from the Jamaican public that Barry and I made it an annual event. Almost the whole island would tune in.

One year Barry G and I battled tune-for-tune on JBC Radio 1 until midnight, and when the contest was over I was collected from the radio station by Arthur Reid – a Jamaican friend from London who was driving me to my Kingston hotel.

We were heading down from the inner Kingston district of Halfway Tree, where JBC was based, when we were flagged over by a serious-looking police unit in blue uniforms. It was a time of intense security and unrest in the Jamaican capital and I recognized the officers as being from the Operation Eradication squad, set up to combat organized crime. They were heavily armed and in full military kit and helmets, sitting in the back of an open-topped jeep.

All I could think of were the lyrics to Eek-A-Mouse's song 'Operation Eradication', which was dedicated to the notorious unit which fired '[M]16 and hot M1' and 'sometime they make mistake, and kill pure innocent one'.

We were stopped because they thought we looked suspicious. What was a black driver doing with a white guy in the passenger seat driving through inner Kingston at that time of the night? They told us to get out of the car and demanded to know who we were, where I was from and why we were out so late. They were mean-looking guys with a lot of firepower, and meant business. I was extremely nervous and had no idea how they were going to deal with me.

Then, like a scene from the children's novel *The Wind in the Willows* by Kenneth Grahame, 'pop-pop-pop', an old British sports car came humming down the road as if Toad of Toad Hall had arrived on the scene.

Only it wasn't Toad, it was Barry G in his open-top British MG. He loved that car. He came sailing down from Halfway Tree and spotted me under interrogation from the Operation Eradication cops. The MG screeched to a halt.

'Good evening, officer, wha' gwaan?'

'Wha'ppen Barry?'

The police recognized him immediately. My sound clash partner slowly climbed out of the MG as the officer gave his account of what was occurring.

'Bwoy, we just find these two man dem and just search them up fi find wha' dem a do.'

'But officer, yuh listen radio?'

'Yeah, mon, mi always listen radio, we love you, Barry G!'

'Yuh listen show tonight, wi'Rodigan from Englan'?'

'Yeah, mon, 'im wicked!'

'Is Rodigan you-a stop, y'know?'

I will never forget the sergeant's face at that moment. He went 'Whaa??' and turned to me and burst out laughing. The other cops were laughing too.

'But we never know Rodigan is a white man! Is you ...
Rodigan?'

To this day people still talk about those annual battles with
Barry.

13

Dancehall

Whereas the outdoor venues of the earliest Ska and Rock Steady sessions were referred to as 'lawns', the home of Reggae was known as the 'dancehall'. This was where the freshest tunes were exposed to the public for the first time.

In the early 1980s, the expression began to be used to describe the music that was made for that audience who would go out to dance and be entertained, as opposed to other genres such as Rastafarian-inspired Roots or the more experimental Dub. Yellowman and Josey Wales were among the early Dancehall MCs – by this time being referred to in Jamaica as 'deejays' – who developed the traditions of U Roy and the original toasters, and delivered lyrics over the classic Jamaican rhythm tracks favoured by the big sound systems.

Their content was more concerned with dancehall life – the latest dance steps, sexual themes, and sound clash boasting – than the socially conscious message of Roots. Bob Marley may have taken Reggae to the world but, by the time of his death in 1981, his studio-created sound was a long way from the Kingston dancehalls.

In the years that followed, with Kingston wracked by political violence, the raw sound of the new deejays, and likeminded singers such as Half Pint, Michael Palmer and Barrington Levy, meant

Dancehall had become the authentic sound of Jamaica. And in 1985, it went digital.

My annual clash with Barry G in 1985 was the biggest of them all.

It's now referred to as 'The Sleng Teng Clash', a reference to the all-conquering rhythm of that year, made from a pre-set pattern built into the Casio MT-40 computerized keyboard. It was Prince Jammy who realized the potential for this new digital sound and cut the track.

Sleng Teng changed the whole direction of Reggae. I still remember the first time I heard it. I was at Capital Radio one Saturday night and somebody arrived at reception and said, 'This is a package from Prince Jammy.' I listened to the recording he'd sent, with this reverberating digital beat, and couldn't believe it. The track was 'Under Mi Sleng Teng' by Wayne Smith. Sleng Teng is a codeword for ganja. I instantly knew the tune was something special. The next day there was a Sunday all-dayer at the Lyceum in the Strand in central London and I went on stage and told the crowd, 'I've just got this dub plate from Prince Jammy in Jamaica and this is the first time you're going to hear it!' I played it and the place erupted with delight.

To this day there's a school of thought that claims Sleng Teng and digital music has been detrimental to Reggae because it removed musicians from the process and brought in computers and synthesizers. But there was something about that song and the way Wayne Smith sang it. He was an unknown young artist but it was one of those bionic records and remains a classic.

The Sleng Teng rhythm was everything in 1985 and Barry G and I took our radio clash to another level in a six-hour battle. For days before we went on air we were going back and forth to the studios to cut dub plates against each other.

I arrived at the station in a coral-coloured American cavalry cap, which was fashionable in the dancehalls at that time. I'd bought three in different colours on a trip to Brooklyn. My dress code was always to look smart – and I liked to tell people that trainers or sneakers were only for the sports field – but when I was younger I also wanted people to see that I understood Dancehall style. I also had a pair of Cuban soldiers' caps, in black and military green, bought from a street vendor at Halfway Tree in Kingston.

The 1985 clash began with Barry and me calling out to all parts of Jamaica and putting them on notice: 'Trelawney, are you ready? Ocho Rios, are you ready? Morant Bay, St Thomas, are you ready?'

We knew the whole island was listening. I sent out a message to my faithful listeners back in London, who would hear the clash on Capital or on cassette tapes: 'Harlesden, Willesden, Wembley, Streatham, Brixton, are you ready?'

The clash started with Barry G phoning Halfway Tree police station in Kingston and speaking to the officer on duty, Constable Bascoe. He asked the policeman to flip a coin and I had to call heads or tails as to who went first.

We'd each recorded dub plates that included introduction comments making special reference to the clash.

'This is the one that's gonna make Barry G sweat, this is going to make him very angry ...' I promised listeners as I cued up my first plate, which opened with the sounds of a formal British accent and the message: 'Good evening, my name is Chief Inspector Knacker of New Scotland Yard, I have here a summons for Mr Barry Gordon, alias Barry G the Boogie

Man, who has threatened to bury Mr David Rodigan in the dub plate clash of 1985. Would you be so kind as to pass on this musical statement to Barry G from David Rodigan's lawyer?'

Then the beat began to 'Rodigan the Gorgon', a dub plate version of Cornell Campbell's classic song 'Gorgon', which I'd cut with the London singer Maxi Priest, featuring the lyric 'Comin' from London with a bag of dub plate, touch a Norman Manley (airport), you know him can't late, him a de gorgon . . .'

For almost the first half an hour of the clash we just played that Sleng Teng riddim over and again, counteracting each other. The first track Barry played was 'Put Your Hand on the Key' by Echo Minott, with the words 'Teach them, Barry G, teach them your stylee!' It was such a killer dub plate that I later heard from friends in London that everybody listening thought it caught me right on the chin and they wondered if I was ever going to get off the ropes. To be honest, I felt that myself.

Barry G had done his preparation.

There was one classic dub intro he played which began with the sound of a knock on the door and an exchange of words:

'Who are you? David Rodigan?'
'I've come to cut some dubs.'
'Ha–ha–ha, you c'yaan cut any dubs, Barry G done cut all the dub plate!'

And then came the sound of everyone laughing.

It was a very competitive contest. Before the clash I remember being at Jammy's studios. The artist Josey Wales

was there and suddenly he announced, 'I've got to go!' I realized something awkward was happening – and then Jammy
admitted to me, 'Josey's going to voice [dub plates] for Barry
G!' There I was sitting in the office and Josey was actually
next door in the studio voicing dubs that were to be used
against me on air.

But there was no animosity. The artists would do one for
me or for Barry – it was whoever got to them first. And the
dub plates were never made in an antagonistic way – it was just
for fun. Barry and I were in the control room with a desk and
a microphone, and the station engineers actually played the
records. They would offer to come in from off duty and work
on these clashes.

Immediately after the clash we asked British Airways stewards to take the recordings straight back to London for broadcast
on Capital Radio, because I was staying on in Jamaica for four
weeks.

The Sleng Teng clash caused such an impact around the
Reggae world that it was the talk of Jamaican communities in
North America. Later that year I arrived at Capital Radio one
evening and the security guard said, 'There's a chap over there
from the United States who wants to see you.'

The man was an American-based Jamaican in a Kangol hat.
He said, 'I've flown from New York for one reason: I want to
book you for a clash with Barry Gordon in Brooklyn. Name
your price and name it now!'

I wasn't sure what to say. I thought of a figure, the sum I
would normally charge for a British dance, and doubled it. He
said, 'Done – and here's your deposit!' His name was Dukie, he
had come laden with US dollars, and he flew straight back to
New York the next day.

I then had to go down to Jamaica to cut dubs for this clash. I arrived on the island in December and Dukie was there from New York doing his work as the promoter, staying in a hotel and stoking up interest. He had cut a deal with Barry G. On top of that he had booked two of Jamaica's biggest artists, Chaka Demus and Tiger, to fly up and perform as part of the same show. It was going to be a huge night.

I was cutting dubs in Jamaica right up to the moment when I was due to leave for the gig in New York. Prince Jammy said to me, 'We are going to do a send-off dance for you in my backyard in Waterhouse.' As the party began I was still cutting plates for the clash with Jammy's assistant Bobby Digital in the dub room; I came out with some of the plates and we tested them on Jammy's sound system.

There's footage of that night on YouTube and I'm wearing a floral shirt and holding the microphone in the thick of the dance, attended by a host of big-name artists including Johnny Osbourne and Josey Wales. I introduced Chaka Demus and Major Worries, who voiced some freestyle lyrics. Then one of the greatest Reggae MCs, Brigadier Jerry, toasted over the Sleng Teng rhythm at the slowed-down speed of thirty-three-and-a-third revolutions per minute. What a send-off!

Just when you thought the night couldn't get any better, Barry G rolled into the dance in his MG. He got a hero's welcome as you'd expect from the number one radio DJ in Jamaica. Suddenly the two of us clash contestants were playing records and Barry was calling for Jammy's partner Mama Iris to bring out some of her legendary bread pudding, which she did. The following day I went back to London, got myself ready and flew out to New York for the main event.

The clash took place a few days before Christmas. I stayed at the very nice Essex House Hotel at Central Park South in Manhattan and Barry G had a room there too. On the night of the clash they sent a limousine to collect us. We were both nervous because we'd never done anything like this outside of Jamaica. It started snowing. We saw queues of traffic. There was a crowd four-deep off the wall outside a large building and the line went round the block and down the street. We commented that there must be some big concert going on that night in Brooklyn, and then Dukie, who was with us in the limo, said, 'It's for you guys!' This was the Brooklyn Empire where we were performing.

We got out of the vehicle with snowflakes falling. It was a complete and utter roadblock. Years later the great Reggae MC Super Cat said to me he was in the crowd that night as a member of the audience. They called security to get us into the dressing room. When we were eventually taken onto the stage I saw the place was packed to capacity. We were both so nervous we could hardly cue up the records – we kept that to ourselves but we could both see it in each other.

I was conscious that Barry is a Jamaican and I'm not – and we were in Brooklyn playing to New York's very large West Indian community. It was 1985 and the first time I'd played in New York. The cassettes of the Sleng Teng radio clash in Jamaica had come to New York and spread like wildfire. That was the reason the dance was rammed and why the Brooklyn crowd already knew my name.

I began by playing a dub plate of 'New York, New York' by Maxi Priest. 'Start spreading the news, Rodigan's in Brooklyn ... If Rodigan can kill Barry G here he can kill him, anywhere ... it's up to you New York, New York!' That was my sign-on dub, voiced by Maxi in the basement at A Class dub studio at Clapham Junction in London with my old friend Chris Lane as engineer.

That was the night when I first played one of my most treasured dub plates – Tenor Saw's 'Ring the Alarm'. It was made for this clash. 'Straight from London to New York City, Rodigan clash with Barry G, they're both gonna play some Reggae music for we . . .'

It was one of the first dubs in the clash and Barry – who realized how special a recording it was – said to me, 'How could you play a big tune like that so early?'

Tenor Saw, who remains one of the most distinctive singers in Reggae, voiced that plate in one take. He died only three years later and hardly recorded any dubs. That one was made at the BFBS Studios in Paddington, west London, directly over the instrumental version of the record.

The Brooklyn clash has gone down in folklore as a 'history dance' because it was such a great night. A recording was made of the night and Dukie, who bought a racehorse with the evening's proceeds, sent the tape to me in fine style – delivered by a courier who flew to London on Concorde.

My contests with Barry G were always friendly clashes; some he won and some I won. The radio ones went on almost every year until 1989 when we agreed it was time to let it go.

We were very close. We were both passionate about the music and he is a natural broadcaster, very fast on the mic and very quick-witted. He has a deep knowledge of the history of Reggae and the great Studio One and Treasure Isle recordings. And he is a very, very proud Jamaican.

One enduring memory I have is of the day after one of the clashes, driving down through the countryside on the way to the Jamaican south coast to do a show in Peter Tosh's home-town of Belmont, with Barry G in his MG sports car and me in my car. In every hamlet we passed through you could hear our radio clash from the night before being re-played on cassette players. It was like being caught in an echo loop.

In Jamaica they burn cane fields deliberately. As I followed Barry to Belmont he decided he would hammer through a cane field, even though both sides of the field were already in flames. We found ourselves driving through a tunnel of fire. I thought it was absolutely crazy but it was an image I will never forget.

We played all over Jamaica. At one big show he played a Josey Wales dub plate that began: 'Run, Rodigan, Run! The Boogie Man a come!' It mashed the place up. We had another amazing head-to-head at Mr Big's, a venue by the seven-mile sandy beach at Negril – but the accommodation wasn't quite so good. The promoter opened a cottage door.

'This is where you'll be staying tonight.'

When he turned the lights on there were cockroaches running everywhere.

'Oh, no, I won't be staying here.'

I did a dance with Barry G in 1985 in Mountainside in the heartland of St Elizabeth, and as I was driving there in a hired car I became aware of all these people walking along the country roads.

As we got nearer to the venue somebody recognized me and people swarmed around the car. They were all heading to this event on foot. We played in a barn and the people danced out-side in a field. I had never seen so many fair-skinned Jamaicans in my life; St Elizabeth is famous for having light-skinned, or 'red-skinned' people as they call them.

It was a strange evening. I stood at the bar and a gentleman stood next to me and said, 'Can I buy you a beer?' I said, 'Yes, I'll have a Heineken.'

He asked me if I knew who he was. I said his face looked familiar. He introduced himself as Dandy Livingstone, one of my teenage music heroes and the singer of such tunes as 'Rudy, a Message to You' and 'Suzanne Beware of the Devil'. I had owned his 'Rock Steady with Dandy' since I was sixteen.

He had left the music business and gone to live in the country. He had virtually disappeared from the scene but was standing in a barn offering to buy me a drink. I noticed people were drinking two or three Heinekens at the same time and holding one while they drank the other. I'd heard they could party in St Elizabeth and, as the sun came up and we emerged from the barn bleary-eyed, there were numerous individuals plastered to the grass in the field.

My first public show with Barry in Jamaica's capital city was at the New Kingston Drive-in Cinema. The famous producer Gussie Clarke helped me cut a dub plate with a cutting machine that was so broken he had to hold it together to cut the plate. It was the classic 'Private Beach Party' by Gregory Isaacs, which Gregory had voiced in the studio the day before. Gussie said, 'You can have that on a dub plate' and I duly took it to the dance.

There was a big crowd. When they announced me you could see there were a lot of surprised faces because I had not appeared in person in Kingston before and I suppose I wasn't what they were expecting – they'd heard me on radio and assumed I was a black Londoner. It was another baptism – the Jamaican equivalent of my first London show at the Apollo club in Willesden.

But the acceptance I have always had in Jamaica has been humbling. Occasionally I have had people there say to me point-blank that I was the only white man they ever felt respect for.

One of the biggest dances with Barry G took place at Walter Fletcher Beach at Montego Bay on Jamaica's tourist-friendly north coast. The event was crammed full with people and I was trying to fight my way inside through a big crowd at the entrance gate when someone tapped me on the shoulder. I turned around and it was the slight figure of Augustus Pablo, one of my musical idols and one of the finest multi-instrumentalists in Reggae.

I asked him, 'What are you doing here?'

'I've come down from the hills and I'm going to play the melodica for you.'

I had to run that one through in my mind for a moment. Augustus Pablo was going to blow the melodica for me . . . in a clash with Barry G on the beach?

In those days when you were clashing, an artist could come on stage and perform for you. I couldn't have asked for a better secret weapon than Pablo.

When the moment came, I said, 'Ladies and Gentlemen, I have a very special guest. Surprise, surprise, you're not going to believe it, Barry G, follow this . . . Augustus Pablo!'

And then he walked out on to the stage, this small man blowing his famous melodica, playing the unmistakable 'Real Rock' rhythm that everybody in the crowd will have instantly recognized. I stood and watched the ecstatic response. It was the key card of the clash and there was no coming back for Barry after a moment like that.

These days Barry is on top form, with a daily show on

Mellow FM in Jamaica. He's a great broadcaster and can speak this incredible livewire jive talk. He will always be Barry G, the Boogie Man, a truly twenty-first-century pacesetter.

I will forever be grateful to Jamaica. The word that first comes to mind if you ask me to describe the country is 'intense'. It applies equally to the fierce heat, to the sweet smell of the island and its fauna and forests, and to the atmosphere in the Reggae dances. It's a place that makes you feel alive. Life doesn't get much better than a day at the seaside at Hellshire Beach. Or eating fish and bammy, which is flat Jamaican bread made from cassava, out at Port Royal, where the old pirates used to hang out in the seventeenth century.

For a while I gave a lot of thought to buying a house outside Kingston or down in Westmoreland, the parish on the far west of the island.

My Jamaica was never about resorts. For me it was about going to see Brigadier Jerry's Jah Love sound system playing in the open air at Spanish Town Prison Oval, or going to the Gemini Club in Kingston's Halfway Tree where I might see Eek-A-Mouse and Ranking Toyan toasting live.

Or maybe going to Sonic Sounds studios and meeting the singer John Holt, as I did on one occasion when he handed me a record with an anonymous white label and said, 'It's a new song; I think you'll like it.' That song was 'Police in Helicopter', one of the greatest Reggae anthems ever. On a white label! That meant it was a rare early pressing; it didn't even have his name on it.

My Jamaica was about playing on Henry 'Junjo' Lawes's Volcano Sound at Vietnam Corner in downtown Kingston, where I was the guest selector alongside Danny Dread, one of the great masters of the art. I was taken to Vietnam Corner by

Gussie Clarke, who became one of my closest friends, a real soul brother. Gussie produced some amazing records, including Big Youth's first album *Screaming Target*, I Roy's first album *Gussie Presenting I Roy*, and the Mighty Diamonds track 'Pass the Kutchie' (which some will know as the inspiration for the Musical Youth hit 'Pass the Dutchie'). Gussie's list of credentials is so long.

Whenever I went down to Jamaica it was non-stop. I wanted to get so much done and I did. I was forever chasing dubs, getting new tunes and going to dances. I wanted to immerse myself in this culture. I was fascinated by it.

I tried to avoid weed if I could. After that disastrous interview with Burning Spear on my first visit to Jamaica – when I got high and could hardly speak – I was always wary. In 1984 I foolishly had a single joint in the back of a car heading up from Kingston to Ocho Rios, and that was the last time I ever smoked. It was so strong it ripped my head off and I felt nauseous and frightened. I've not touched a spliff in more than thirty years since.

Of course a lot of the artists smoke. I remember being in Sugar Minott's studio in Chisholm Avenue in Kingston and Jah Stitch built up a chalice pipe and I had to go outside because I was getting high on the smoke in the room.

But what many people don't realize is that there are many Reggae artists who refrain from using marijuana. Contrary to popular belief, it's most definitely not an integral part of the Reggae music scene. Sly Dunbar and Robbie Shakespeare are good examples of this. When I got to Jamaica I realized that there were a good number of Reggae musicians who did not indulge in weed smoking at all.

One of my most memorable Jamaican moments came at

Coxsone Dodd's legendary Studio One. Johnny Osbourne was singing on the microphone that day and I was in the studio listening with Coxsone himself.

In between recording I started singing along with the tune, 'Lend Me You Sixteen', and Coxsone shouted out, 'Johnny! Rodigan can sing!' With that, Johnny came out and grabbed me and put me into the studio alongside Jennifer Lara on harmonies. You can hear someone shouting out 'Bo!' and that's me, I'm afraid to say. I was pretty embarrassed. Very few people know I was singing on it. It was released as a single and I have a copy, though I'm not a big fan of the tune. At least I can honestly say I've made a record at Studio One – not many people can claim that.

All this time I was riding two horses: I was immersed in the world of Reggae and enjoying success as a DJ but, at the same time, I remained committed to being an actor and my thespian ambitions had taken me onto the small screen.

I think my mother's dream was that I would one day be on *This is Your Life*, the biographical show with presenter Eamonn Andrews. I made it onto the show, not as its subject but as a guest for the actress Nyree Dawn Porter, who I had appeared with in an ITV television series called *For Maddie with Love*.

This series was significant because it was the first of the UK's afternoon soaps. I played a police detective. It also featured Ian Hendry, a well-regarded actor. He gave me one of my first big compliments in acting when he said he liked my style.

For Maddie with Love was my start in television, followed by a strange series called *Horse in the House*, starring Pete Postlethwaite as the father of a girl who was crazy about her horse. It reminded me of my teenage relationship with horse-mad Alison Archer back in Kidlington. I played a vet and Pete became a good buddy during the filming.

They say you shouldn't act with animals but it was a part opposite an exotic bird with a colourful bill that got me more recognition than anything else I performed in. Guinness had decided to use a toucan – having used images of this distinctive species in its historic poster advertising – as the star of its new television campaign. I was cast to play alongside my new feathered friend.

A real-life toucan arrived every morning, perched in the back of a chauffeur-driven Volvo with its owner. It was ridiculous – the toucan was taken care of better than I was.

Each day we filmed a different one of the ads from the series and they were very popular. But after the campaign went on air I couldn't go into a pub without someone shouting out, 'Wa-hey, it's the toucan guy!'

A TV campaign was a big deal and in those days you were paid repeat fees, so by the end of the run I'd earned a considerable amount of money. It was the sort of cash I'd never had before and it enabled me to put the deposit down on my first house in Streatham Vale, south London. I moved in the day Princess Diana and Prince Charles got married in 1981. I'd left the flat in Barnes and bought a three-up, two-down terraced house, and it had been paid for by acting with a toucan.

The acting work I'm most proud of was for *Shackleton*, a serious series for the BBC in 1983. David Preston got me the audition. David Schofield played the polar explorer Sir Ernest Shackleton and I had the part of Frank Wild, his first in command. Another member of the cast was Kevin Whately, later well known for his work in TV shows such as *Auf Wiedersehen,*

Pet and *Inspector Morse*. I knew Kevin from working together at the Victoria Theatre Company in Stoke.

Shackleton was a four-part drama documentary on BBC2 and involved a year's filming, mostly up in Greenland, with other locations being in Edinburgh and Bath. There was disappointment that we didn't have penguins in Greenland but I got very good reviews.

Something I wasn't so proud of was doing a farce called *The Office Party*, which was like the saucy *Confessions of . . .* films, where the star is typically a window cleaner who gets off with the au pair. I asked my agent, 'Who's in it?'

He said, 'How about Diana Dors, is that good enough for you? And Alan Lake, her husband, they're playing the leads and [*Coronation Street* actor] Johnny Briggs is in it and Andrew Sachs [who starred with John Cleese in the hit TV sitcom *Fawlty Towers*].'

Even though the cast sounded good, the film was a bawdy farce. I was cast as an office junior and, thankfully, didn't have to do anything untoward. Artistically it was garbage but it was a job for a jobbing actor.

Not many actors can say they've been on television playing opposite Sherlock and Doctor Who, but I can. Unfortunately, my Conan Doyle adaptation was only a forerunner to Benedict Cumberbatch's global hit: a 1984 ITV series called *The Adventures of Sherlock Holmes* in which I played a grumpy detective called Inspector Forbes who had little time for Holmes (played by Jeremy Brett). Wearing a Victorian brimmed hat of a style that wouldn't have looked out of place in a Reggae dance, I marched into the room and told him, 'Mr Holmes, I'm a very busy man – I have other cases besides this one.'

My most notable TV part, in terms of a show's profile, has to be my role in *Doctor Who*. I'm not sure how many 'Whovians' remember the character Broken Tooth. But that was me. My big moment in one of the world's best-known science fiction dramas ended up with me getting exterminated by a giant robot.

My chance came during the era of Colin Baker, the sixth incarnation of the Time Lord. It was 1986 and *Doctor Who* had been in danger of being canned by the BBC when it returned to the screens with *The Trial of a Time Lord*, its twenty-third season and still the longest-running story in the fifty-year-old series. I was in the opening four episodes, a segment called 'The Mysterious Planet'.

Equally exciting, I got to perform with Joan Sims, the great British actress best known for her roles in the *Carry On* comedy films. In *Doctor Who*, Joan was cast as Queen Katryca of the Tribe of the Free, the Doctor's latest mortal enemy, and I was chosen to play the commander of her armed forces on the planet Ravolox. I didn't have a lot of lines but I'd have taken any part to get inside the Doctor's famous Tardis time-travelling machine.

Playing Broken Tooth required me to go to Harley Street, not to have the expensive medical treatment that you expect from that address, but to be dentally disfigured. The horrible craggy teeth I ended up with were absolutely disgusting. I had to wear a bushy beard and a mane of red hair. Dressed in medieval-type clothing I looked like the haggard old hermit character who lives in a hole in Monty Python's film *Life of Brian*.

Much of my part in *Doctor Who* involved running around the same corridor at the BBC where Broken Tooth was eventually killed off at the end of the story. But other scenes were shot in the Hampshire woods, and while we filmed them we were staying in a country hotel. Towards the end of one day's shoot, Joan completely forgot her lines and announced, theatrically, 'Oh, I'm sorry, I've dried.' No one minded – we were so enamoured of the one and only Joan Sims, already a movies legend.

In the hotel that evening she said to me, 'Oh, David, dear boy, you're so lovely, come up to my bedroom and we can just go through the dicky birds, because they're not really working.' I said, 'Dicky birds?' And she said, 'The dickies? The words, dear! I've got to get them *off the page,* dear.'

I loved her. So I went up to her hotel suite and she said, 'I'm going to have some salmon sandwiches and tea sent up.' We started going through her lines but then, the next thing I knew, the great Joan Sims had fallen asleep and I was sat there looking at this famous actress as she snuffled away. Delicately, I left the room.

14

Legends

It's frustrating that so many people think that Reggae died with the great Bob Marley. Jamaica has produced so many other wonderful artists whose brilliance and originality has sustained decades-long careers and who deserve to stand in the worldwide pantheon of music legends.

My privileged position as a radio broadcaster has given me direct contact with so many of these greats, not least the other two members of The Wailers: Bunny Wailer and, when he was still alive, Peter Tosh.

I became increasingly involved in bringing the biggest Jamaican artists to the UK to perform live, which meant that I got to know the real people behind the on-stage stars.

Superb artists such as Alton Ellis and Bob Andy became my personal friends over many years. Some of Reggae's most eccentric characters, such as Yellowman, are warm and charismatic figures off stage.

I thought a great deal of King Tubby, and was deeply affected by his sudden death.

And although my listeners never knew it, I had serious worries concerning my own life that threatened to bring my broadcasting career crashing down.

The Wailers was not merely a band, it was a triumvirate of three very powerful individuals: Bob, Bunny and Peter. There was a unique fusion of talent.

Of the three, it's Bunny I have got to know best. Bunny Wailer is truly an icon of Jamaican music but securing an audience with him can be a delicate negotiating process.

The first time I saw him was in January 1979 as he was coming out of Harry J studios in Roosevelt Avenue in Kingston and getting into his Land Rover jeep. I approached him and asked if I could take a photograph and do an interview. 'Not right now,' he said, then he got into his jeep and zoomed off.

A little later, during that same three-week stay in Jamaica, I saw Bunny at Cash and Carry records in Orange Street, the downtown hangout of so many of the island's music makers. Big Youth and Gregory Isaacs were there too, and so was Junior Delgado, who acted as my intermediary because he had spent time in London and I knew him.

Delgado approached Bunny for me and said something like, 'This is David Rodigan, a bona fide radio DJ in London who is doing a lot for our music.' Bunny agreed to a short interview and I asked him for a copy of a promotional poster that Solomonic Records had just made for him – a striking head-and-shoulders portrait photograph. I asked if he'd autograph it and he agreed, but only on the condition that it would be displayed in the foyer at Capital Radio, so he shrewdly signed it: 'To Capital Radio, Bunny Wailer, One Love.' It was displayed at Capital and it's now on the wall of my music room at home.

I persuaded Bunny to give his first performance in London as a solo artist, which he did for Capital Radio at Brixton Academy. It wasn't straightforward. I flew to Jamaica with John

Burrows, Capital's head of music promotions, and we spent three days waiting and waiting for the great man to meet us at the agreed place, an open-air rehearsal area called 'Zinc Fence' in New Kingston. We finally got our audience and he took us down to the end of this small field surrounded by a corrugated zinc fence. We sat on some stalls near where a fire was burning and held a reasoning session with Bunny about why he should come to England to perform.

Neville O'Reilly 'Bunny' Livingston agreed to come and when he arrived in England I was able to get another radio interview. This time it lasted three hours and left me spellbound. He has phenomenal presence. He is a strict Rastafarian and watches his diet, so there's not an ounce of fat on him. To see him perform and leap in the air defies belief. How can anyone do that at seventy years of age? Bunny has the most amazing rich tone of voice, and what he's got to say about music and life and the politics of Jamaica is a revelation.

During that interview I asked about what I assumed to be a tough childhood in the Kingston slums. 'As a young boy in Kingston, what was life like?'

'Just enjoy!' he responded without a trace of bitterness. 'As a youth, y'know, you don't have any problems. You don't even get tired, you don't know what it feels like to be tired or even to be hungry because you have so much things to do, marble[s] to play, gig to play, kites to fly, football, cricket, table tennis, you name it. You could go to the beach ... so many things to do as a youth in Jamaica!'

He discovered his talent for music when still a small boy. 'At about seven, I used to make guitars out of bamboo and old sardine tins. We used to get the wire from the electric wires – cut the outside and get the fine strong wire that runs inside, take that and make the strings. You could really have fun, draw a lot of crowd.'

And he told me how he recruited Peter Tosh to the group that he and Bob were putting together. 'Well, Peter was also in Trench Town and he used to be a man that could play guitar. Now and then he would pass through singing his old religious songs, "Go Tell It on the Mountain". I told Bob that I know of a guy who can handle a guitar and can handle his voice properly so he said I was to bring him. We all sat down and started singing and that was it.'

When it came to describing The Wailers' time at Studio One, Bunny was far less charitable towards Coxsone Dodd's treatment of the young group than Bob had been when I spoke to him in 1980. 'What was it like working with Coxsone Dodd at Studio One?' I asked.

'Like working on a slave farm,' he said. 'You just had to work for nothing. So it was like working on a plantation. But then again, if you enjoy it, it takes away some of the burden. We were enjoying what we were doing, we were satisfied because we were relating to other people's problems and they reacted in the way that they should to accept The Wailers in the way that they did. We were for the people and the people were for us. That was where the whole binding between the people and The Wailers started because we were pleading the cause of the people and that happened because of the environment where people were struggling – peasants and the lower class of society in all the towns – Trench Town, Jones Town, Denham Town – all those [Kingston districts] are where the poorer class of people live and we were experiencing the same thing.'

That interview became a three-part documentary in the mid-1980s on Capital Radio. And I became even more of a fan of Bunny's. I just thought he made the most amazing music. I've said this a hundred times, but his masterpiece, *Blackheart Man*, is one of the greatest Reggae albums ever made. It's such an important document in the development of Jamaican music; the musicology, the structure of the rhythms, the haunting quality of the arrangements, the orchestration of the horns and flutes, even the artwork.

I have since met Bunny more than once in Jamaica on the street, usually outside a studio, and he has always had time for me. He has a very distinctive laugh.

The most memorable meeting was when I arrived at the airport in Kingston in 2005 to be told by a close friend, Henry Lewis, that I had urgent business at Anchor Studios where Henry worked. I wanted to go straight to my hotel but I trusted Henry, who has been instrumental in helping me to work with so many Jamaican artists. We screeched into the Anchor car park and Henry said, 'Come, come' and took me into one of the studios. I opened the door and who was standing there? Bunny Wailer! He was dressed in camouflage trousers and a camouflage top – and building a big spliff. He proceeded to voice two specially recorded dub plates for me – 'Rodigan is the Conqueror' and 'Run for Cover'. I couldn't have asked for a better welcome to Jamaica.

I met Peter Tosh briefly at Miami Airport when we were both in transit and found ourselves walking towards each other. I recognized him and walked up to him. He knew who I was. We shook hands and he said, 'Yeah, mon, respect for what you've done for Reggae and keep up the good work.' It was a brief encounter but a lovely thing for me, hearing that he knew what I had done.

Tosh was known, after one of his early songs, as the 'Stepping Razor'. 'Don't you watch my size, I'm dangerous', went the lyric. He was very tall with a powerful presence – vocally, musically and lyrically. He was an accomplished session musician as well. Among The Wailers in their earliest days he was *the* musician, a self-taught guitarist.

Peter was forthright and absolutely militant. The police beat him to a pulp because, when a plain-clothes officer approached him as he stood on a street corner in Kingston smoking a spliff, he said, 'What's it got to do with you?' His classic song 'Legalise It' remains an anthem. So does 'Equal Rights', which Barack Obama has quoted from.

When you're alone in a radio studio with a turntable and a microphone you don't know who is out there listening. So for someone as politically hard-core and musically influential as Peter Tosh to know about the show was really humbling.

It has always touched me deeply, as an outsider from another culture and another country, that Jamaicans at home and abroad have given me love and respect. It means so much to me that I'm not seen as a 'band-waggonist', just hitching my horse to the latest musical fad to benefit my career before moving on to something else. I couldn't ever divorce myself from Reggae – it's been with me since I was a boy.

My position on Capital, and my experiences in Jamaica, meant that I had the opportunity to bring many of the top recording artists to the station. In 1980, I was delighted to get the chance to conduct a proper interview with Burning Spear, after my attempt the previous year had descended into gobbledygook because I couldn't cope with the potency of his marijuana. This time, in the Capital Radio studio, I had the chance to do a more professional job, and Burning Spear, who is a very quiet and reserved Rastafarian, conducted himself with great dignity.

I managed to persuade Alton Ellis to be my guest on *Roots Rockers* in 1981 and he was a gentleman too. I desperately wanted to tell the whole Alton Ellis story. He agreed to the idea and, after we had spoken on the phone, he came to my house in Streatham, south London, and we spent an afternoon mapping out the narrative so I could get all the background from him.

It turned into a very special two-hour show, because Alton was a lovely storyteller with a wonderful memory and a rich supply of anecdotes.

Alton Ellis is one of the most soulful singers in the history of Jamaican music. He had a wonderful repertoire of hits made at Duke Reid's Treasure Isle studio and for Coxsone at Studio One. One example would be 'Chatty Chatty People', a brilliant song which he wrote. Another would be 'Let Him Try', a cover version which he made his own. He was a generous, warm-hearted man and we would speak regularly over the phone. Alton epitomized the traditional element of show business where the ego was on the backburner and what was important was the music. He was simply born to sing.

People often ask me to name my favourite Reggae artists. I always put Bob Andy near the top of the list – even if he doesn't get the public recognition he deserves. I got to meet him early in my Capital Radio years around 1981 when I was introduced to him at a house in Ladbroke Grove, west London. Beforehand I was a nervous wreck – it was almost worse than going on stage for a major gig.

I've always loved Bob's work. The first song I became aware of from him was 'I've Got to Go Back Home', which I heard as a teenager back in Oxfordshire on a compilation album called *Put It On It's Rock Steady* on Island Records. The cover art was a cartoon image of a boy and a girl, and Bob's song was credited to 'Bob and Andy', in the way that Reggae records often mangle the names of the artists.

Bob Andy became better known in 1970 when he recorded 'Young, Gifted and Black' with Marcia Griffiths as Bob and Marcia. He is one of the great Jamaican singers and had been a member of the wonderful vocal harmony group The Paragons before leaving them in 1966.

During my student years, Bob Andy songs such as 'Life' and 'You Don't Know' had a profound impact on me. 'Feeling Soul' became almost like a prayer to me, a psalm I would sing along to for consolation, encouragement and strength. It's a song of great humanity, about being kind and gentle to each other, to give your best when it's asked of you. It's just so beautiful.

Chris Lane played a big part in making me aware of the importance of Bob Andy. I have to thank Chris for so much that he has done as a Reggae pioneer in Britain. He got on a plane and went to Jamaica and stayed with Lee Perry and hung out at King Tubby's studio before anybody else from Britain. He set up the Dub Vendor record stall in London with John MacGillivray. But just as importantly, he wrote a Reggae column for *Blues & Soul* magazine that I never missed. I've still got a scrapbook with all his articles.

In that column I read about this Bob Andy album *Song Book*, which Chris argued was deeply significant. I was in awe of Chris, and when I was working in Lee's record shop there were a couple of guys who came in who I thought might be him, but I didn't have the guts to ask: 'Are you Chris Lane?'

I bought *Song Book* at Peckings record shop in Shepherd's Bush and fell in love with it, every song. Bob hadn't recorded it as an album so much as a fantastic collection of singles.

Bob came to Capital Radio and did an interview. His greatest strength is his song writing and he exposes his soul when he sings, reverberating feelings of pain, heartache and loneliness or man's inhumanity. One of his greatest songs is 'Unchained'. I defy anyone to listen to the lyrics – 'Take these chains away and set me free' – and not be deeply moved.

I had briefly seen Sugar Minott on my first trip to Jamaica but I really became friends with him when I helped promote his career by play-listing 'Good Thing Going' on Capital before it became a British chart hit in 1981.

I put it on the playlist because it had a wonderful flavour to it. People knew it as a song that was originally made by The Jacksons, but Sugar's version was sung so well. I knew he was a red-hot artist – cool and chilled and with an unrivalled underground following. He had been in a group called the African Brothers and then worked at Coxsone Dodd's Studio One as a solo artist before breaking away to form his own record label called Youth Promotion.

We put on Sugar Minott's first British concert, which was at the *Roots Rockers Roadshow* at Hammersmith Palais, west London.

At Capital, I was always trying to give a live platform to Reggae music. I had the idea that we could do live performances as live broadcasts. The first big one was Yellowman at the Picketts Lock Centre in Edmonton, north London.

At the time, Yellowman was a phenomenon. As an albino deejay, he was a cult performer and incredibly popular. To this day he is referred to as the 'King' by the Jamaican music fraternity.

I met him in Jamaica and decided to bring him to London. I took the idea to John Burrows, Capital's head of music promotions. John was a forthright Yorkshireman with a passionate love of classical music, but he supported me and negotiated the deal.

We couldn't find a location, so we booked Picketts Lock, a glorified gymnasium. We weren't sure how many tickets we would sell but there was a fever as soon as we announced it: 'Capital Radio presents . . . Yellowman!' I went into the station, the 'Rocking Tower' on London's Euston Road, and saw the management standing on the first floor looking down on the box office in the foyer and a queue of black people – with some white people too – stretching out of the door and down the block to the Thames Television building. We expanded from one night to four and they all sold out.

King Yellowman was wonderful to be around and we all loved him. We treated him with the respect he deserved and put him up in a suite at the plush Kensington Gardens Hotel, west London. I was Master of Ceremonies at the gigs and he name-checked me on stage every night. An album was made that his management released in Jamaica, *Yellowman Live at the Picketts Lock Centre*, and you can hear me introducing him to the crowd.

Yellowman is a fantastic entertainer. He does rock and roll, he does doo-wop, he does ballads – and he's a great dancer. He is also the ultimate professional and doesn't drink or smoke. All he wanted to do during his time in London was to buy clothes for his wife Rosie and their children.

The car brought him to the stage door every night, and he got out of the car and went straight into the wings just as they were doing the warm-up medley of rhythms for his show.

He had it timed to perfection. After he had done his curtain call he was into the car and straight back to the hotel. There was no party and no hanging out. It was the complete opposite of his reputation for singing sexually explicit lyrics as the so-called 'King of Slackness'.

The whole project was so successful that we then did the *Roots Rockers Roadshow* from the Academy in Brixton with Frankie Paul. That was his first concert in London. We had a recording studio at Capital Radio where we did live band sessions with an incredible array of artists.

My radio shows were always live and guests included Delroy Wilson, Augustus Pablo, Dennis Brown, Prince Buster, The Skatalites, Johnny Osbourne, Cutty Ranks, Ranking Joe, Josey Wales, Brigadier Jerry, and British artists such as Papa Levi and Tippa Irie. Not to mention Bob Marley. It was like a Who's Who of Reggae. The show ran throughout the eighties. Unfortunately Capital Radio doesn't have an archive of the material but I'm very proud of the body of work.

Tim Blackmore, the head of music at Capital Radio, supported me loyally, as did Aidan Day, the programme controller. I produced the show myself but the engineers were devoted to it.

I worked on the Capital daytime and night-time schedules and sometimes as a floating DJ, dropping in here and there. I told Aidan I didn't want to be a full-time radio DJ because I was determined to continue with my acting career. I would do the drive-time show or the late show when people were on holiday, 'depping' for great broadcasters such as Dave Cash, Kenny Everett, Mike Allen, Michael Aspel, Greg Edwards and Nicky Horne. These people were my buddies and really backed me.

As well as the *Roots Rockers Roadshow*, Capital staged another live event, *The Best Disco in Town* at the Lyceum, by The Strand in central London, on Friday nights. It was a guaranteed roadblock and as a Capital DJ you were invited to perform on rotation. One night in 1982 I was there and a young act was brought on stage to sing their new song. It was George Michael and Andrew Ridgeley, with their backing singers, Dee C. Lee and Shirlie Holliman. 'Give a warm welcome to Wham!' They threw records out into the audience.

After the success of the *Roots Rockers Roadshow* concerts by Yellowman for Capital in 1983, John Burrows said, 'Wow, what can we do next?'

In 1984 we introduced Sunsplash, the iconic live Jamaican Reggae festival, to a British audience for the first time.

It was one helluva line-up. We had The Skatalites, featuring Prince Buster, topping the bill. Also performing were Dennis Brown, Black Uhuru, Aswad, Leroy Sibbles, Lloyd Parks and We the People Band, King Sunny Ade and his African Beats, and the great drum and bass 'Rhythm Twins' of Jamaican music, Sly Dunbar and Robbie Shakespeare. I was Master of Ceremonies, alongside my great friend Barry G from JBC Radio in Jamaica.

I'd been down to see Sunsplash in Jamaica and got to know the people who were running it. We cut a deal to put the festival on in London as part of the Capital Radio Jazz Festival. The Sunsplash management in Jamaica brought the whole thing over here, including their logo.

It took place on 7 July at Selhurst Park football ground, the home of Crystal Palace in south London. The crowds were enormous, with tens of thousands packed onto the pitch and the standing terraces. We charged £10 a ticket or £12 on the day. The gates opened at 1 p.m., with the show starting at 2 p.m. and going through to 8.30 p.m.

Afterwards we released a video called *Splashin' the Palace '84*, featuring some of the concert's special moments, including 'Al Capone' by Prince Buster, 'Guess Who's Coming to Dinner' by Black Uhuru, and 'Redemption Song' by Lloyd Parks and We the People Band.

After the show I got to meet Prince Buster and interview him on Capital for a three-hour special, divided into segments. He had so many wonderful stories. In the period when Buster was ruling the music scene in the sixties it wasn't just the songs he recorded as an artist but the ones by other artists that he produced for his own labels. He was his own man and completely independent, a trendsetter with his own business and record shop.

After the success of *Splashin' the Palace '84*, the second year's Sunsplash took place at the same stadium, this time at the end of July. We had Sugar Minott topping the bill above another stunning line-up that included Gregory Isaacs, Ini Kamoze, Third World, Smiley Culture, Arrow and, once again, Sly and Robbie.

It was a wonderful event but unfortunately there was a violent incident outside the stadium and the local authority used that as a reason for not holding Sunsplash at Selhurst Park for a third year. To my mind it was the sort of incident that can happen when huge crowds gather – there were 22,000 people at the show. Old rivals meet up and there was a stabbing – there wasn't anything the organizers could have done to stop it. But the council came up with all the other usual reasons for objecting, such as people using residential gardens to take a leak. The truth was they didn't want Sunsplash any more, so they stopped it.

It was a nervous time for me and my wife Elaine, who I had met through the music industry, because we were expecting a child. Our eldest son Jamie was born in Chiswick hospital in London on 5 July 1985, one of the proudest days of my life.

I'd hoped Sunsplash would become a fixture in the calendar, but it wasn't to be. We tried moving it to Wembley Arena, north-west London, which was an altogether different atmosphere because it was indoors. It just wasn't the same. The following year, 1987, we did it outdoors as a free event on Clapham Common, south London, and it was a lovely warm day, but that was the last one we did. Once again the local authority took against us – it's a recurring theme for live Reggae events. That was the end of Sunsplash in Britain for twelve years.

The Capital Radio show was so helpful in my career. There was nothing else around by way of Reggae on the radio at the time, apart from Tony Williams' show on Radio London and a show on BRMB in Birmingham. Urban pirate radio had not yet taken off, with one exception being the Dread Broadcasting Corporation in Ladbroke Grove, west London.

Because of the success of the radio show and the Gossips nights in Soho, I started to get invitations to work from across the United Kingdom. The bookings mostly came from Caribbean communities around the country; such as the West Indian Centres in Manchester and Leeds and the Marcus Garvey Centre in Nottingham.

I would get letters from distant listeners saying things like, 'I drive to a car park on a hill outside Northampton so that I can pick up your show in my car – give me a shout on the air next week.' The show was an appointment to listen, and people would record it on cassette and send it to friends and relatives in various parts of the country or overseas.

I was also still doing my weekly Reggae show on BFBS, which would run for almost twenty-five years. What with the Capital shows, the BFBS broadcasts, Gossips on Saturday nights and organizing so many big live events, I was pushing myself to the limit.

I thought I could take it. Then, one day in 1988, I found out otherwise.

I was stretched out on the concrete floor of the underground car park at Capital Radio not knowing if I would live or die. The physical pain that overwhelmed me was like nothing I'd experienced before. I felt like I had been hit by a truck. Every breath had to be strained for – as though I had the weight of an elephant on my chest.

I knew I couldn't stay where I was. I crawled onto my feet and dragged myself up the staircase to the Capital building to find help. I probably owe my life to the fact that University College Hospital was directly across the road from the studios. My colleagues helped me into the Accident and Emergency area and the medical staff took one look at me and went straight into action.

It was the first time I had been in an emergency medical situation and I was very frightened. A few minutes later a young doctor was wheeling me towards the operating theatre.

'I'm going to save your life,' he told me. 'But you must promise me never to smoke again.'

'How do you know I smoke?' I stammered from the hospital trolley.

'Oh, you smoke all right . . .'

He gave me an injection and it was the biggest legal high I have ever had. I was sent into outer space, spiralling higher and higher. The pain started to fade away and I was in another place. Dreamily, I asked him if I could have another shot.

I had nearly lost everything. You're nothing without your health.

That day, in July 1988, had begun so well. My son Jamie was at nursery and had been part of a little drama production that I had gone along to see.

Being a dad had brought new responsibility, which I felt very strongly. We had moved into an old house in west London, which we were renovating, and, as a husband and father, I had a very traditional sense of needing to provide for my family.

I was working flat out. Not only was I broadcasting for Capital Radio and BFBS but I was gigging all the time, at Gossips on Saturday nights and at venues all over Britain and Europe. I was putting myself under a lot of stress. Most ominously, as that young doctor correctly surmised, I was chain smoking.

Benson & Hedges was my brand and I was a twenty-five-a-day man. I didn't turn to cigarettes as a way of coping with work stress, it was just something I really enjoyed. In those days there was no problem with lighting up inside a venue and I would have a cigarette on the go while cueing up records at a gig and even in the radio studio when I was on the air.

But I wasn't always a smoker and had given it up entirely during my student years. It was only because of an acting part, in which I was required to puff on a cigarette on stage, that I rediscovered the taste for nicotine. I was cast as an army officer in the war story *Seagulls Over Sorrento*, a production at The Crucible in Sheffield. Each night I lit it up and took a few drags but never inhaled. As the run went on I found myself having a single cigarette with a pint in the pub after the show. Then, in 1976, I became a hard-core smoker.

I was unrepentant at the time, and took the view that since I was going to die from something eventually it might as well be from a practice that gave me immense pleasure.

Payback came twelve years later. As I left Jamie's nursery to drive into work, I felt the first twinges of discomfort in my left arm. During the journey, that pain steadily grew worse until, as I climbed out of the car at Capital, I collapsed onto the ground. The next time I saw Jamie was on the ward at University College Hospital as he ran towards me holding out a present.

'Is that your son?' asked another of the doctors.

'Yes, it is.'

'If you want to see him grow up then you will have to stop smoking.'

I thanked the doctor for those harsh words because I was learning a lesson. The gift Jamie gave me was a wash bag, and inside was a teddy bear which I had bought him in Germany and which he wanted me to have because I was unwell.

After three days in intensive care I'd been moved onto a ward where the sight of some of my fellow patients did me an enormous favour in coming off cigarettes.

One man walked around everywhere with an oxygen canister because he could hardly breathe. But still he hauled himself along and went out of the ward with his canister for a smoke.

Then the guy next to me was visited by some hospital staff who erected a screen round him and cranked up the angle of his bed. Through a gap in the screen I could see his head was hanging over the edge of the bed and he was having his back massaged and pummelled until he coughed up this revolting brown sludge from his lungs. I realized that, like these men, I'd had a very close call, but I vowed to myself that I was going to do something about it.

Lying there in hospital I was frustrated that I now wouldn't be going to the big Michael Jackson concert at Wembley Stadium that we had tickets for and had been looking forward to for months. John Peel later described it as a show 'I do not expect to see equalled in my lifetime'.

I remained in hospital for a week because, although I had experienced many of the classic symptoms of a heart attack, the doctors were having trouble in determining exactly what was wrong with me. Tim Westwood, by then a presenting colleague at Capital, was kind enough to come and visit me, as was Richard Park, the head of the station.

I was taken to another hospital for tests. They pumped some dye into me and tried to see what the cause could be. Using a camera they found a narrowing of the artery on the left-hand side of my heart. The medical analysis concluded that I was suffering from arterial spasm caused by smoking and stress.

My lifestyle, spent largely in nightclubs, was a deeply unhealthy one. I was so consumed by my music scene that I wasn't doing any sport or even exercising.

I immediately gave up smoking and, belatedly, tried to look after my body. Having someone tell me they were going to save my life had left me shocked, but I thought I had learned from the warning and my confidence gradually started to return. I was still in my thirties and a young man, I told myself.

Then, at Easter weekend, it struck again. I was in the bedroom in the early evening and the same awful pain came crashing back. I collapsed at the side of the bed. An ambulance took me to the Central Middlesex Hospital in west London. This attack was even more terrifying because I had stopped smoking. What was happening to me? I remained in hospital for the whole of the Easter holiday. I was advised I needed complete rest and so we jumped on a plane and headed for a family holiday in Bermuda.

These arterial spasms around my heart became a constant fear. Twice more I was struck down. The next time, ironically after my earlier trip there for rest and recuperation, came in Bermuda just before I was due to perform at a big show. I was hospitalized again. Then I suffered another attack in Portsmouth when I was playing a gig at the pier with Papa Face. I was helped off stage and taken to hospital, where I went into A&E and was given an injection.

Subsequently I was given a nitrate spray and told to carry it with me at all times as a back-up to relieve the pain if I suffered again. The fear of a subsequent attack is something I have learned to live with for twenty-five years.

I often get asked how I maintain my energy levels at live shows after a long career of performing into the early hours of the morning. The fact is I have a very strict regime.

I gave up alcohol a decade ago because it was making me sleepy. It's very easy in this business to get caught up with ganja or champagne or whisky. I realized it was a road I didn't need to walk down and I'm certain that has allowed me to be more energetic on stage. Drinking creates a false sense of euphoria but within an hour or two you can feel rather tired.

Whether I'm playing in London, Berlin or New York, I follow a well-practised routine. I always have a good sleep at my hotel beforehand, what I call my disco nap. It's a rule I live by. I will eat my dinner as early as I can, usually by 7 p.m., and then hit the bed. I will settle down with a good classic novel, a Charles Dickens or a Thomas Hardy say, or my favourite magazine, *Private Eye*.

The trick is to try and stay awake by reading – if you just put the light out you will never fall asleep. After a while reading, I feel the sandman crawling over me and I'm passing through to a place where I have complete peace, that wonderful nirvana moment just before you drop off. I always manage a couple of hours, because at home I wake up at 5.20 a.m. each day and am tucked up in bed by 10 p.m. when I'm not working.

My pick-up time to go from the hotel to the venue will be at midnight or 1 a.m., and I set the alarm for forty minutes beforehand to allow time to freshen up.

Then, wherever possible, I will try to order an espresso. That's my high. The idea of weed or drink or cigarettes, that's all gone.

I have been fortunate. In 1989, the year after my first life-threatening attack, I received news of a friend that rocked me to my core.

Almost exactly ten years after my first visit, King Tubby was murdered outside his house. In a state of shock, I found myself producing a programme dedicated to him on *Roots Rockers*.

I began the show with a tragic news flash:

> Tonight on Capital Radio we pay tribute to King Tubby, the Dub inventor and the Dub master who was tragically shot dead last Monday the sixth of February. He was returning from his studio in Waterhouse to his home in Duhaney Park, it was ten past one in the morning, his wife was asleep when she was woken by the sound of Tubby parking his car on the driveway.

As he got out, a lone gunman confronted him and pointed the gun at his chest. He demanded that Tubby handed over his own gun, which he did. The next thing a single shot rang out and one of Jamaica's greatest musical legends was dead. The gunman then stole Tubby's chain, his gold chaparrita [bracelet] and his wallet and fled into the darkness.

Tonight between now and midnight we pay tribute to the Dub Master.

Years after I had first visited him in 1979, Tubby had created a proper recording studio at the back of Dromilly Avenue. He built the place almost single-handedly, selecting every single plank of wood from the Kingston wharf. I have treasured memories of going to the new studio and cutting dub plates of the 'Tempo' rhythm, one of the most popular in Reggae. I became a good friend of his and we would sit and talk, what the Jamaicans call 'reasoning', putting the world to rights.

On one occasion he invited me into a room at his house and I saw that he had an extensive collection of Jazz records. That was when it hit me that King Tubby's genius for Dub was founded on his great love for Jazz. He had become a kind of Jazz engineer. In the sense that Jazz can have multiple themes and change into something else, King Tubby was making a kind of Jazz when he was creating Dub. He was breaking things down and going against the norm; he wasn't doing things that were expected, he was echoing things out to oblivion, highlighting a phrase or a vocal, dropping everything out and bringing it back in again and making special sound effects. He was creating something completely different from what you had when you bought the original song.

As I played the great man's music after his murder I tried to convey the significance of the loss. I told listeners that the 'consensus of opinion from Jamaica' was that the only motive was to steal the producer's licensed firearm.

'King Tubby was one of the most dearly loved and highly respected people in the Jamaican music industry,' I concluded. 'Occasionally you do hear derogatory things said about producers but never, never about King Tubby. Everyone loved Tubbs.'

I feel honoured to have spent time in his presence.

15

Ragga

Suddenly everything was in bright colours and high definition; the beats, the lyrics, the costumes and the dancing became more flamboyant and more outrageous.

This Jamaican sound that emerged at the end of the 1980s was not Reggae; it was something new. In Britain it was dubbed 'Ragga' after the 'ragamuffin' street hustlers who seemed to epitomize the new scene. In Jamaica it was still referred to as 'Dancehall' or as 'Bashment', a name which captured its brash style and digitally produced rhythms.

It wasn't just Jamaicans but all West Indian communities that embraced the new vibe. Ragga's electronic pulse had a strong affinity with the frenetic rhythms of the Soca music found in Trinidad and loved by other Caribbean islands. This was not music for Rastafarian elders.

I championed the exciting new sound and in 1990, as Ragga was hitting the mainstream, I left Capital and became part of one of the most exciting adventures in the history of British radio: the legal launch of a pirate network.

But there were elements to the Ragga culture that I found hard to deal with …

I felt part of history on the day Kiss 100 FM launched in London and changed the sound of radio around the world.

It was 1 September 1990 and I was in the studio when the first record went on air. The place went mad – everybody was jumping around in the room because we knew how important that moment was. The debut track was perfect: 'Pirates' Anthem' by Home T, Cocoa Tea and Shabba Ranks.

Not only was 'Pirates' Anthem' a Reggae hit of the moment, it was also the ideal signature tune for a network that had been operating outside the broadcasting laws for five years and had finally been granted a legal licence. The lyrics couldn't be more apposite and go straight to the issues, even managing to reference the Department of Trade and Industry (DTI), the UK government body responsible for policing radio stations.

> *Them a call us pirates*
> *them a call us illegal broadcasters,*
> *Just because we play what the people want.*
> *Them a call us pirates*
> *them a call us illegal broadcasters,*
> *DTI try stop us but they can't.*

For weeks before the launch you couldn't go anywhere in London and escape our distinctive logo of a hot red puckered-up mouth and the slogan 'Kiss 100 FM – the station on everyone's lips'. The papers and magazines fed the frenzy of anticipation.

I was so pleased to be part of it. After spending the whole of the eighties on Capital Radio, giving Reggae music the attention I felt it deserved, I was now joining this hot new station, just as Ragga, the latest colourful incarnation of Dancehall, was taking off.

Kiss was a dance station. As well as embracing genres of black music that had previously been under-represented in mainstream radio, it was championing the UK's new 'Rave' culture that grew out of the Acid House 'Summer of Love' in 1988 when warehouses and fields became the scenes for vast all-night parties.

The Rave culture, with its hunger for huge sound systems and towers of speaker boxes, shared a lot in common with Reggae. I'd always thought the best Reggae parties took place outdoors, which was the Jamaican tradition.

The illicit status of many Acid House events – with organizers and ravers being constantly pursued by the forces of law and order – tallied with the cat-and-mouse experiences of Kiss and the other pirate stations as they sought to evade the DTI. Now Kiss was going above ground just as the whole of mainstream youth seemed to be taking to dance culture. The name Kiss was inspired by a famous station in America, and we secured a frequency on the dial that you couldn't beat: 100 FM.

I agreed to join Kiss after being courted by the station's bosses during several months of negotiations. The face of Kiss 100 was Gordon McNamee – known to everyone as 'Gordon Mac'. I had my first meeting with Gordon and his colleague Grant Goddard early that year in the Camden Brasserie on Camden High Street, north London, near where Kiss opened an office.

Leaving Capital was the right decision for me but it wasn't an easy one.

My show had been moved from the plum Saturday-night slot that it had held for years to Friday nights, coming on air at midnight. There was no doubt this made it less accessible. I've always been fiercely protective of the music whenever I felt it was being marginalized.

I knew the station boss Richard Park understood the significance of Reggae and had even commissioned a Reggae show in Scotland when he worked at Radio Clyde. Park's logic at Capital was that Hip Hop was becoming very important in the culture of young London and he wanted Tim Westwood's Rap show to be the centrepiece of Friday night, with my Reggae show following afterwards.

I was flattered by the interest of Gordon Mac and Grant Goddard, who said they were big fans of my broadcasting and of Reggae music in general. They were keen to bring me into the Kiss daytime schedule and present a show which featured a cross-section of black music. The idea appealed to me and I'd brought with me some cassettes of my BFBS forces radio show, which was broader in musical styles than Capital's *Roots Rockers*.

The Kiss bosses were also offering me a second more specialist Reggae show. I was very interested in the package of the two together. The early negotiations had to be conducted in secret. Rumours that I might leave Capital surfaced in the music paper *Record Mirror*, which wrote an article saying, 'London's Kiss FM seems likely to be gaining the services of a certain superstar Reggae DJ when it comes on air in August.'

I had a new agent, Adrian King, who I'd known since my days at drama college. Adrian worked under the name AKA (Adrian King Associates) and had been social secretary of the Students' Union at Rose Bruford College when I was the union president. He later started working part-time for my theatrical agent David Preston, and when David died, Adrian took on some of his clients, including me. We talked over the move to Kiss at great length.

His view was that it was a good idea because we were expecting our second child, Oliver, and needed a more stable income. A two-show deal with Kiss would make me better off financially, rather than the arrangement I had with Capital, where I was trying to juggle my broadcasting career with acting jobs. 'It's difficult for you doing both,' Adrian told me. 'Acting or radio – it's time for you to make a decision.'

I chose radio. Kiss was a big challenge because it was a new urban dance music station which I felt was going to be very important. To be given a position as a daytime presenter meant that I would have an involvement in choosing the station's music, and that too was an important responsibility. Always at the back of my mind was my health after the arterial spasms I had suffered to my heart. I knew I had to manage my stress but I was also conscious of needing to provide security for my growing young family.

I was nearly forty years old but I had loved pirate radio since I was a boy. Growing up in Oxfordshire, my connection to Soul and Reggae music had been through pirate stations such as Radio Caroline and Radio London, broadcasting from out in the North Sea, beyond the reach of the authorities.

I'd seen the growth of a new generation of London-based pirates such as Kiss, LWR, Starpoint, TKO and WBLS, which tended to work from secret locations using aerials on high blocks of flats. They played black music. The Dread Broadcasting Corporation had been set up in the early eighties in Ladbroke Grove, west London, and Ranking Miss P, whose brother Leroy 'Lepke' Anderson set up DBC, went on to have her own Reggae show on BBC Radio London. Miss P is a really good broadcaster with a lovely voice and a deep knowledge of the music.

The pirates were definitely making an impact on Capital and the commercial radio market in general. Legal radio was dominated by Rock, Pop and Classical music but this upstart Kiss, which in its pirate days only played at weekends but operated very professionally, had built a reputation on the street and shown there was an under-served audience for the music I loved.

It was just a question of me telling Capital I was leaving. I broke the news on 1 August. Richard Park acknowledged the logic of my decision and told me he wouldn't have expected me to walk away from such an opportunity. He is one of the most senior figures in the British radio industry and understands how it works. To my disappointment I wasn't allowed to do a farewell show – Richard doesn't believe in them. But he gave me a farewell party downstairs in the Capital Radio music room and, after eleven years on the station, it was an emotional send-off.

I had another big boost in 1990. At the age of thirty-nine, I finally overcame my phobia of swimming. After seeing my five-year-old son Jamie swimming with joy and confidence in the hotel pool on holiday in Montego Bay, Jamaica, I realized I had to overcome my fear. It struck me that Jamie was about the same age as I was when I got into trouble off the coast of Libya. I was also deeply aware that I needed to stay fit to avoid more problems with my heart. We returned home and I started going to Porchester Baths in west London three times a week. It took three months but one morning I was treading water for the first time. I was hugely relieved, because it's terrible to live with a water phobia like that. It's so important to me that I get up at 5.20 a.m. to go swimming most mornings.

Life was changing. After getting its licence, Kiss, which had previously been operating from secret locations in the back streets of Finsbury Park, north London, came out of the shadows and opened new studios nearby in a building it named Kiss House, overlooking the busy Holloway Road. This location was right on the street and in the heart of the community – a world away from the Capital headquarters in London's commercial centre.

The weekend after Gordon Mac played our first record, 'Pirates' Anthem', Kiss had its big public launch with a huge live event just up the road in Highbury Fields. The line-up was extraordinary. LL Cool J and Tony! Toni! Toné flew in from America and the British artists included Aswad, Caron Wheeler and Maxi Priest. Most amazing of all was the size of the crowd.

I jumped into a car for the short drive to the show, but the streets around Highbury Fields were filled with traffic and everyone was tooting their horns in support of the new station. There were supposed to be 20,000 present but the numbers were far greater. It was such an important moment, the most significant radio station launch since 1967 when, after the government's long battle to close down Radio Caroline, the BBC set up BBC Radio 1 as a legal popular music network.

The early days of Kiss were so exciting. There was freedom in what you were allowed to play – even in the daytime schedule. DJs were given 'Free Choices', where they included their personal selections alongside the station's playlist. This was revolutionary in commercial radio.

Gordon Mac wanted the listeners to see Monday night as Kiss FM's Reggae night, so I had a three-hour show from

7 p.m. until 10 p.m. with the first hour being dedicated to a Reggae chart rundown. For the rest of the show I mixed up hot new releases, classic revivals and competitions. We always recorded live.

Of course I would have preferred that it was on a Saturday. When I'd decided to move to Kiss I'd presumed that was the plan because I had been on Capital Radio on Saturdays for almost all those eleven years. But Gordon had his vision. Kiss wanted Saturday nights to have a different musical structure and Nick Mannasseh's Dub-based Reggae show was scheduled for the wee small hours of early Sunday morning. Looking back, it was for the best – Monday nights for Reggae meant I could have the weekend with my young family.

I admired Gordon for what he was doing. By choosing premises on Holloway Road he was avoiding the rates he would have had to pay in Soho, which would have been the obvious central London location for a dance music station.

There was a big contrast in atmosphere with Capital Radio, which had become part of the establishment. Capital's roster of DJs had been round the block a few times and the station had its own recognizable broadcasting signature. Kiss was young, hungry, angry and volatile. Weekly playlist meetings reflected this. They were open to any DJ to attend and could be very emotional. Champions of different musical genres would be shouting, 'I want this, we need more House, we need more Techno', as they tried to get their songs onto the playlist.

The original staff at Kiss shared an extraordinary passion, which was embodied by the station's slogan: 'Music is Life'. Everyone was an obsessive, right through to Gordon Mac himself. For the people who set up the station this was their dream coming true. When I first met Gordon he was very reserved and didn't say a great deal. But later he showed me a photograph of himself wearing a '*Roots Rockers*' sweatshirt he had once bought from the Capital Radio foyer. It told me how much he loved Reggae.

There were so many DJs with so many great shows on Kiss. The early programme listings were amazing: Trevor Nelson, Steve Jackson, Graham Gold and Dave Pearce, to name a few. Beyond the full-time staff there was a part-time DJ roster of top names like Judge Jules, Colin Faver, Colin Dale, Norman Jay, Jazzie B, Paul 'Trouble' Anderson, Patrick Forge and Danny Rampling.

They had way too many DJs but that was the concept of a pirate station. It was a legal business but it still stood for the values it embraced as a pirate. I felt sorry for Lindsay Wesker, who was head of music and had to keep all these DJs happy, ensuring that all genres were featured in the playlist. Lindsay did so much to try and satisfy everyone.

Being at Kiss and feeling the enthusiasm of the staff and listeners made me realize that, far from being this isolated music obsessive that I had often thought myself to be when I was younger, I was actually part of something much bigger. There are so many of us! Some people don't understand it and their attitude to obsessive music collectors is that they should 'get a life'. But I look at my record collection and remember how I scraped and scrimped for the money, making all those trips to Peckings record shop in Shepherd's Bush on the number 9 bus from Barnes to buy three singles. The shop owner George Price had been a personal friend of Coxsone Dodd in Jamaica and I became very close to him and his wife, Miss Gerty, and their sons Chris, Duke and Trevor. I often visited the family on Sundays to eat rice and peas and drink carrot juice. I used to play those records from Peckings again and again and again. It was a serious addiction to music – but I was not alone in having it.

Ragga came with a remarkable ghetto fabulous look; crazy costumes, lots of gold chains, and girls wearing tiny shorts known as 'batty riders'. You would see black girls wearing blonde wigs. Lots of women organized themselves into crews, which would compete to wear the most outrageous outfits or perform the most original dance moves.

To stand on the dancefloor at one of these sessions you had to look the part. The focus was very much on the ladies – what they looked like and how they danced. And with this came the advent of the video camera and the concept of the red 'video light' which would appear in the middle of the floor as an entrepreneurial cameraman made his way through the crowd to film the best dancers and release the footage as a film for sale. Previously there had only been demand for audio recordings.

The most famous woman on the scene was Carlene Smith, who was known for wearing a white wig and supposed to have invented the extravagant 'Butterfly' dance, with legs apart and dipping of the knees. Carlene had a relationship with the DJ Beenie Man, one of the most successful Jamaican artists of all time.

A feature film, *Dancehall Queen*, depicted this culture by telling the story of a poor single mother trying to win an amateur dance contest while facing the physical threats of Kingston ghetto life. Beenie Man performed the title track and had a role in the movie, which was co-directed by the British filmmaker Don Letts.

If Carlene was the Dancehall Queen then the King was Bogle – no one could match him on the dancefloor. He created his own 'Bogle' dance, a bodily contortion during which waves of energy appear to pass through the torso. The move went round the world and was celebrated in numerous Ragga anthems, such as Buju Banton's 'Bogle', in which he instructed fans to 'Fling yuh hand inna the air, then you rock, then you dip, move to the drum and make your body kick, step forward and come up back way . . .'

For a time no Kingston session was complete unless Father Bogle – or Gerald Levy to give him his real name – had graced the floor.

The Stone Love sound system in Kingston was at the heart of the new scene. They were one of the first sounds to play without a break between records. They used special effects to create a collage of sound. With their selectors Rory and Cancer they catered to the dancers; it wasn't about clashing. Stone Love's magic formula was about songs played in the right order with just a sprinkling of dub plates. They knew just how to pace a dance, playing a mixture of Ragga, Soul and Roots music.

I'd seen the origins of this new Dancehall sound back in King Jammy's yard in Waterhouse in downtown Kingston in 1985, when the electronic Sleng Teng rhythm built from the Casio keyboard altered the energy of the entire Reggae world by introducing a new digital sound.

Reggae before then had been the slower 'chunka, chunka' sound of the snare-driven One Drop beat created by session musician Winston Grennan and developed by Carlton Barrett, the drummer of Bob Marley and The Wailers. Or else it was the Steppers sound, where the bass drum is played every quarter-beat of the bar. The new beats were of a much higher tempo and quickly championed by drummer Sly Dunbar and bass player Robbie Shakespeare, the famous 'Rhythm Twins' who have done so much to shape Jamaican music. The producer Dave Kelly, who ran the Madhouse Records label, was at the forefront of the scene.

The rhythmic energy of Ragga was very exciting. It was epitomized by songs such as 'Murder She Wrote' by Chaka Demus & Pliers, for which Carlene starred in the video.

The hits kept coming and they crossed over into the mainstream Pop charts because they had this tremendous dance appeal. Although earlier Jamaican music genres such as Ska and Rock Steady had been created with dancing in mind, the Reggae styles of the seventies were different. One of the problems that some people had with Reggae was: 'How do you dance to it?' The new rhythms were made for dancing, the tempo was almost four to the floor, and even if you didn't understand the lyrics you could feel the beat.

Even though I was now approaching forty I fully embraced the revolution. It was young, fresh and new. Some of the music elders didn't agree with it because they said it wasn't Reggae. And they were entirely right, it wasn't. It was a new chapter in the evolution of Jamaican music – everything had changed. It was no longer about the One Drop and the serious or romantic message in the lyric. Dancehall was party music and the lyrics were often about very little, other than simply having a good time.

For me, as a DJ, this new musical explosion allowed me to switch genres without moving away from Jamaican music – you could go from One Drop to Dancehall and back, and you were no longer dependent on Soul music for the change of pace.

Some of the performers became superstars. Shabba Ranks emerged at the end of the 1980s with his gruff voice and an ability to 'ride a rhythm' by rapping or deejaying lyrics over these pulsating electronic beats. Shabba is unmistakable and the impact he had is difficult to underestimate. The rhythm for his track 'Dem Bow', part of his 1991 album *Just Reality*, became the staple of an entire musical genre: Reggaeton, the new soundtrack of the Spanish-speaking Caribbean.

Shabba was an international star and in 1991 he was signed by Epic, an American label within the global Sony music empire. He had countless hits in the Jamaican charts but released his biggest international record 'Mr Loverman' with the singer Chevelle Franklyn in 1992. It was re-released the following year as Ragga was enjoying a surge in mainstream popularity and reached number three in the UK charts.

The United States took a renewed interest in the vibrant Jamaican music scene and American record labels began looking at artists. Another fast-talking mic specialist, Lieutenant Stitchie, signed to Atlantic Records as early as 1988 – the first Jamaican MC to be signed to an American major label. Super Cat signed to Columbia, another Sony imprint, in 1992.

As a Jamaican in New York, Super Cat played a key role in forging even closer links between Dancehall and Hip Hop, which were already entwined in their musical roots. Both genres were originally inspired by the early Jamaican sound system culture and the microphone skills of originators such as U Roy, the deejay I obsessed over as a student in the early seventies. The 'Stalag' rhythm, one of the most important in Reggae, has been sampled in more Hip Hop records than I could add up. And during the early 1990s you would hear more and more snippets of Jamaican jive talk and slang sampled into American Rap.

Ragga took Jamaican music worldwide once more. It took off in Germany, Italy, France, Belgium, Holland and in Scandinavia to the point where young artists in those countries were starting to experiment with making the music themselves.

The new rhythmic structure brought in an audience that knew little of Reggae or Ska. Sean Paul, who arrived at the end of the 1990s, was the figurehead. At the start of the new century, his albums *Dutty Rock* and *The Trinity* were two of the most successful and influential in the story of Jamaican music.

Even though Ragga was party music, this modern Dancehall sound has lasted longer than many predicted. You can play any of those 1990s rhythms from producers such as Dave Kelly or Steely & Clevie in a dance session now and people still go crazy.

Sadly, it's also associated with other less positive things.

The controversy over homophobic lyrics has followed Ragga culture for many years and badly damaged the careers of several artists. Tours have been cancelled and songs banned. Back in 2007, when a campaign called Stop Murder Music was at its height, a number of performers signed a Reggae Compassionate Act promising not to perform or record songs which advocated violence against gay people – but the issue has never quite gone away.

I don't defend homophobia, how could I? But there are two sides to this story and some of the media sometimes fails to recognize this. We have to look at the significance of religion in Jamaican life. It is said that there are more churches per capita in Jamaica than anywhere else in the world. Religion and devout belief in the Bible has been part and parcel of Jamaican culture since Christianity was introduced to Africans taken to the West Indies as slaves. I know from many visits to

Jamaica that people will quote from the Bible categorically, arguing that homosexuality is unacceptable behaviour in the eyes of God.

This is a part of the island culture in the way that it was in the United Kingdom when I was growing up. We should remember that it wasn't so long ago that you were arrested or even went to jail in Britain for being homosexual. Even John Gielgud, one of Britain's greatest actors, was persecuted for his sexuality and arrested on the charge of 'importuning for immoral purposes' in 1953. So if we are going to talk about homophobia let's also remember the levels of homophobia in England until recent times. That's not in any way a defence of homophobic lyrics or comments by Reggae artists but it's putting the issue into a wider context. Homosexuality is now regarded as acceptable in society in England and in most of Europe. In the West Indies that is still largely not the case.

It's my belief that there can be no place for homophobia in Reggae. The essence of the music is love. It has always appealed to me because it has constantly stood up for humanity and fought against injustice and inequality. It speaks out against the shackles and chains of mind, body and soul. To remember this we only have to think of songs like 'Unchained' by Bob Andy or 'Slave Driver' by Bob Marley and The Wailers.

Reggae's message is that Babylon devours poor people. It teaches of the origins of the motherland of Africa and preaches humanity, love, tenderness and respect for society. This is the very reason why it is so universally appealing – it speaks out for the underprivileged. That's why people in South America, Asia, Native Americans and all those who have suffered injustice can relate to it.

Given those foundations, how can a Reggae artist possibly

take a bigoted attitude? Some might say that Reggae has always stood by the words of the Bible but the Bible also says 'Judge not, that ye be not judged', and 'He that is without sin among you, let him first cast a stone'. The teachings of Jesus Christ in the Sermon on the Mount included the message of doing to others as you would have them do to you.

I was brought up in the Christian faith and I have power-ful memories of my devout mother clutching my hand firmly as she took us to Mass in Libya. In her other hand she had an immaculate Roman Missal liturgical book, with a hard cover made from mother-of-pearl, glistening in the sun. By my own bedside I have a King James Bible with a zip cover, which was a present from a Christian community which I met during a student trip to Scandinavia and stayed with for a week in Oslo. I slept on the floor in my sleeping bag in their church meeting hall. They were very kind and generous people, originally from Oregon in the United States, and it was a nice way of ending my Scandinavian trip. I still draw comfort from that Bible.

The King James Version has a beautiful linguistic structure and rich language. West Indian music has a deep religious tie in it, and I am always seeing in this King James Bible quotes used in Reggae songs, such as 'The Beatitudes' by Slim Smith, based on the Sermon on the Mount. The Book of Proverbs refers to 'the wine of violence', which is used in a famous Freddie McGregor song.

How can any musician justify advocating the causing of harm to someone who is not of their sexual persuasion? Reggae is a music that has never supported violence but sup-ports humanity and endorses love.

Ragga or Dancehall has also been accused of celebrating firearms. For decades guns have been rife in the downtown

Kingston districts where Reggae music's heartbeat sounds loudest. And for years there has been a strange fascination with different weapons and their ballistic capabilities. To some it's a legacy of the popularity of Western films, referenced in director Perry Henzell's Jamaican movie *The Harder They Come*, in which Jimmy Cliff plays the gun-slinging gangster anti-hero Ivanhoe Martin. People argue that gangs and guns and violence are simply part of society's problems worldwide.

But why would you glorify in song lyrics something that causes suffering among fellow members of the human race? Why would you endorse a culture that says it's cool to kill someone or intimidate people because your gang is more powerful? How does that bring love and humanity? What if it leads to your brother killing your best friend? I can't support that.

Almost inevitably, guns sometimes find their way into live events.

There was a dance session I performed at in the 1990s in Toronto where gunmen came in and started firing bullets all over the place. I had to run for my life, as we all did.

It started out as a very pleasant evening. I played my set and the Jamaican sound system Stone Love was performing to a crowd of at least a thousand people. Next thing, the side doors flew open and gunshots started going off. The gunmen were firing into the air and no one stayed around to find out why. There was screaming, shouting and crying and women's shoes everywhere on the floor as everyone fled for the exits. I got caught up in the stampede and ended up tumbling on top of the Stone Love sound system, with its owner – 'Wee Pow' – falling down on top of me.

I've had some adventures in the United States. In Houston, Texas, they sent a stretched limo and two guys as minders to

collect me from my hotel. On the way to the venue the minders both took their guns out in the back of the limo and started
comparing them. One of the weapons was a chrome Magnum
with a mother-of-pearl handle. I was shocked and asked them
what they were doing. Matter-of-factly, they informed me
that I was in Texas and that comparing handguns was perfectly
legal as long as the ammunition clip was not in the weapon.
We arrived at the venue, which was in the middle of nowhere
in the outer limits of the city. The roof of the building was
burnt off and you looked up through the charred remains of
the roof and saw the stars twinkling in the sky. The promoters had got hold of this fire-damaged venue somehow and
decided to put on a Reggae show with me.

On another occasion, in Baltimore, I found myself asking
the driver why I wasn't being taken straight to my hotel and
was told there were orders to bring me to 'see the Boss'. I was
taken across the city to a semi-derelict building where a guy
was eating his lunch out of a takeaway box. He was seated at
a fold-up table surrounded by plastic chairs. But he was the
Boss and he wanted to meet me personally before the night's
big show. It was like a scene from *The Wire*, which of course is
set in Baltimore.

In the dancehall, you have to be prepared for everything.
One evening in 1985 I was playing with my old rival Barry
Gordon at Ashanti Junction in downtown Kingston. He had
this big tune called 'Rewind' by Johnny Osbourne, which is
a cut of the 'Stalag' rhythm which Prince Jammy had built. I
didn't have that tune and Barry was getting big crowd responses
(known as 'forwards') whenever he played it.

What I had managed to do was cut a dub plate special
with Junior Reid on this same 'Stalag' rhythm, with a great

customized lyric: 'Your sound look good but your dub plate nah ready. Listen Rodigan gon' set the dance steady'.

I took the mic and said, 'Barry, you've been mashing me up with your cut of the "Stalag" rhythm, but I've got a counteraction.' And I played the Junior Reid special, to the crowd's delight.

'Piaow-www!'

I heard a bullet ricochet and felt the thud of it as it hit some corrugated iron. Everyone in the crowd roared and then I heard someone scream out.

'Leee-gal! Leee-gal!'

That basically meant a police officer had fired the bullet – it was a legal gunshot. It was my first ever 'gun salute', which meant that the shot had been fired as an endorsement of the song that had been played. That wasn't much consolation at the time – I was terrified. But that was how it was; plain-clothes policemen would come to dances as fans, carrying their guns on their waists.

One Jamaican gangster was apparently so impressed with my clashes with Barry G that he started calling himself 'Rodigan'. When he was exposed as a gun smuggler he fled to New York and, much to my embarrassment, was involved in a series of shootings that took place in the Jamaican community in Brooklyn during the 4 July celebrations one year. The Jamaican newspapers picked up on the news and under the headline 'Rodigan Shot in New York', the *Gleaner* reported that the 'now infamous Jamaican community "don" known as "Rodigan"' had taken three bullets to the lower body. To make matters worse, I was in New York at the time. There was nothing in the article to distinguish me from this character and the headline ensured I had many calls from Jamaicans wanting to know if I was safe. This "Rodigan", whose real name was Robert Davis, died with three others in another shooting in Los Angeles in 2016.

Some shady characters were actually supporting events I was booked to play at. I suppose it's always been the way in the nightclub industry. In New York, I came into contact with the real wise guys.

'I've got you a gig at Hot Tree,' the New York promoter told me proudly in his thick Jamaican accent. It was a big event, playing alongside the top American sound system King Addies. We drove over to the venue and I was warned in advance, 'Don't mess with Nick', the club owner. Nick was an Italian-American. 'When he pays you your money, don't count it in front of him.'

We got to the club and there was a giant sign on the front of the venue: 'Act Three welcomes David Rodigan'. I had misunderstood the Jamaican accent and it wasn't called Hot Tree at all.

Inside the office of the club it was like a scene from *The Sopranos*. When I left the club at the end of the evening – having taken my money but not counted it in front of Nick – they sent a decoy vehicle in front of me to drive up outside and pull off – just to make sure I wasn't carjacked for my earnings.

But I have always felt at ease in the dancehall. I've consistently maintained that my purpose was only ever to share the music, and I wanted to do it wherever I was invited. So I felt I had nothing to fear and I don't believe I did.

After forty-odd years in the dancehalls I've become used to looking a bit different.

I have my own dress code. You'd never catch me in the extrovert clothing that some of the dancehall patrons like to show up in. But, like them, I do enjoy making an effort. Traditionally I've always worn suits. Back in the 1980s that was the standard dress code for a professional DJ, and I took pride in my appearance. You couldn't turn up for a booking in muck order wearing a T-shirt! A DJ always wore a suit on a Saturday night, and turning up in trainers was unheard of.

Denzil, the mic man for Lloyd Coxsone's Sir Coxsone sound system at some of my early dancehall experiences down in London's Carnaby Street, always wore a suit and a shirt and tie. He was what Jamaicans call a 'Dapper Don'.

Even in the 1990s, when everyone was wearing American sportswear, I would still make a point of wearing suits. I was taking a leaf out of Gregory Isaacs's book – he wore suits no matter what. He would often purchase a suit just for one show and I thought there was something cool and elegant about that. Unfortunately it came to a point where I realized a suit made me look over-dressed at some events, so I cut back to casual wear.

In the grand scheme of things, of course, none of this is really important. Who are we? We are just record selectors. But we are enabling people to relax and to find happiness and a release from the day-to-day boredom of jobs they might not want to be doing or situations they don't want to be in. Gregory Isaacs once told me why he wrote his song 'What a Feeling'. He said that Saturday night was the one time of the week when the working man and his woman could escape and have freedom with a dance, a beer and a spliff. His words make me think of the ambience of the open-air dances in Jamaica, the fragrances and the special feel of music played in that setting. That to me is the true spirit of the dancehall.

16

Jungle

The frenetic dance sound that emerged in London in the early 1990s was so rooted in Jamaica that even its name is said to have come from the 'Junglists' of the 'Jungle' neighbourhood of downtown Kingston, who are frequently referenced on live sound system recordings.

Early Jungle tracks sampled Jamaican artists from Black Uhuru to Jigsy King and combined Hip-Hop-style breakbeats and a fast-paced London energy. Many of the artists, such as the Ragga Twins, had come from the UK sound system world.

It was instantly exciting and the essence of what Kiss FM was all about in reflecting the music of the streets. I related to it and supported it. But at that time it wasn't my music. I was immersed in the world of sound clashing and being asked to compete in increasingly hardcore events.

But radio was my bread and butter, and in that broadcasting world I could see the first signs that commercial pressures on Kiss FM were stifling the music I loved.

I loved 'Incredible' by M-Beat. It was a Jungle anthem and featured vocals by the unmistakable London-based Dancehall artist General Levy with his hiccup-style delivery.

This was a new UK music movement, a Reggae and Dancehall-inspired genre that would later became known as Drum & Bass. I played that Jungle track in the daytime Kiss output because I thought it was an infectious record with great potential. Sure enough, it became a Pop hit and reached number eight in the UK chart.

Jungle and Drum & Bass grew to become one of the most important stories in modern British music – and Kiss played a big part in that. I could get excited about songs or new musical styles and influence how much success they had.

A number of the MCs singing on Jungle tracks were well-known Reggae performers, like General Levy and Tenor Fly. I could see strong similarities between Drum & Bass and the Dub music of the sound systems I first used to listen to in London, such as Jah Shaka and Sir Coxsone. Drum & Bass had huge basslines and big drops and the driving energy of a fast drum beat.

DJ Hype was one of the big players in the Jungle and Drum & Bass scene and I got to know him well when we worked together at Kiss. I liked his passion for life and his knowledge of Reggae. I met him once when I was cutting dub plates at Music House studio in London. Exclusive dub plate recordings were also a part of the Drum & Bass culture, something which it carried over from Reggae.

It was a shame the music nuts couldn't remain in charge of Kiss forever but the station was employing a lot of people and had to run as a business. Emap, the company that would later take it over, was involved from the outset as shareholders. Its interest was genuine but it was an East Anglian publishing house making a first foray into broadcasting and it was on a big learning curve.

With its legal licence, Kiss inherited responsibilities. Bills had to be paid and commercial viability had to be the aim. Lorna Clarke was brought in as programme controller and was very successful. She was very good to work for and commanded a great deal of love and loyalty. She always had time for people and helped the station to run smoothly.

But the heady early days couldn't go on forever. There was a big cutback after a pretty short time and a lot of DJs fell by the wayside because costs had to be reduced. Kiss turned from a party into a business.

It still had the evening specialist programmes from 7 p.m. onwards. Those were the station's biggest assets and made it stand out from everything else on the radio dial. Even when the reality of budgeting seriously kicked in and spending boiled down to the gravy, Kiss maintained specialist shows from the evening through to daybreak, although the watershed was nibbled back from 7 p.m. to 8 p.m. to 9 p.m. as daytime-style programming leaked into the evening schedule.

During the next decade I worked through the daytime schedule myself, hosting the breakfast, morning, lunchtime, afternoon and drive-time shows. I thoroughly enjoyed every job, especially the relationship you could build with audiences as you tried to be each listener's companion. It was a great challenge and gave me an opportunity to push Reggae to a wider audience.

I became aware that these shows gave me the chance to break records into the Pop charts. One example was 'No, No, No' by Dawn Penn. Then there was 'Oh Carolina' by Shaggy, 'Who Am I? (Sim Simma)' by Beenie Man and 'Heads High' by Mr Vegas. We championed all those breakthrough hits.

I pushed hard for these tunes – initially Kiss didn't want to put 'Oh Carolina' on the playlist because they thought it was unsuitable. But I was playing it daytime in my free choices and eventually the station play-listed it and it went to number one in the UK chart. I was very fond of the original Folkes Brothers version of 'Oh Carolina' produced by Prince Buster in 1960 but I thought the producers of this modern remake had done a brilliant job in rebuilding the rhythm. Sting International, a producer based in New York, was the brains behind the project and Shaggy supplied a distinctive deep vocal. I wasn't surprised when it went to number one because it had all the elements.

When I joined Kiss I'd hoped to bring back the live events that we had done at Capital, such as the UK Sunsplash and something akin to my *Roots Rockers Roadshows*. The latter – which included shows by Yellowman and Bunny Wailer – must have appealed to Gordon Mac, with his '*Roots Rockers*' sweatshirt. But it never happened. We managed one special Kiss Reggae show in south London with British-based artists but it was never repeated.

There's always been a stigma attached to live Reggae events and I've never understood why. I never worked out how you could have 40,000 people going to a football match to support rival teams and often being quite antagonistic to each other but the authorities apparently could not cope with a smaller crowd of people going to listen to music, which is mostly about peace and love. Was it a problem for the police or for the council? There always seemed to be an issue.

Ask promoters and they will say that in terms of festivals and major events there are invariably problems in getting permission simply because it's Reggae. But this music, as far as I'm aware, never encouraged gang violence in the way that you hear of problems occurring in some other genres, where events have been shut down before they have begun due to fears of retribution attacks. I don't want to be too negative because we have had so many big live Reggae shows at major venues, especially in London where Bob Marley's performances at the Lyceum and the Rainbow have gone down in music history.

After Emap became outright owner of Kiss, the company started buying other radio stations and extending its power base as a major broadcasting player. But Kiss began to lose its status as the sound of the streets.

Under the new Kiss programme controller, Andy Roberts, the station chased higher audience figures and installed a computerized playlist which was not to be tampered with in any way, shape or form. It became almost impossible to bring your own musical background to daytime broadcasting.

To me, free choices meant you could colour your programme with shades of the music that you loved. There was once a time when listeners would tune in to a particular daytime broadcaster because they knew what they might play. Everyone who followed Capital's long-standing *Drivetime* host Roger Scott knew they were likely to hear a Bruce Springsteen record because he was such a follower of 'The Boss'. If you listened to Dave Cash, another legendary Capital presenter from the seventies and eighties, you knew you would hear Doctor Hook. Radio stations weren't homogeneous.

Modern commercial radio stations prefer to be so focused that listeners know they are going to get the same music, whoever is presenting. It's the consistency advertisers want. Presenters became voices on sticks. They were not invited to playlist meetings. This became the format at Kiss. Those of us who joined the station at the start, when it had the ethos of a pirate station, tried to challenge the process but were told it was a management decision and it was final.

Things came to a head for me in 1999. It was almost 6 p.m. on a Friday evening and, following the instincts of a career at the turntables, I dropped a record from the computerized playlist and instead inserted 'Who Am I? (Sim Simma)' the Beenie Man hit, well known to Kiss listeners for its memorable line 'Sim Simma, who's got the keys to my Bimma?'

I'd championed the track on my Reggae show and made it a UK Pop chart hit the year before. When I came off air at 7 p.m. I was informed that Andy Roberts had commented on the fact that I had dropped a playlist record and substituted a free choice. I'd been caught!

'You do realize that no presenter has any more free choices on this station?' I was told.

'Yes, but what was wrong with my choice when it was a record we championed here on Kiss?'

I was seething. If ever a song reflected urban radio it was that one by Beenie Man. By 1999 it had the status of a classic. Any fool could see that. Why was it not acceptable? I was told the track had been 'strategically positioned' to be played on what they called 'lower recurrence'. I asked sarcastically if that meant it could only be played at 4 a.m.

We agreed that it was time to talk.

It became clear to me that some members of the Kiss management team thought it was time for David Rodigan to move on. I was one of the few remaining original DJs but I'd been on the station for almost ten years and had enjoyed a good run. That was their reasoning.

I spoke with Mark Story, the managing director. I'd worked with him at Capital when he produced the Roger

Scott show and knew him to be a devout radio professional with boundless passion for the medium. It turned out he still had faith in me.

'You are not leaving this radio station,' he told me. 'Over my dead body!'

But from my point of view, it looked as though it was time to walk away. We discussed alternative possibilities and Mark suggested I consider a position as a daytime presenter on the sister station Magic, which was known for playing mainstream chart hits.

I didn't want that.

Story and Roberts insisted that, whatever happened with my daytime show, they wanted me to stay at Kiss with my weekly Reggae show. I'm grateful to them for that. In the end we agreed that because I was having real difficulty with the axing of freedom of choice it was time for me to stop doing daytime.

I didn't feel animosity so much as frustration. After ten years of broadcasting across the whole schedule I had played my part as cast.

I knew that I couldn't pass on any bad feelings to the listeners. I learned many years before that you must sound fresh and bright at all times. You're there to entertain the audience, and listeners are not interested in miserable, self-obsessed presenters talking about themselves. They want you to play good songs and be a good companion.

The impact of Kiss on radio is undeniable.

It championed the new urban dance styles that followed one after another, from Drum & Bass to UK Garage, and forced the broadcasting world to change – especially the BBC.

BBC Radio 1 was given a complete overhaul, with Tim Westwood being poached from Capital to present a Rap show in 1994, followed by Chris Goldfinger's *Reggae Dancehall Show*, which launched two years later and ran for thirteen years. In 2002, twelve years after Gordon Mac pressed play on 'Pirates' Anthem', the BBC admitted they had ignored the urban dance audience for too long and created a new station, BBC 1Xtra. That is part of the Kiss legacy.

17

Sound Clash

Sound clash is the ultimate environment in which to play Reggae music.

From the earliest days of sound systems there has been intense competition – and when two sounds go to war at the same dance that's a sound clash.

It's a battle that can last all night. The rival sounds compete for the adulation of the baying crowd – a bit like the gladiator contests in the amphitheatres of ancient Rome.

Clashing has developed its own strict rules. Typically, contestants play their best records in 'rounds' of half an hour each that are judged by the audience. Then the rounds are shortened to fifteen minutes before a final duel in which the performers alternately play their rarest and most precious dub plates, 'one for one', until a winner is declared. Strategy is crucial and the best sound clash combatants combine the wiles of a good chess player with the ring courage of a boxer.

Throughout the rollercoaster of my time at Kiss FM I was pursuing this other working life of sound clashing.

For me to get involved in this world was highly unorthodox. Clashing was for the 'sound bwoys' who played on the big systems, not for radio broadcasters such as me. Even less for radio broadcasters who'd grown up in rural Oxfordshire.

But my 'friendly clashes' on the airwaves with Barry G had led me
into an arena which can be intoxicating but also humiliating. In sound
clashing, there's nowhere to hide.

I'd fantasized about having a sound system since the days when
I was a young actor in Sheffield, commissioning my one giant
speaker box and name-stamping all my records. But I never
really thought I'd be sound clashing. Even when I became
known in the Reggae world I was always a radio DJ, not a
sound man.

That all changed in 1991, the year after I began working
at Kiss.

Bodyguard was the fresh sound system from Jamaica that
everyone was talking about. It was set up by two school
friends, Courtney Singh and Big Mac, and based in May Pen,
Clarendon, in the heart of the Jamaican countryside. They
cut serious exclusive dub plates with big-time artists and very
quickly established a reputation as a fearsome sound. They
were red hot and when they came to England to do their first
set of shows everyone wanted to see them. At one of these
events Courtney Singh approached me.

'Next time you come to Jamaica why don't we do a clash,
me and you?'

'What do you mean? Me clash against Bodyguard ... the
sound system?'

'Why not?'

Bodyguard were well aware of my clashes with Barry G
and their popularity in Jamaica. But I knew that clashing on
the radio was very different. Barry and I were two friends who
loved broadcasting and Reggae music and we were just having
fun. Bodyguard was a sound system, which meant they made

their living from clashing. They were professionals and their sound was the best around.

I really liked Courtney and I thought his proposal over. I decided it was a helluva challenge and that I was going to do it.

The clash was set for Big J Lawn, an open-air skating venue in May Pen, Bodyguard's home turf. When I arrived in May Pen, a bustling market town, there were crowds on the street and packed onto buses. It was incredibly busy near the venue and we couldn't get there by car, so had to walk.

I was with Courtney Singh and asked him, 'Why are there all these people?'

'They've come to see you and it's going to be a roadblock.'

It was all because of those shows I had done with Barry G in the 1980s on the radio. My name was still known to Jamaicans and this was a major event in the heartland of the island. This wasn't Kingston or Montego Bay. This was Clarendon, one of the garden parishes, and people were coming off buses from the surrounding countryside, eager to be entertained.

The sound system at Big J Lawn was phenomenal and Bodyguard and the people of May Pen made me feel very welcome. We played on a roof looking down on the auditorium.

One of the biggest dub plates I had cut was of the Mighty Diamonds song 'Bodyguard', which starts with the lyric: 'Who's going to bodyguard you Mr Bodyguard?', and I got the Diamonds to customize it against Bodyguard sound.

But I was nervous about the whole thing and became further bemused when, in the second round, the whole sound system apparatus kicked out and broke down. It just stopped. Normally in a situation like that everyone in the crowd would just go home, but they sat down on the ground, or squatted or leaned. No one left. They waited for the sound system to be rewired. Courtney Singh and Big Mac told me the people wanted to see 'Rodigan from England', they wanted to know what he looked like and what he had to say.

With Bodyguard it wasn't an acrimonious clash; there was fierce competition but there was no disrespect on the microphone.

People back in the UK had warned me, 'Bodyguard will murder you', but the Clarendon people gave me a warm reception. I saw a lot of people just gawping at me because I must have looked so odd – a white Englishman clashing with the hot local sound system. This was rural Jamaica – 'country' – and the people hadn't seen anything like it before. I was doing it for fun but I did it properly because it was an exciting challenge. I was in a different league, playing a musical chess game. It was very different from being in a club playing records.

We repeated the exercise the following year and my clashes with Bodyguard remained popular and friendly. It didn't really matter who won. Ahead of the second one in 1992, Cutty Ranks voiced a dub for me customized with a suitably disparaging lyric, ordering Courtney and the crew to do some menial work – 'Bodyguard, wash off mi car'. By coincidence, Courtney Singh was in the studio in Ocho Rios and heard the dub plate being made by Cutty, but he didn't prevent it getting to me, which was typical of his generosity. The dub was duly delivered to me in May Pen just in time for our clash.

The clashes became annual events, relocated to nearby Bamboo Lawn in May Pen and always taking place on Jamaica's

Scratch: With the inimitable Lee Perry.

Coxsone: With the great producer Clement 'Coxsone' Dodd, founder of the famous Studio One, where this picture was taken.

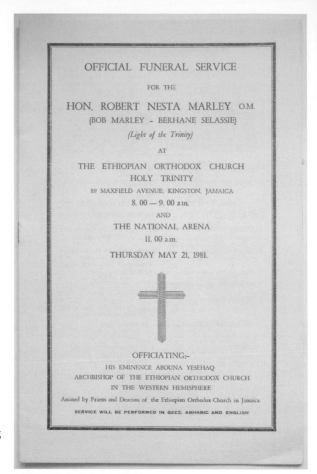

Bob: When the Hon. Robert Nesta Marley passed in 1981 I was among the 6,000 mourners at the National Arena in Jamaica.

Scratched: Lee Perry came to visit me at my London flat and I asked him to sign one of his albums – this was the result.

Clash history: Jamaica was transfixed in 1983 when I clashed tune for tune with star presenter Barry G live on JBC Radio.

Beach clash: My contests with Barry G became legendary – Augustus Pablo came along to represent me at this one on crowded Walter Fletcher Beach.

Dancehall stylee: Wearing a Cuban cap and gold chain, the height of Jamaican style in 1985.

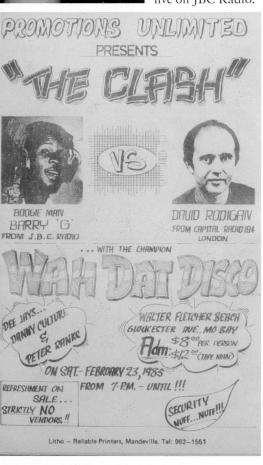

Yellowman: With the king of the dancehall after I brought him to London to play live. Note the *Shackleton* t-shirt, related to the BBC drama series I had recently performed in.

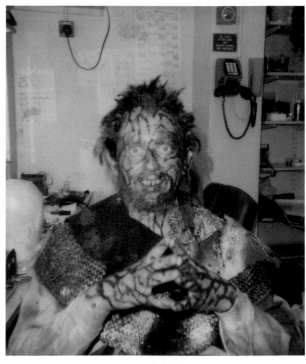

Shackleton: On the set in Greenland, filming the story of polar explorer Ernest Shackleton for the BBC.

Doctor Who: Made up to play the part of the Doctor's enemy 'Broken Tooth' in the most famous sci-fi series of them all. Taken in the dressing room at BBC TV Centre after my death scene.

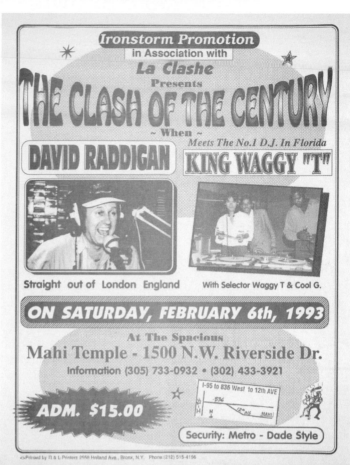

Sound clash: Flyer for one of my first big clashes, against King Waggy T in Miami.

World champion: With the trophy after being crowned winner of the world sound clash in New York in 2012, with my mixer Pee-Wee *(left)* and promoter Chin *(right)*.

Festival life: Standing on the mixing desk at the packed Parklife festival in Manchester in 2015.

Bunny: In the studio at BBC Radio 1Xtra with Bunny Wailer, holding a copy of *Blackheart Man*, one of my favourite albums.

Goldie: I have a great relationship with the Drum & Bass crowd. The multi-talented Goldie presented me with this magnificent portrait.

Rebel Sound: With my compadres Chase & Status and Shy FX when our newly-formed Rebel Sound won the Red Bull Culture Clash in 2014.

Junior Gong: On stage with Damian Marley at the Notting Hill Carnival, shortly before he told me to tell the story of my life in Reggae.

Music room: Today with my collection of 7-inch vinyl Reggae records.

Tools of the trade: My 7-inch record box, with a Studio One selection, and my 12-inch record box, with my precious dub plates.

Trophy cabinet: The prizes of my sound clashing career.

independence weekend at the start of August. One of the most memorable was in 1994, when I took part in a three-way clash with Bodyguard and Stone Love. The Clarendon County Show where Jamaican farmers would show their produce was taking place the same weekend across the road in the agricultural showground. There was a tremendous energy all around May Pen that day. It was the perfect combination of independence weekend, the county show and the big clash.

At all the big Reggae dances in Jamaica you would see wires coming out of the sound system belonging to professional cassette men who recorded events and sold the tapes from their stalls on the street corners in Kingston. The Bodyguard clashes were so popular that the cassettes swept up out of Jamaica and into New York and Miami. I soon began to get invitations to clash in the United States.

One of the most significant in my entire career was in Miami with King Waggy T, the number one selector in Florida. Miami is known as Kingston 21 or Little Jamaica, because of the massive Jamaican communities there and in nearby Fort Lauderdale. Waggy T is a Chinese-Jamaican who moved to Florida. He has the most amazing collection of dub plates and is well known for his seamless mixing when playing tunes. He was a selector who famously never spoke – he employed an MC to do all his talking.

This was billed as 'The Clash of the Century' and took place at the Mahi Temple, a Miami nightclub, on Bob Marley Day, 6 February, in 1993. There were around three thousand fans inside the place.

'Tonight is going to be a night of musical pleasure . . . I've flown 6,000 miles to clash with King Waggy T, Florida's ruling champion,' I told the audience.

'Tonight you are going to hear music you have never heard before. Tonight, Miami, you are going to hear the most cantankerous, poisonous dub plates you ever heard!'

The hot Dancehall producer Dave Kelly, who runs the Mad House studio in Jamaica, was crucial to me beating Waggy T. He arranged for a killer dub plate to be delivered, literally on a plate, in the wings of the auditorium just before the 'one for one' finale. A guy gave it to me and said, 'This is for you, from Dave Kelly.' The dub was 'No Retreat, No Surrender' by the hot Dancehall artist of the moment, Daddy Screw. And it won me the clash.

That was the night when I first started to experiment with recorded sketches and the theatrical side of my sound clashing. It helped me get the upper hand – even though Waggy T is a great selector and a tough opponent. I recorded a newsflash in BBC style saying Waggy T had died in a sound clash at Mahi Temple. It was so well received that I started writing more funny scenarios that I would use in clashes.

I used a similar newsflash theme a few months later in Washington, DC when I clashed with Emperor, the ruling sound from the American capital. When I beat them it caused a sensation in the Reggae sound clash world and people really started to take me seriously. My clashes with Barry G and Bodyguard had been friendly affairs but taking on Emperor was different. This was a hard-core ghetto dance with no prisoners taken and Emperor had a big reputation.

I flew out there on my own and the club was absolutely packed. Clash audiences are highly knowledgeable and there are strict rules – you automatically lose if you play a song already played by your opponent. When I beat Emperor everyone who followed sound clash culture knew it was a big deal.

After the early popularity of my recorded newsflashes people came to expect them of me. Skits on the themes of James Bond characters and spies became a particular speciality.

Then I took it to the next level by appearing in fancy dress. I was drawing on my theatrical roots – but it's a long way from the Rose Bruford School of Speech and Drama to the heat of a sound clash in the vast cavern of Club Jam Roc in New York.

Inside that venue hordes of hard-core fans from the United States, the Caribbean and even the UK had come to see me do battle with the toughest sound system in all Jamaica; the mighty Killamanjaro from downtown western Kingston (named after Mount Kilimanjaro in Africa) was taking on David Rodigan from Kiss FM in London.

But I proved that night that some theatrical talent can be a valuable secret weapon in a sound clash.

As we prepared to take to the stage, my opponent Ricky Trooper, who was selecting the records for Killamanjaro, could not believe his eyes as I appeared before him dressed in an Indian turban.

'What are you doing?' he asked me.

Trooper is the fiercest and most competitive character you could meet in the sound system world. But this time he was completely thrown. I just laughed – he'd find out soon enough.

The clash was billed as 'Jamaica versus England' and the crowd was hyped up. They must have been as confused as Trooper by my Sikh costume.

As soon as it was my turn to play I picked out a specially recorded skit in which one of my actor friends spoke as a broadcast newsreader. It started to play:

CNN headline news. Tonight's top story. Rumours have been confirmed that David Rodigan, the sound system serial killer, has landed in the New York area.

Police and Immigration authorities have confirmed reports that Rodigan is disguised as a Sikh Indian taxi driver. *(Cheers and laughter from the crowd)*

He was last seen driving a yellow taxi in the direction of the Jam Roc club in Long Island. Police are warning members of the public not to approach him as he is armed and extremely dangerous.

There are many Sikh taxi drivers in New York and suddenly the turban made sense. People were falling about laughing. I had the crowd on my side.

After the news flash, I started playing my real dub plates, but still with the Sikh turban on. I began with an a cappella of 'The Lion Sleeps Tonight' by the Jamaican vocal group ARP.

'In the dancehall, the mighty dancehall . . . Rodigan's gonna kill a sound tonight.'

This was all part of my approach to sound clashing, which can be a very aggressive environment. I like to remind people that, first and foremost, it's entertainment.

Costumes are a sound clash trademark for me and I take them seriously. I bought the authentic turban from a theatrical costumer in Camden, London, which I used during my acting career when I appeared in the BBC drama *Shackleton*.

I took the dressing-up to another level when I clashed in Brooklyn against Bodyguard. This time my theme was horse racing, which is a big thing in Jamaica, where they have the historic Caymanas Park racetrack. I had my strategy all planned – I would come on stage dressed as a jockey.

I decided to cut a special dub plate of the classic 'Long Shot Kick De Bucket' by The Pioneers, with its opening line: 'What a weeping and a wailing, down at Caymanas Park . . .' Long Shot was a famous Jamaican racehorse who died – kicked the bucket – on the race track.

So I had the song customized to kill Bodyguard in New York with the lyrics: 'What a weeping and a wailing, in New York tonight, Bodyguard flop . . . and Rodigan win the clash'. I went to the costume shop and got the full horse-racing outfit, the jockey's silks and cap. Everything was proper. I couldn't get The Pioneers to voice the dub plate because they had broken up but I got Mafia & Fluxy to rebuild the rhythm and re-voice the track with my chosen lyrics.

But in sound clash, things don't always work the way you plan. I came on stage in New York wearing my jockey's silks and the place collapsed with laughter. So far, so good, and I could hear them thinking 'What's he doing this time?' But then I played my dub plate, thinking everything would make sense to the crowd.

The trap door opened that night.

For some reason the New York audience did not recognize the song. It had been a big hit in the UK in 1969, a favourite with the skinheads and a chart smash. To me it was an absolute classic tune. But clearly it had not crossed the water to America and was pretty much unknown in the large Jamaican community in New York. Plus it was 1994 and the older generation that might have known it was apparently not present at that dance.

The silence was deafening. The dancehall stage can be a lonely place when you're not getting a favourable crowd response. I stood there and my world fell in. It was good night, Brooklyn and I had already lost the clash.

Bodyguard, my opponents, thought it was hilarious. They knew the tune of course but what the selectors and hard-core collectors know isn't necessarily what the general public knows. Sometimes you can be too clever and get hoist with your own petard. It was a lesson I should have learned all those years earlier at my very first gig, the so-called 'Tribal Hot 100' in High Wycombe, where I'd pressed cutting-edge dub plates at Mr Magoo's for the dance and no one had a clue what I was playing.

But my theatrical skits were generally so popular that I had other sound systems asking me if I would voice intros and write sketches for them. I agreed to do some recorded sports-style commentary for Bodyguard when they competed in the World Clash competition of 1993. I got into trouble for that.

I wasn't taking part in the World Clash but it was staged in London and featured the British sound system Saxon among the contestants. My commentary was based on the football World Cup and I was talking about the Bodyguard selector Johnny putting the ball in the back of the net. It went down a storm on the night but I had some stick from the Saxon supporters who said I shouldn't have done a favour for a Jamaican sound competing against a British one.

The greatest opponent in my sound clash career has been Killamanjaro. 'Jaro', as it's known throughout the business, is one of the great heavyweight sound systems in Jamaica, perhaps the biggest of all. In Reggae culture it is deeply respected alongside historic sounds such as Volcano and Jah Love.

My first encounter with Jaro was in 1993 at the Mahi Temple in Miami, shortly after I battled with King Waggy T. Jaro had legendary dub plates and had just hired Ricky Trooper, a hot young selector with a lot of energy, who got his name from having once been in a marching band in Jamaica.

I prepared hard for the clash and persuaded Prince Buster – who never previously made dub plates – to cut me specials of two songs, 'Hard Man Fi Dead' and 'Ghost Dance', both made over rhythms rebuilt by Mafia & Fluxy. I thought these dubs – which were recorded in Miami – would win me the night, but 'Ghost Dance' was met with silence. The crowd didn't recognize it because it hadn't been a hit in Jamaica, only in England in 1967. Killamanjaro won the clash by playing what seemed like the ultimate weapon – a Bob Marley 'dub plate' of his song 'Bad Card'. We only found out later it was Bob's son Ziggy singing the vocal – but the crowd thought it really was Bob.

There's great controversy over whether Bob Marley ever made a dub plate for a Reggae sound system. I have my own special mixes of 'Sun is Shining', 'Get Up Stand Up' and 'Natural Mystic', because I've been allowed access to the original multi-track recordings, and good friends such as Ashley Beedle, Dave Hill and RS Digital have done the production for me. I don't have a Bob dub plate – though some think I do. That stems from the only time I played a Bob record in a sound clash. I was competing with Killamanjaro in New York in 1997 and I knew that Ricky Trooper loved the classic 'Cuss Cuss' Studio One Reggae rhythm and often used it when recording dub plates. So I asked Island Records if I could have the a cappella of 'Iron Lion Zion' and persuaded Seani B, an amazing DJ from west London and master of the remix, if he would put the Marley vocal on the Cuss Cuss rhythm. It took him eighteen hours because 'Iron Lion Zion' was originally sung live with real instruments. Seani adjusted and adjusted until the mix sounded right. And that night I won the sound clash after I made a little speech – 'Ricky, I know you love the Cuss Cuss rhythm; well, how about this . . .?' – and in came Bob's voice with the lyric: 'I'm on the rock . . .' People still think Rodigan's got a Bob Marley dub plate because this was a unique recording, but it wasn't voiced as a dub plate and he doesn't call my name in it.

I clashed against Trooper again in London and Fort Lauderdale, but the biggest contest was that night in November 1997 when I dressed as a Sikh taxi driver in Long Island. Unfortunately the evening didn't end with the same good humour that accompanied my arrival in fancy dress.

It turned into an epic clash that went on for around four hours. There was a clock on the wall and we started at 1.30 a.m. It was round after round after round.

Ricky is an inspiring selector and very difficult to beat. Even when you have really given it to him he can make a speech which suggests to the audience that the tune you just played was of no significance.

But that night in Long Island the dance was going in my favour and he couldn't take it. So he drew the race card at the end of the clash.

He played a dub plate 'Jaro have no white God' and then made a succession of comments about skin colour. He called me 'some little white boy' who 'nah brush oonuh bloodclaat teeth'; he said the 'black man originate toothpaste and toothbrush' and 'when Rodigan talk to me, mi smell him breath through the bloodclat speaker'. He then lined up a record, shouting, 'Ayy! White bwoy!'

He played a track by Goofy, a jokey song about bad oral hygiene called 'You brush yuh teeth', and as it finished he shouted, 'Stand up with Jah!' – a righteous cry that also punned on the 'Ja-ro' nickname of his sound.

I was seething.

'Stand up with who? Stand up with Jah? After bullshit like that? You're a hypocrite! Now hear this.'

I then played Prince Buster.

'Yuh pick him up, yuh lick him down, he bounce right back, Rodigan's a hard man fi dead.'

But I was furious and made a speech.

'I've got one thing to say to you. This was a sweet dance until you started on this colour thing. You know what you've done? You've just brought the whole thing down into the gutter. And you've spoilt the night! You've taken away the spirit from the dance, because you're bad mind and mi finished with you!'

He tried to stand his ground even though people were starting to boo him.

'Nuff man want to see Jaro dead. It not my fault that I have better tune dan dem and me is a better selector.'

I couldn't understand why he had gone down that route after we had been playing for four hours. I suppose he was clutching at straws because I was winning and he knew that. It didn't do him any favours because the crowd was perfectly well aware of the fact that I was a white man and Jamaicans know me as someone who has a passionate love of their music. Because of that I was never disrespected in my career, which made this lone episode hard to take.

Ricky left the dance and the revered owner of the Killamanjaro system, Noel 'Papa Jaro' Harper, apologized to me and said he had tried to stop Ricky as soon as he started talking about race. Mr Harper, who founded the sound in 1969, naming it after Africa's highest mountain, is a veteran of clashes over many decades and he knew that tactic wasn't going to work.

Years later I got to know Ricky better. When he wasn't doing that nonsense he was a great selector. He said to me that I didn't realize how tough it was for him. I was a white man from England and if I lost a clash I could go back home undamaged because people would know I was first and foremost a radio DJ. He asked me to consider his position. If he lost and returned to Jamaica as a black man playing on the legendary Killamanjaro sound, he would be taunted with: 'Bwoy, you let white man beat you?' He said it was much harder for him.

'Yeah, but you didn't have to do that,' I said.

A couple of weeks later we had a rematch called 'Come to Settle a Score' in Fulham Town Hall in London. It was another epic struggle and was eventually declared a draw. I pulled a wicked dub plate on Ricky recorded for me by the Dancehall artist of the moment, Red Rat, who had a huge hit called 'Wrigleys', which was another jokey song about dental cleanliness. The dub was customized and told my opponent, 'Trooper, don't chew on my name like Wrigleys!' It ripped the town hall apart.

I rate Trooper for his ability to choose records, his energy, his speeches, and in the history of sound system culture he is a very important player because of the persona he brings to the stage – especially in sound clashes. He and the late Kevin

'Squingy' Bennett from the Bass Odyssey sound in Jamaica are two prime examples of selectors who have extraordinary power as MCs on the microphone. Ricky can pull the tunes, play them and make a speech as well. On form he is phenomenal and will bounce around from foot to foot.

But although I rate him as an inspired selector, another criticism I have always levelled at him is that there are times when his knocking of other people's songs is invalid and unkind.

At our clash in Fort Lauderdale I played a dub plate of 'Who Could It Be?' by Luciano on Bob Marley's 'Natural Mystic' rhythm and Trooper grabbed the mic and said, 'That nah work, it nah good!'

I was shocked by the comment and told him so.

'How could you make such an unpleasant comment about a song when you say you are the one who champions Luciano? I know that song is good and everyone else does too – what's up with you?'

I really had a pop at him.

I was often out of kilter because, unlike all the other sound clash selectors, I would give compliments if I thought they'd played something exceptional.

'That was an amazing tune! Nuff respect to you for that.'

People would question why I'd want to compliment an opponent in a bear-pit environment like a sound clash. I was warned that it was a hard, tough game and you can't be a nice guy to someone you're trying to take out. Only big knocks knock down big doors, I was told.

But I say it's an entertainment form and that's the way I think it should be.

There are all sorts of tricks of the trade in sound clash but for me it was never about winning at all costs. I have always played fair and I felt people would judge me on that. I've had positive feedback from the artists because of the way I selected and played their music.

People who see me leaping about on stage at these big events probably don't realize that there was a time when I lacked all confidence to go into these clashes. I would make all sorts of excuses about not being able to do big speeches or to mix records.

I conquered those fears because of people like Valerie Robinson, the owner of the Nottingham-based sound system V Rocket, and Irish & Chin, the promoters of the World Clash events in New York. They persuaded me I could do it and said I should have more belief. They had total faith in me and really pushed me.

When I clashed at the start of the nineties I was able to operate on my own. But at the big World Clash events there would be lots of different sound systems competing in the same venue and the tracks would be played so fast that you needed really polished skills on the turntables. Irish & Chin encouraged me to get someone who could mix my tunes. That was how Pee-Wee became my mixer in New York and we went on to win so many clashes together, with him mixing and bringing his ideas to the table.

You have to prepare for a big sound clash. I'm fastidious about the way my dubs are recorded and notorious for it in the Reggae world. They have to be really, really good, and if the dub plate recording is inferior to the record, then I will play the vinyl. When I commission a dub I have always tried to emphasize this to the artists and engineers working in the studios.

I've been fortunate in having trusted friends to support me in cutting dubs. Many recordings in my dub plate box have been mixed for me by RS Digital. I always insisted they were 'split', which meant the voice was recorded separately from the instrumental rhythm so that I could then put that voice on other rhythms for remixes. RS Digital is a very good recording engineer and a fanatic for Rock Steady music. When he was younger he was a DMC Mixing Champion.

I also had David 'Henry' Lewis on the ground for me in Jamaica. I first met him on the island in 1997 and he became a good friend. I realized he was somebody who I could trust implicitly with my recordings. This enabled me to buy a lot more music because I didn't have to fly down to Jamaica every time I needed dubs. Henry became my right hand in Jamaica. He worked at the famous Anchor Studios and because he knew how fastidious I was, he wouldn't rest until a dub was recorded just as I'd asked for it. He demanded that it be made with enthusiasm and gusto and he would encourage a vibe in the recording session in order to achieve this. Some of the artists – especially the hot acts of the moment – are recording dub plates on rotation and can easily fall into a trap of going through the motions. That's not good enough – a dub plate has to have energy – they are called 'specials' and they need to be special. Every dub plate has to be worth its place in the record box. As the saying goes: 'In the abundance of water the fool is thirsty' – the worst thing you can have as a selector is too much choice and too many dubs to pick from.

A key contact in the United States was Philip Smart. Back in Jamaica he was called Prince Philip. He was Tubby's protégé and worked as an assistant to Errol Thompson at Randy's Studios on North Parade. He was there when Errol T engineered Augustus Pablo's first recordings, which I used to covet in the window of Lee's Sound City record shop.

I met Philip in New York, to where he emigrated. He ran HCF Studios in Long Island, a real old-school multi-track recording studio where Shaggy and many other New York Reggae artists made their best work. Philip was the go-to man in New York for getting stuff done because he had a warm gracious personality and a lovely sense of humour. He didn't pressure people but was very attentive to detail. He recorded some of my best dubs – by Johnny Osbourne, Shabba Ranks, Shinehead and Phyllis Dillon. I never heard a bad word said about him.

The prices for dubs vary from $100 or $150 up to $2,000 for a single track if it's what I'd call a Premier League prime dub by a top artist. A red-hot tune such as 'Driver A' by Buju Banton, from 2006, will command top dollar. When Bounty Killer's 'Look Into My Eyes' hit the streets in 1999 the demand was impossible to meet.

When numerous sound systems have dub plates of the same hit song you have to be more creative by also recording the vocal on a different backing track, such as a classic old Studio One rhythm.

Many of the most precious dubs I have were given to me as gifts. On several occasions I've offered artists money for specials and they have refused to take it. It had been a gesture of thanks from them and they seemed almost insulted that I'd wanted to pay.

Bunny Wailer has never charged me. Prince Buster didn't want any money for those dubs I used against Killamanjaro and neither did Tenor Saw, Bounty Killer or Damian 'Junior Gong' Marley. I was on the radio and playing their music at live events and that was enough for them. In the early years the dub was really a gift and another way of spreading the music.

I've never made a point of playing dub plates on the radio because I maintain that serves no purpose since it doesn't help record sales. I would only use them in the context of a live dance or a sound clash.

Nowadays you can buy dub plates on the Internet and it's an online industry. You have studios set up in Jamaica with the sole purpose of providing an international dub plate service. 'The best customized dub plate service in Jamaica', they will claim. I get emails from them quoting one price for the standard lyrics of a song and another to personalize it with your own words.

In days gone by there would have only been a few of us selectors out in Jamaica competing for the dub plates from the big artists. It's very different now with the Internet. On the whole I think that's a good thing. It means dub plates are no longer beyond the reach of potential new young sound boys and girls who are trying to develop their careers. It's difficult for young people in distant parts of the world to afford to get to Jamaica but the age of the online dub plate has brought new possibilities. Some old timers argue it has devalued the currency of dub plates but I would beg to differ. It has made the culture more accessible.

Just as importantly, Reggae artists are living from this. Music revenues have fallen to almost zero in terms of vinyl sales and this is a way by which music makers can put food on their tables.

There is a certain code among sound boys. We see records as the tools of our trade and we look after each other and help each other when we can.

There was only one instance where someone tried to steal my records in a dancehall and that was at a gig in Germany. I placed the records at the back of the stage and I was feeding from the box when I realized that some of the records had gone. There was a curtain and someone had got behind and put his hand in the box and taken some of them. I stopped the dance and made them put on the lights.

'Ladies and Gentlemen, something has happened that has never happened in my life; someone has actually stolen some of my records.'

Security closed the doors and they found the person that did it. I didn't want to see him or talk to him. He had tried to stash the records away – for what reason I don't know.

Finding the right record when you are in a dark dancehall or club is a matter of instinct. Every selector or DJ must know his box and mine is carefully divided.

I have a seven-inch record box divided into four sections; the left-hand side is for the oldies, with separate sections for Coxsone Dodd Studio One and for Duke Reid Treasure Isle productions. The front-right section is new and fresh tunes, and then there is some Soul on the back at the right if I need them.

In my twelve-inch box there are the dub plates at the front, and then the ten-inch dub plates, and behind those the new twelve-inch releases with, right at the very back, the older twelve-inch records that still get a good crowd response.

An instinctive quality that you have to learn is when to change gear. You just sense it in the crowd. Sometimes they are hyped up and then later you might have to bring them down; change gear and go to a Lovers Rock selection. In an intimate club like Gossips, the Lovers Rock sequence was a key part of the evening because people would be on dates and wanted to get close. This changing gear was a lesson I learned in my early days from mentors such as Captain Ken at the Bouncing Ball club in Peckham.

I know this sounds a bit funny but the records kind of talk to you. A tune will almost say 'Play me' – that's the only way I can describe it. You are looking through the box and almost feel that the song is calling out to you. I've always trusted and relied upon that instinct. Sometimes in a two- or three-hour set I will find myself thinking, 'Where am I going to go next?' But then certain songs leap out at you and you know they will work. Those are the instincts that keep you alive in a sound clash.

The sound clash arena can be very intimidating.

Using humour – by creating a character, scenario or spoof of a horserace or a boxing match – is a very effective way of entertaining the audience and at the same time taking the sting out of the tail of someone who thinks they will use aggression to take you out. Announcing an opponent's death at the hands of a 'sound system serial killer' – who happens to be a bald-headed white man from London – is ridiculous enough to get the crowd laughing.

It's pointless for me to try to fight fire with fire against the most warlike selectors. Humour neutralizes the impact and firepower of your adversary. At the same time it proves that the sound clash, which can be a very aggressive environment, doesn't have to be about shouting, screaming and threats. It's primarily about music, which will speak volumes if you allow it to do so.

Part of the creativity of recording a unique dub plate can be scripting a funny intro. It is one of the things that has given me a reputation – the use of humour as opposed to just being a bad man sound boy.

Many times I have called on acting friends to voice a dub plate introduction posing as a BBC or CNN announcer or impersonating a well-known voice such as John Arlott, the legendary cricket commentator, telling the crowd how Rodigan has just smashed Jaro for six. The pukka-voiced radio presenter Richard Astbury was among those who would record intros for me.

For clashing with Barry G, I used a fellow broadcaster at BFBS to do a clipped English accent to let listeners know that 'David Rodigan has landed at Norman Manley Airport with a selection of dub plates that have been specially cleared by customs.' For one Jaro clash I had a sound-a-like for ITN newsreader Trevor McDonald, along with the Big Ben bongs and music which signal the start of the *News at Ten* bulletin. I had a *Star Trek* intro specially scripted for a clash with Bass Odyssey.

These intros became my signature and the clash crowds have come to expect them of me. I recorded a special one for a big clash in Jamaica against the broadcaster GT Taylor, aka 'The Dancehall Master'.

That was a massive event. It was a Millennium clash in 1999 and GT Taylor was the number one Dancehall broadcaster in Jamaica with a late-night radio show that everybody rated. He was a later version of my old friend and musical adversary Barry Gordon and a promoter decided to put me and GT Taylor up against each other in a clash at Windsor Lawn in St Ann's Bay, just outside Ocho Rios.

There was heat inside the place that night!

When it came to the final decision as to who had won and

who had lost there was a discrepancy in the voting over how many hands had gone up. The MC said there was only one way finally to resolve this.

'If you think GT Taylor won the clash, go to that side of the lawn. And if you think Rodigan won, go to the other side of the lawn.'

That's when you could clearly see that more had gone to my side than GT Taylor's and it was obvious that I should get the trophy.

I was dressed all in black, including a fedora and silk shirt. The crowd put me up shoulder high and it was a big deal.

GT didn't take it very well. After he complained that it wasn't fair, an article was published in the Jamaican press saying 'GT – Stop Cry Man'. It asked if he really thought Jamaicans would allow a white man to come to their country and beat a Jamaican if they didn't think he had done so fairly. It was a crowd decision. The message was 'take your licks'.

At the end of the day it was show business. We got to laugh about it afterwards and did another show together up in Canada. GT is a highly professional radio DJ and he's been around the block.

The special intro I recorded was of a courtroom scene where GT Taylor was charged with the attempted murder of Mr David Rodigan using metal dub plates. I found out that The Dancehall Master's real name was Gordon Taylor, so that got a mention in the dub plate, in order to weaken him a little. That's all part of sound clashing. The dub gave a name-check to Madden's, the famous eighty-year-old Jamaican funeral service company that I knew most people in the crowd would have heard of.

Of course, sound boys try their own stunts to weaken my

position. It is a competition after all. Because I would wear suits or smart clothing I would come in for teasing about it, suggesting I'm not tough enough, and not close to Dancehall culture.

The Japanese sound system Mighty Crown – run by Simon and Sami T – caught me out once by very publicly offering me a drag on their spliff. They got me there, to be fair to them. It was during a clash in Hartford, Connecticut. Knowing my reputation for using fancy dress, they came on with Sami T dressed in a Kung Fu outfit. Then they played a big marijuana anthem, 'Joker Smoker' by Tristan Palmer, and they passed me their spliff as if to say, 'How come you don't smoke, David, if you're such a big fan of Reggae?'

I wasn't going to puff on their spliff. Smoking had nearly killed me after all, although Mighty Crown weren't aware of that. I just had to laugh and smile and take that one on the chin. That was a smart move on Mighty Crown's part, using a theatrical element in their performance that I had used many times myself.

That was the night the rap star Wyclef Jean from the Fugees turned up to support me and I defeated Mighty Crown – even though they'd just been made world champions, after winning the World Clash in November 1999.

Wyclef drove all the way from Brooklyn to bring me the crucial dub plate personally. He came in a convoy of cars and his people had to arrange for him to get into the building unnoticed by the crowd. You can imagine how hard that was – a superstar like Wyclef with a big long fur coat on, coming into a packed club. I had got to know Wyclef in London when he appeared on the Kiss FM stage at Notting Hill Carnival and we met back stage.

Now in Connecticut he was standing in this little side room near where we were performing and his bodyguard Beast was in the wings, gesturing to me to come over. I thought, 'What's Beast doing here?' I went into this little room and behind the door was Wyclef.

He said, 'Do you know what the number one tune is?'

'No.'

'"Maria Maria". It's produced by me.'

'Oh, congratulations.'

'Here's the dub plate. Play the second track.'

Mighty Crown couldn't recover from that Wyclef dub. 'Maria Maria' by Carlos Santana and the Product G&B was number one everywhere at the time. Wyclef had produced it and he'd made a dub with my name and a derogatory mention of Mighty Crown in it! I knew it was bona fide because Wyclef was handing it to me, so I just played it blind without having heard it. That dub received one of the biggest 'forwards' I've ever been given! You heard the roar start at the back of the room and it swept forwards in a wave. We call that a 'rolling forward'.

To be fair to Mighty Crown, when we had a rematch in New York the following Easter they chased after Wyclef and persuaded him to cut a counter action dub plate for them, which they used on me and won that clash.

Wyclef is a great student of sound clash culture, as I realized when he came to headline UK Sunsplash, which finally returned for a one-off event in 2001 at Victoria Park in east London. It was a big day and Wyclef was top of the bill. They also had Goofy, Buccaneer, Red Rat, Mr Vegas, Ali Campbell from UB40 and Jah Shaka performing. During Wyclef's performance he played dub plates in a sound system style, including an exclusive Whitney Houston dub that paid tribute to the great Dennis Brown, who had just died. After the show, Beast asked me and my son Jamie to come to the dressing room and Wyclef said I had inspired him to cut dubs.

For many years I had a club night every Wednesday at Subterranea in west London called Rodigan's Reggae. One week I had a call from Wyclef, who was in London and wanted me to put him and a friend down on the guest list for that night. I laughed and said, 'Of course.'

We were on stage playing when he emerged from the crowd and approached me with Beast and asked if I had a CD player. I told him we hadn't because we were playing vinyl but that the engineer had a CD player upstairs on the gallery. At which point Beast jumped off the stage, walked across the dancefloor at Subterranea, climbed up a trellis to the upstairs gallery and handed a CD to the engineer, telling him to play it.

Wyclef took the microphone.

'Ladies and Gentlemen, this is a very special moment tonight. I want you to hear a special dub that I have just cut,' he said.

The CD started to play – it was the 'Heavenless' rhythm, which was a Dancehall classic of the moment. Wyclef said he wanted to present to them the singer who provided the vocal they were about to hear. And onto the stage of this small London club walked none other than Tom Jones, an artist more usually seen headlining in Las Vegas.

The dub plate was extraordinary; a medley of Tom Jones hits sung by the most famous of Welsh baritones in a Dancehall style to kill an opponent soundboy! 'Green, Green Grass of Home' was the main cut – with the customized lyrics warning all the sound boys that 'come to meet me'. Wyclef had written all the lyrics and told Tom to sing them, and the dub plate was name-checking Wyclef and his sound system.

The place went crazy. Tom Jones just stood there centre stage and smiled and waved back to the audience. To this day people still struggle to believe that we saw Jones the Voice at a Reggae club night, but I can assure you we did.

18

World-a-Reggae-Music

Reggae is Jamaica's great gift to mankind and this music is so contagious that it has spread to all corners of the earth.

Not surprisingly, it's a culture that is shared by the other islands of the Caribbean, to which I am a frequent visitor.

But it is much less known that there are vibrant Reggae movements in Germany, Italy and Switzerland, and I have been fortunate enough to be intimately involved in these scenes from the outset.

From California in the West to Japan in the East, Reggae music has been my passport to travel the globe.

My BFBS show for the British Armed Forces had extraordinary consequences which I never foresaw.

My original intention in 1984 was to entertain British troops, especially those with Caribbean roots or those who had developed a love of Reggae back in the UK. What I didn't expect was my two-hour Thursday-night show becoming required listening for a cohort of German teenagers as they did their homework.

Since the end of the Second World War, the British Army has had a presence in western Germany with barracks in

North-Rhine Westphalia and Lower Saxony, where I was born in the British Military Hospital at Hanover. The BFBS signal could also be picked up across large parts of northern Germany and young Germans realized the music we were playing was something very different from their mainstream stations.

I was only made aware of the impact of my show years later when I was invited to play in Essen and somebody tapped me on the shoulder and spoke to me.

'What's it like to see all your children in front of you?'

I was confused. 'What do you mean?'

'Most of these people were teenagers when they discovered you on a Thursday night on *Rodigan's Rockers* on BFBS. We heard this guy playing Reggae but it wasn't just the Bob Marley and Peter Tosh that we knew.'

I hadn't thought that young Germans might be listening. I was entertaining British soldiers who knew the music – and so I would drop a wide range of Roots and Culture artists alongside the latest Dancehall releases, and pepper the show with personal anecdotes. There was nothing like that in Germany.

Word spread. And today Germany has its own phenomenal sound system culture and one of the strongest Reggae scenes anywhere in the world. I like to think I played a part in that process.

Three teenage lads who used to come to my gigs at Neons in Bielefeld used to stand at the front all night, staring and watching the records play. They went off and set up their own sound system called Soundquake, and it's one of the biggest and most successful in Germany. They also have a record label and an online mail order company.

There are now many sound systems in Germany. The founders of the Pow Pow sound system in Cologne are former listeners to the BFBS show. That sound has been going for over twenty years. Cologne hosts Summerjam, which is one of the biggest Reggae festivals in the world and has been going since 1985, and the city is home to Gentleman, who is one of the finest Reggae singers to come from the European continent.

In Berlin you have another great scene, thanks to the likes of Barney Millah and Panza from the Supersonic sound. In Stuttgart, there is Sentinel sound, who I thought were so good that I put their name forward to take part in the World Clash contest in New York in 2005 against the big Jamaican systems. Sentinel duly brought the trophy back to Germany!

The German Reggae scene, more than those in most other European countries, is influenced by the Dancehall culture of contemporary Jamaica. They try to keep right up to speed with the latest trends. But its origins are in BFBS radio, which introduced German youth to music that they hadn't heard before. Charles Foster, who ran the network, was very loyal to me. As BFBS chief executive and head of radio he showed unswerving support for Reggae, and my show lasted twenty-five years from 1984 through to 2009.

Italy has become another home from home. For many years I've celebrated my birthday there by playing Reggae on the beach in the Bay of Naples.

The Italian scene is a little more laidback than the one in Germany. There's an element of Dancehall but in general they prefer the traditional Roots Rock Reggae and the One Drop beat.

The first time I was invited to play there on a sound system was in 1997 when I was contacted by One Love Hi Pawa sound system from Rome. They was a group of about six university students and one of them, Duccio, had a doctorate in Philosophy. They were deeply in love with Reggae and probably had the first sound system in Italy. They booked me to play in a fort in Rome.

I'd played in Italy once before, five years earlier. There was an open-air event to celebrate the 500th anniversary of Christopher Columbus reaching the Americas. It took place at Villa Borghese, the great public park in the centre of Rome. I played over two weekends in the park and as I approached the record decks there was a Rastafarian Italian called Lampa Dread playing Reggae and he shook my hand. Shortly afterwards he became a selector with One Love.

Duccio and the crew brought me out to Rome on a regular basis. The sound system became well established in the Italian capital and had its own record shop, One Love Music Corner. On occasion, they told me about a place down in the south of Italy where Reggae parties took place on the beach and the people spoke in a dialect so strong that they as Romans couldn't understand them.

Then one Friday night back in London in 2002 I had finished playing at a bar in Battersea when I noticed a man and woman standing outside at the end of the evening. They had arrived late and looked a little lost but I could tell straight away that they were heavily into the music.

I asked them if they were OK. They said they were from Italy and had come down specifically to listen to me, so I asked their names. She was Fabiana and he was Lele. It turned out that he was an MC who performed as Rankin Lele. They told me how much they loved Reggae and said they were visiting a friend in London. They came from Salento, in the far south of Italy, right on the heel.

'Salento!' I said. 'That's the place where you have Reggae parties every summer!'

They told me I had to come down and experience it. And I did. The first year I played in a bar in the fishing village of Casalabate. It was such a great night that I was presented with a silver plaque by Papa Gianni, one of the founders of southern Italy's Sud Sound System. He made a speech in the local dialect.

The next year I played on the beach alongside the bar, and the year after that it was on the promenade. Now it's an annual event with 10,000 people. It's free and is the most incredible gathering of Italy's Reggae fraternity. There are so many Reggae events that happen in that Puglia region – but that one on the first Saturday of August has become a date in my diary for over a decade.

As a result of playing in Rome other bookings came through from the major towns of Italy where there is a similarly deep love and appreciation of Reggae. I played in Milan each year and in Bologna, Modena and many other cities.

The growth of this Italian scene was partly driven by the fantastically successful Rototom Sunsplash festival, which I played at on a couple of occasions when it was based near Udine in northern Italy. After sixteen years it moved to its current location at Benicàssim, north of Valencia on the coast of Spain, where it takes place over eight days and attracts nearly 250,000 people.

Every summer on the weekend nearest to 24 June, I would go to Italy to celebrate my birthday with a Reggae party on the beach. My friend Fabio opened the first Reggae bar in

Naples and, together with Doc Scott, he runs the Kinky sound system. The first birthday party we held was on the beach itself but we held others at lidos owned by various powerful Neapolitan figures, shall we say.

The Bay of Naples is vast, the beaches are endless and the dances we did there included some of the biggest I have ever played at. I'll never forget one particular moment of kindness from Doc Scott, when we were performing together. He played a track called 'Tropical Land' by The Melodians. It's a particularly beautiful song and one of my all-time favourites but I had never owned it – my only copy was on a Various Artists album. He was playing it on a vinyl seven-inch and I stood there watching it going round and explained to him the importance of the song to me. As it finished he took it off and gave it to me and said, 'It's yours! Now you own it.'

I have had so many great nights playing in Italy. One year I did my birthday party on the beach at Ostia, an hour out of Rome. I also performed in the open air at Mercati Generali, an incredible nightclub at an old wine press in the countryside outside Catania in Sicily.

So many young Italians are into Jamaican music and the culture, which many of them experience in the network of community centres (*centri sociali*) which exist in the big cities. I think they saw in me a reflection of themselves, someone who was from outside the Jamaican culture but who is passionate about the music.

One night the One Love Hi Pawa crew introduced me to a guy who they said had taken a boat from the island of Sardinia just to be at this dance I was doing in Rome. He had taken photographs to record his journey; leaving home, crossing the sea to the Italian mainland and making his way to the Eternal City.

There are now many Italian Reggae fans living in Jamaica. I think a lot of British and American people would be astonished by that. But if they go to Jamaica they will find Italians working as teachers or working in the music business, some of them as sound system boys or girls. Like a lot of Germans they have embraced the world of Reggae and its culture so much that it has become the central part of their lives.

There are numerous Italian recording artists making Reggae-influenced music. Brusco, who is from Rome, is a good example of someone who raps in Italian and in Jamaican-English patois. Alborosie is the figurehead of the Italian Reggae movement. I really rate him because he is an incredibly gifted multi-instrumentalist.

Alborosie was born in Sicily and moved to Bergamo in the north of Italy, where he joined a Reggae band at the age of fifteen. He decided to move to Jamaica to further his career and left his mother in Bergamo in tears, telling her he had to do what he was born to do. He worked as an engineer at Jon Baker's Geejam studio on the north coast at Port Antonio and from there he moved to Kingston and started working as a recording artist.

He has built his own recording studio and has a collection of memorabilia connected with the historical origins of Reggae – from King Tubby's spring reverb unit to Jackie Mittoo's keyboards. The sound that he has managed to achieve recreates but does not merely imitate the Rub-a-Dub sound of Jamaica from the seventies and early eighties.

He has used samples from great artists such as Eek-A-Mouse and Dennis Brown but done so respectfully as an indication of where the music has come from. He has a distinctive tone of voice and something to say lyrically. The fact that he does so much of the production himself is indicative of his total commitment to the music. He has produced and mixed a Dub album and uses students from the Jamaica College of Music, who he takes on tour with him. So he is living in Jamaica and encouraging new talent, giving performers an opportunity to play live in Europe. He has completely embraced the culture and come up with several albums which have been significant stepping stones in the story of Jamaican music made by people who are not Jamaican by birth.

Switzerland is another vibrant scene. Every year for twelve years I have played at Rote Fabrik, a red-brick former factory in Zurich, on the last Saturday before Christmas. It's always packed to the rafters and it's a very big place. One year I turned around and there was Lee Perry himself standing right next to the DJ table. He hadn't come far because he lives in Zurich.

The Rote Fabrik events are organized by a guy called Buzz from the Swiss sound system Boss Hi Fi. Buzz is a great DJ himself, a diehard music fanatic with a very serious record collection. He has a shop in Zurich called 16 Tons which specializes in second-hand records, clothes and furniture. It's not just Zurich – I've seen the strength of the Swiss Reggae scene in Biel, Geneva, Lausanne and other cities too.

Thanks to the clashes I'd done with the Japanese sound system Mighty Crown, I became friends with the owners, the brothers Samuel and Simon Tse (Sammi T and Masta Simon). They invited me to come and tour their homeland.

The Japanese have been into Reggae for a good thirty-five years and I was aware of their fascination for the music in the 1980s, because you had Japanese Dancehall artists even then.

That first tour with Mighty Crown was fascinating. They had so absorbed Jamaican culture that when we played at a small-town venue Mighty Crown told me, in all seriousness, 'This is a typical country dance.' It was exactly the way that someone might have described a rural Reggae session in Jamaica.

Mighty Crown are from the city of Yokohama. To perform on their home patch was an incredible experience and on the first night I played in Yokohama Bay I could see the excitement in the eyes of the young fans. I felt like I was looking at my young self, attending my first Ska and Reggae shows back in Oxford. I could sense that same fever you have when you first go out to listen to music and are desperate to hear the big tunes. They gave me a tremendous reception.

We played in the north, in Sapporo, and at three or four other shows. I did another Japanese tour that included Tokyo and Hiroshima, where I signed on with 'I Know a Girl from Hiroshima' by Third World. Unfortunately hardly anyone in the crowd seemed to know the song, which surprised me because Japanese audiences are incredibly knowledgeable.

In Osaka I visited Drum and Bass records, which is a well-established shop where the collection of music is just astounding. It was like going back forty years because of the meticulous way the shop was laid out. I saw albums in there I have never seen before. It was collectors' stuff with wonderful Japanese reissues of classic and rare recordings. There was extraordinary attention to detail in the presentation.

Aside from Jamaica I have played in a number of the other Caribbean countries, such as St Lucia and Trinidad & Tobago. I have a strong affinity with Antigua, which I started to visit following an invitation from Jazzie B, the frontman of London's Soul II Soul music collective – the famous 'Funki Dreds'.

I've known Jazzie since 1990 when we were colleagues at Kiss. He left a DAT tape for me that he had produced of the American soul singer Teena Marie. There was a message attached: 'Rodders. Listen and play!' When I was playing my Monday-night Reggae show on Kiss I would hand over to Jazzie.

Soul II Soul started out as a sound system and was well known for its events at the Africa Centre in central London. They started to make their own music, signed to Virgin's Ten Records, and achieved worldwide fame with their debut album *Club Classics Vol. One*, which topped the British chart, the American R&B chart, and won two Grammy awards. The Soul II Soul slogan was 'A happy face, a thumpin' bass, for a lovin' race'.

Jazzie's family roots are in Antigua and he has a home on the island. In 2004 he invited me to come out and play at a special series of parties under the banner 'Back II Life'. I was one of four DJs, alongside the BBC Radio 1 presenter Trevor Nelson, BBC London's Norman Jay and Jazzie himself. All of us had worked at various times on Kiss FM.

Back II Life took a crowd of music-loving British holidaymakers to the Caribbean for a week in the sun and a series of great parties. My event – which took place at Nelson's Dockyard or at the Shirley Heights vantage point overlooking the historic English Harbour – was always open to the Antiguan public and I tried to mix a selection of classic anthems by the likes of Bob Marley and Maxi Priest with a few hard-core dub plates that some of the locals had come to hear.

I went back in 2009 for a great clash with the local sound system Poison Dart at Millers by the Sea beach bar in the capital, St John's. That has become a smash hit on YouTube. In the 'one fi one' best-of-ten dub plate finale, I went into a 3–0 lead with dubs by Barrington Levy ('Murderer/Sound Killer'), Dennis Brown ('To the Foundation/Rodigan's Going to Get Himself Together'), Half Pint ('Substitute Lover/Substitute Selector'). I then told the young Poison Dart sound that I had a personal message for them from the singer Cocoa Tea. I climbed down from the stage and joined the crowd on the beach as Cocoa sang:

> Now this one is dedicated to all just come selectors, who want come test David Rodigan, Lord! Ay-ay!
> Soundbwoy! Won't you go home, go home to your nana, your nana!

The crowd erupted in delight and I was soaked as drink flew through the air. I could smell champagne on my clothes. That was 4–0. I climbed back up on the stage and finished the clash with Johnny Osbourne ('Dub Plates Playing in the Ghetto Tonight') and Garnett Silk ('Keep Them Talking'). Six–nil and game over.

Of all the places I have played music, one of the most beautiful has to be Horseshoe Bay in Bermuda, which has been rated one of the top ten beaches in the world. The phone call came in 1995 from a guy called Tiko who wanted to book me to clash against the Bermudan sound system Souljah 1 on the beach.

The Bermuda archipelago is not actually in the Caribbean – it's in the North Atlantic Ocean off the east coast of the United States. This place is picturesque beyond belief. It's immaculate – there's no litter anywhere. But it has long had a strong affinity with Reggae and there's been significant Jamaican immigration to the islands in addition to its own majority population of African descent.

Big international sound systems had played there before me, notably Saxon from London and King Addies from New York. So I was keen to go.

When I got to Horseshoe Bay, on the south coast, I couldn't believe what I was seeing. There were thousands of people but the scene was just idyllic; there was a moon above the sea on the horizon. I had never played anywhere quite like it.

Because it was over-subscribed and people couldn't get on to the beach itself, many others had decided to watch pro-ceedings from out at sea. All-evening boats arrived from other parts of the island into Horseshoe Bay, getting as close as they could to the event on shore. You could see people bobbing up and down on board.

Before I started playing I cued up an anthem by Bob Marley and The Wailers.

'Let us just bless the session with a tune that says it all,' I told the big crowd. 'If you listen keenly you will hear a bassline bouncing off the ocean onto the beach. When you hear that bassline I want to see every torch go up, I want to see every lighter go up, I want to see the most noise on this beach. When you hear that bassline . . .'

An unmistakable bassline dropped and it was indeed as if it was bouncing off the ocean. As it reverberated, I implored everyone to illuminate the scene, shouting, 'Torch! Torch! Lighter! Torch! Robert! Nesta! Marley! Bermuda!'

And then Bob's voice took over: 'There's a natural mystic blowing through the air . . .'

It was an amazing night and the talk of the island for weeks.

There were so many people on the beach, both white and black. I was told afterwards it was the first really significant gathering of white and black youth on the island – they were sharing their love of Reggae.

Afterwards I was about to board the aircraft to go home when I was called to the phone at the airport. The caller was a man called Choy Aming. He had been pointed out to me before because he was such a distinctive elderly gentleman; partly Chinese and with wispy hair that made him look like a mad professor.

'I want to bring you back to Bermuda and put on your show myself,' he said.

Choy Aming was almost a traditional entertainment agent with a roster of bands which he booked for the hotel circuit. He was the man who would bring the big stars to Bermuda. I was flattered that he was interested. He was as good as his word and in subsequent years I returned to play against big Jamaican sound systems such as Bodyguard and Stone Love on that beautiful beach.

Bermuda's most successful Reggae artist is Collie Buddz, who came to fame in 2006 with the hit 'Come Around'. I'm glad to say that I championed him from the off after my friend Pee-Wee played me the track and I knew I had to record a dub plate. Collie Buddz is a special talent. He is a white Bermudan who was working as a recording engineer but decided he could actually voice songs himself and started recording dub plates for local sound systems.

The mix of cultures and races was something I really liked about Bermuda. There is a large black population as well as people of all sorts of different heritage: Portuguese, Italians, Asians – and a lot of Scots. I felt very at home there.

Sound clashing had taken me to the United States early in my career and I have always had a warm welcome there.

In 2006, I was booked for a celebrity sound clash in Queens, New York. It was probably the high point of my fancy dress antics. I was to play against Ninjaman, the Dancehall artist. Ninjaman is a Jamaican superstar, a legend in the country's music history. He's a larger-than-life character with a tremendous stage persona.

As an MC he is famous for being able to use his voice to 'ride' a rhythm, but he also has extraordinary freestyle technique. I considered it a massive compliment, an honour, to be put up against him in a celebrity clash. But I knew he could bring all his stage skills into his performance as a clash selector and that he would be a formidable opponent.

It was a much-anticipated night. Our event was a finale to the earlier 'World Clash' show, a big annual contest between international sound systems that attracts a massive crowd and global interest for weeks afterwards.

At first I was going to come dressed as a Ninja warrior but then I realized that was too obvious – if Ninjaman also wore a Ninja outfit I would be the one who ended up looking stupid.

As it turned out, Ninjaman had been thinking more about my outfit. He knew I had a reputation for dressing smart. If I wasn't in fancy dress I would normally wear a suit. So Ninjaman, instead of his usual Jamaican street gear, went out and got an amazing bespoke suit. When he came on stage at the famous New York venue, Club Amazura, he looked a million dollars.

Fortunately I had planned something completely different. I had the idea when I was travelling on the Bullet Train in

Japan on tour. There was a man in front of me on the other side of the carriage watching a TV show on his laptop. The host of this chat show, who was Japanese, had the most outrageous Elvis Presley hairstyle, straight out of Las Vegas. I thought it looked fabulous.

That evening in Japan I was having a pizza in a restaurant when I heard the song 'Suspicious Minds'. When the lyric dropped, 'You're caught in a trap', the inspiration hit me like a rocket. I decided I was going to do the New York clash dressed up as Elvis Presley. And I was going to sing on my own dub plate.

I went back to London and ordered the Elvis suit in white satin with a red sash. I picked up a big Elvis wig and some 'Tanfastic' foundation cream to get that bronzed Elvis appearance. I wanted the whole look.

Then I went to the UK Reggae singer Peter Hunnigale and got him to rebuild the melody with the correct chord progression of 'Suspicious Minds', and I rewrote the lyrics. 'Ninja, you're caught in a trap, you can't get out . . .'

Peter Hunnigale sang the harmonies and I sang the song as the Elvis character. I recorded one version with my singing and another cut with just Peter's harmonies, leaving space for me to sing my part of the song live.

When I emerged from my hotel room in New York that night my driver and New York buddy Alex King Mellow had the shock of their lives. We headed out to Queens and Club Amazura. I was following a game plan. I had invited Pee-Wee – who has a sound system from Queens called Pretty Posse – to play my tune selections so that I could be right out front on the stage, working the crowd. I told Pee-Wee I wasn't coming straight into the venue because I didn't want anyone to see me. Instead I remained outside in a van parked near the stage door, dressed as Elvis and with a jacket on to keep warm. I had to wait for the end of the World Clash event before I could emerge.

Finally the World Clash finished and the MC for the night announced the big Celebrity Clash: 'Ninjaman versus David Rodigan.'

In sound clashes it's traditional, as it is in a sports contest, to flip a coin to see who starts first. The MC was looking around for me but I'd told Pee-Wee to take the coin and that I would turn up a little while afterwards.

Outside in the van I knew that people in the crowd would be thinking, 'Where's Rodigan?', and wondering whether I would turn up at all. Ninjaman was to play first – which was perfect for my big entrance. For the next twenty minutes or so he was playing his tunes in his bespoke suit and wondering what was going on, while I waited in the van, watching the clock and sending texts to Pee-Wee.

With a few minutes to go I climbed out of the van and started banging on the stage door. The bouncer opened up, took one look at me in my white suit, big wig and 'Tanfastic' face, and shut the door, thinking I was some sort of freak.

So there I was standing outside in Queens, in the middle of the night, dressed as Elvis with a giant wig and a false tan. I shouted through the door, 'I'm Rodigan, please let me in!'

Someone inside must have persuaded him to do so, because he relented and opened up and I then hid again behind another door so that no one could see me before I went on stage.

Ninjaman played his last tune. Then I heard Pee-Wee play a dub plate that I had made especially for the night, with a formal announcer telling the audience: 'Ladies and Gentleman, we regret to announce that David Rodigan is unable to perform this evening . . .' The plate concluded with the news that 'we have sent a substitute selector from Las Vegas'.

At which point, Pee-Wee cued up one of my most treasured dub plates – 'Rodigan is not a substitute selector' by Half Pint. While it was playing I rushed onto the stage as Elvis and the place was going nuts. I took the microphone and turned to Ninjaman as he was standing there, shaking his head.

I told Ninja that he couldn't kill me in the sound clash because, as Elvis, I was already dead. Then I told him, 'Duppy know who fi frighten', a Jamaican proverb meaning a ghost (i.e. me dressed as Elvis) knows who to pick on. The audience was loving it and so I went into the big tune of that year, 2006, 'Crank That' by Souljah Boy. It wasn't a Reggae record but everyone knew it because it had spawned a dance that even big company CEOs were doing in clips posted on YouTube. I'd rehearsed the Souljah Boy dance and performed it in my Elvis guise while that record was playing. The New York crowd loved that too.

I turned to my 'Suspicious Minds' dub plate. As the instrumental version was playing with Peter Hunnigale's harmonies I asked Ninja if he could identify the song from the melody. And then, as he paused, I asked him to allow me to sing it for him. 'Ninja, you're caught in a trap, you can't get out . . .' It was a hilarious moment and even he could see the funny side of it.

I eventually won the clash and Ninjaman was a great sportsman. Ninja has had a hard life. He followed a drugs road that others have walked down and went to prison, but was released in 2012 and has campaigned against the dangers of drug abuse. He's a reformed character and I love him greatly.

A great old musical adversary based in the US is Tony Screw, aka 'Downbeat'. He is known as Downbeat because that was the original nickname of the great Studio One producer Coxsone Dodd, and Tony Screw was famous for his Studio One dub plates. His collection is unrivalled because he was such a close friend of Coxsone's and had access to original tapes and rhythms that nobody else could record. Alongside that, he has a deep knowledge of the music and is an inspired selector.

We came together for a massive clash in Brooklyn, New York, in 2006. We were of a similar age and it was a serious showdown with a lot at stake over our reputations. There were many famous artists in the audience, including Sammy Dread, Glen Washington and Johnny Osbourne. And before the clash, Downbeat had been on New York radio's Hot 97 to say he was going to give me the beating of my life.

I signed on by playing a vinyl cut of Billy Joel's 'New York State of Mind'. It was a bit of a gamble to play a Pop song, and to this day people still talk about that – how on earth did you sign on in a Reggae sound clash with Billy Joel?

It annoyed Downbeat; it really pissed him off. He complained later that rather than just playing acetate dub plates I had played vinyl, which he thought was somehow against the rules.

But I had said in my opening speech, 'I am going to play three songs that reflect what this evening is about. And they're all on vinyl.' My justification was that in the beginning of this sound clash game it wasn't just about having exclusive dub plates with your name in them, it was about songs, selection and message. I was playing in the traditions of the music.

Before I pressed play on the record I asked how many Jamaicans had left New York to go and live in Atlanta,

Miami and other cities. I appealed to the hard core in the crowd.

'If you're a true New Yorker and you love New York and you're not leaving – this is for you!'

When 'New York State of Mind' started, you could see people thinking, 'What is this?' And then the significance of it hit them.

Then I said that Tony Screw was the big tree in New York – it was his home turf – but I was the small axe who would cut him down. And I played 'Small Axe' by The Wailers. It wasn't a dub plate with my name in it but it was a different mix of the song that the crowd wouldn't have heard.

I narrowly won the early rounds but it still came down to the 'one for one' dub plate finale, which was best of seven. Things were getting sticky for me when I trailed 3–1. But then I lined up two of my hardest dubs, 'Golden Hen' by Tenor Saw and 'Don Dadda' by Super Cat, to even things up.

For the final round I took the microphone and made a short speech.

'I have one more tune to play. This tune is by Jamaica's first ever superstar. [In] 1964, when he came to London . . . road-block! No sound in the world can play this! Rodigan's last tune! Buster!'

As the instrumental kicked in, lighters burst into flames and klaxons sounded as my exclusive Prince Buster 'Hard Man Fi Dead' got a huge forward. It was more than a match for Downbeat's last dub, 'Dancing Mood' by Delroy Wilson.

It was a great night, described by the MC as the 'most decent clash in history'. At the end I gave thanks to Downbeat as 'a true sound system father, the mighty Tony Screw'. But playing that vinyl was a thorn in his side for a long time. He was sore but the clash was based on points scored at the end of the night and it was indisputable. Later, we did a clash in London, a kind of rematch, which he won.

We worked together again in California at the famous Dub Club in Los Angeles. I didn't even know he was going to be on the bill until I saw the flyer and so when we were in the wings together I spoke to him.

'Tony, whatever you do don't start the clash thing in here because it's not going to work. Tonight is an exhibition and we will play our best dubs and watch what happens.'

I knew it wasn't the kind of venue or crowd for a clash. That warm Wednesday night in California we had a ball. We just played our big dubs and the audience loved it. You don't have to clash, as I told Tony. It doesn't always have to be about the competition.

Reggae music has taken me around the globe, but the early years of the new Millennium were a strange and confusing time for me back home at Kiss. The departures of the station's founding figures such as Gordon Mac, Lorna Clarke and Grant Goddard had brought a lot of transition.

I had left daytime presenting but the Reggae show I made with my producer Chris Blacklay frequently had good audience figures, and with Sean Paul leading a new explosion in Jamaican Dancehall which began in 2004, fusing the Soca beat of the Caribbean islands with Reggae Dancehall traditions, the music was back at the forefront of street culture under the name Bashment.

In 2004, to my great surprise, I was named Music Broadcaster of the Year at the Radio Academy Awards, the Oscar ceremony for the industry in Britain. It's a huge event in the ballroom of the Grosvenor House Hotel in London and I only knew I'd won when they read my name out on the night. My heart stopped because I'd never had that recognition before and very few of the presenters at Kiss had won an award. When your peers in the radio industry decide that what you have done is special it means everything.

One of the happiest people that night was Mark Story, the managing director of Kiss, who had told me that I would leave the station only over his 'dead body' during the row over me playing Beenie Man during daytime in 1999.

'My judgement on you has been vindicated!' he said.

I was proud but even more proud for the music I had loved all my life. It was Music Broadcaster of the Year, so people were really reviewing the music and my music was Reggae. But at the same time I was conscious that Kiss was marginalizing my show to a later slot.

Then in 2006 I was inducted into the Radio Academy Hall of Fame. The ceremony took place at a lunch in the art-deco surroundings of the Savoy Hotel, off the Strand in London. It was so humbling because I thought of how much radio had done for me during my childhood and teenage years, schooling me in a trade that I later earned my living from. I was back at the Radio Academy Awards in 2009 to win Specialist Music Broadcaster of the Year, and was also nominated as Music Broadcaster of the Year.

All this sudden recognition meant a lot to me because I had been fighting hard to maintain the quality of the show after Kiss had cut it in length.

It was all very strange. Winning awards and travelling the world, it felt like I was getting more and more interest from outside of Kiss, while the station itself was pushing me to the edge of its schedule.

19

Dubstep

So many of the musical sounds of urban Britain have their origins in Reggae, whether it's the Jungle and Drum & Bass sound that emerged in the early 1990s, or later scenes like Grime, the UK's take on Rap.

Dubstep is another classic example of London's deep affiliation with Jamaican music. This ground-breaking and experimental hybrid uses samples and breakbeats, and elements of many UK sounds from Drum & Bass to 2-Step and Grime.

Just as Reggae is best appreciated when it's performed live in a dancehall, so listening to Dubstep on headphones in your front room is just not the same as hearing it played live. You have to really feel the music as part of a crowd as it responds to the slow build-up, the break and then the almighty bass drop when the place just explodes.

Light and shade is very important in the way Dubstep is created. It's very atmospheric and generates unique audience responses that you can see if you go to a gig by big artists such as Skream or Benga. You can feel the power of the music in the faces of people in the crowd. Dubstep has a more energized tempo than Reggae and in that sense it's easier to dance to.

To be part of this scene was a thrilling new direction in my career. But just as Dubstep was getting big, and inviting another young *generation to seek out its Reggae roots, so my radio bosses seemed more intent on pushing our music into the wilderness of the twilight hours of the schedule.*

Dubstep changed my life. I was in my fifties, presenting *Rodigan's Reggae* show on Kiss FM, playing live in Reggae clubs and doing sound clashes, and had come to the view that I worked in a closed-circuit world.

Then I discovered the music of a younger generation and my horizons were utterly transformed.

I found Dubstep and it found me. It began when Breakage, the name of a Drum & Bass and Dubstep DJ called James Boyle, sampled my voice on a track called 'Hard', featuring the grime rappers Newham Generals. That was in 2009. My eldest son Jamie heard it and told me about it and when I first listened to the recording I could hardly believe it. Midway through this frenetic, exciting track was the unmistakable sound of my own voice as I made one of my Dancehall speeches:

> Keeping up the theme of hard-core music,
>> The music is what it's all about,
>> I love it, just like you love it,
>> That's why you're here,
>> I'm here cos I love to play,
>> You don't come, I can't play – and I love to play,
>> So I won't make too many speeches cos it's all about the
> music,
>> You just heard a hard-core sequence of hotshot dub plates
> from down Jamaica way,
>> Right about now we're gonna start to change the pace
> and change the style,

> During the course of the night we switch and we swap
> and we ride around the track together . . .

At which point the voice of Newham Generals rapper Footsie cut back in:

> I said to myself go harder . . .

I was transfixed. They had found this speech on a recording of one of my sound clashes. To my delight the track really took off and went from being an underground Dubstep hit to a mainstream dance hit that lots of people knew. The BBC Radio presenter Zane Lowe even used my clip from the track for the opening of his show on Radio 1.

Then I was approached by a young man called Caspa, who was at the forefront of the Dubstep movement.

Caspa asked me if I would consider doing an intro speech for his 2009 album, *Everybody's Talking, Nobody's Listening*, which I agreed to do. I was amazed because I didn't think that these young people, devoted as they were to other types of music, even knew what I did. I felt honoured when I saw a clip of Caspa being interviewed on YouTube saying the thing he was most happy about on the album was getting Rodigan to voice the intro.

'Everybody's talking, nobody's listening', my twenty-five-second segment began.

> It's all about the music. From King Tubby's echo chamber in
> western Kingston to the Dubstep phenomena out of London.
> Who's hot and who's not, we don't care. Dark rooms with
> heavy basslines, full of fans who are only there for the music

and selectors who not only play it but create it. Are you listening? Because Caspa's playing!

That same year I played at Caspa's Dub Police event at Fabric,
the huge London nightclub famed for championing Drum &
Bass and similar styles.

I was given encouragement by Shaun Roberts, the promotions manager at Fabric.

'You have really got to do this,' he said. 'You have to come
and perform.'

I travelled down to the club with my CD pouch, half a
dozen dub plates and half a dozen albums with important
sleeves – one was the album *King Tubby The Dubmaster*, with a
picture of the great Osbourne Ruddock on the cover.

There was phenomenal energy and excitement in the
venue and a constant flow of young people, all hyped up as
if they had just been let off a leash. There are many levels
to Fabric and the sound system is amazing. It's an incredibly
vibrant place. I'd played there once years before with Jazzie B
from Soul II Soul for a midweek gig, but this was a wholly
different experience.

They brought me into the main room and it was pitch-
dark. I could hardly see. I was incredibly nervous while The
Others, the DJs who were on ahead of me, were playing. I
could see it wasn't my normal Reggae crowd. This was a sea
of young white faces and the music they were dancing to was
all Dubstep.

I was looking around at the air-conditioning system, the
smoke machine and the amazing light show, and my last thoughts
to myself before the lights came up were: 'What the hell am I
doing here?' 'What am I going to play?' 'Why did I agree to this?'

Once more I had put myself under a lot of stress.

My son Jamie, who was into heavy-duty Dubstep by the likes of Digital Mystikz, had told me about the sound and played me some of it.

But I felt very insecure and uncertain as I nervously cued up my first record. I made a speech and held up the record sleeve of *King Tubby The Dubmaster*.

Caspa had assured me the Dub Police crowd would know me from my contributions to his album and the Breakage album.

As I held aloft King Tubby I said there is a direct connection between this man and the music made in Jamaica and the music that you love – Dubstep.

I then played some Dub instrumentals – 'The Roots of Dub' by King Tubby, and a couple of dub plate instrumentals. To my relief, the crowd loved it and the place just went off. Then I played Damian Marley's 'Welcome to Jamrock', Barrington Levy's 'Murderer/Soundkiller' and 'Hard' by Breakage, all on dub plate.

For me this was the dawning of a new age. I lined up what I like to call my 'Salute to the Veterans', running through Reggae classics such as 'You Can Get It If You Really Want' by Jimmy Cliff, '007' by Desmond Dekker and, 'Rudy, a Message to You' by Dandy Livingstone. The young crowd knew every syllable.

Shaun Roberts told me later that Fabric's management received a phone call about the event and was shocked to learn that 'My Boy Lollipop' was being played in this famous Drum & Bass club. When they heard it was me who'd chosen it they understood, he reassured me.

There was no one in the club over the age of twenty-four. But my selections worked well and although the crowd had come to hear a range of Dubstep DJs this was a nice change of gear. They really responded to me as I was jumping around on stage, pulling up the needle on tunes, and playing them again to shouts of 'Re-wind!'

At first I was astonished by the response of young people to these Reggae classics, but I realized that the music that I play is very much part of their lives because it is so much part of our British music and culture. It didn't just pop up the other day; it has stood for the best part of fifty years.

At the height of its popularity from 1968 to 1970, it was Pop chart music. All these songs are staples of British Pop radio and are played on Radio 1 and Radio 2. 'Israelites', by Desmond Dekker, was a British Pop chart smash in 1969. In 1970 'You Can Get It If You Really Want' got to number two. The Specials did their cover version 'A Message to You, Rudy' (changing the title of the Dandy Livingstone song) in 1979 and got to number ten, and everyone knows that 'Red Red Wine', written by Neil Diamond but also a Reggae classic sung by Tony Tribe, was a huge number one for UB40 in 1984. These songs have become part of our daily lives, just as much as those by Oasis, The Beatles and the Rolling Stones.

This was the music that many of these young people would have heard played by their parents – or their grandparents. Virtually every home in the country has a Reggae compilation album because it's good summer music.

I think some of this younger audience might have known me from Ram Jam FM, the radio channel I had on *Grand Theft Auto*. That was a lucky break. I'd received the offer by email but the name *Grand Theft Auto* meant absolutely nothing to me and I deleted the message. When I spoke to my sons they asked me if I was crazy and told me it was the biggest computer game in the world. I went back to my inbox only to realize the email wasn't there.

Luckily they contacted me again and flew me to their headquarters on Broadway in New York, where they were the perfect hosts while I recorded the phrases and chose the records for Ram Jam FM, which you can listen to in your virtual car while playing the game.

After that night at Fabric I became a big fan of Dubstep, which was at its height of popularity. When I heard it in context – on that big sound system – I completely got it and instantly recognized the origins of the music.

I told myself that this interest I was getting from the Dubstep crowd was probably no more than a brief moment in time that I should just enjoy while it lasted. But it only grew. The following year Shaun Roberts asked me to make a Fabric Live compilation album, part of a long and well-known series of recordings that the nightclub has commissioned.

I fell in with the Drum & Bass crowd too. I'd followed that genre since we first began to play it on Kiss FM around 1993, when it was still talked about as Jungle. My contacts within the scene grew when I met Jon Bailey (aka D&B MC Jon Wrec) and made him my manager. Nicky Culture, the promotions manager for Jah Shaka, got in touch and said, 'Jon Wrec in Brighton wants to contact you and he's a bona fide guy.' I didn't know he was a Drum & Bass MC but the show he booked me for on the South Coast was very successful.

Jon, and Marc Sheinman, his partner at SEG International management, said they would like to give my live events a branded feel, putting me on in places where I wouldn't normally play. That was how my Ram Jam live events started.

We've been working together ever since and I owe them a great debt of thanks. They took me out of my comfort zone by the scruff of the neck and put me into arenas I would never otherwise have performed in.

Hospital Records, the Drum & Bass label run by Tony Colman and Chris Goss, booked me to play at their Hospitality event at the Matter nightclub at London's O2. I have to admit I had no idea who Hospital Records were. When Jon asked me what I thought 'about Hospitality' I assumed he was referring to the rider of refreshments which venues provide for performing artists and asked for some Coca-Cola, some peanuts and a bar of chocolate. Jon explained Hospitality was one of the biggest names in Drum & Bass.

I did the Hospitality Tent at Lovebox festival in London's Victoria Park in 2011. It was mid-afternoon and it had started to rain. I promised the crowd it would stop raining and played Bob Marley's 'Natural Mystic' and – guess what? – it stopped raining. A woman came to the front of the stage and threw her bra on. I took the mic and told her she had made an old man very happy as I threw the bra back into the crowd and saw this young lady attempting to put it back on.

I've become good friends with Goldie, one of the great icons of the Drum & Bass world. I met him for the first time at a Red Bull Music Academy event at Fabric in May 2012 when I gave a talk and played some of my favourite dub plates to celebrate thirty-five years of working in the business. There was a gig afterwards in the club's VIP room. It turned out Goldie had been following my career for a while, and he presented me with a magnificent portrait painting.

I never believed I could be a DJ in a dance music club for the simple reason that I have never have been able to mix records, a fundamental skill in that line of work. When I was working at Capital Radio and mixing started to become all-important with the growth of House music in the 1990s, a producer called Simon Harris gave me a mixing lesson. 'You count your beats,' he told me. I'm afraid I wasn't terribly good at it and there wasn't much Simon could do for me. Reggae is hard to mix because of the pace. I always thought the best mixer in Reggae and Dancehall was Rory, the selector of the Stone Love sound system. In England, Chris Goldfinger of the Asha World Movement sound system, who went on to become a presenter on BBC Radio 1, was very good. Selectors like Rory and Chris developed the 'Juggling' style of playing music, moving from one track to another without speaking on the microphone while cueing up the next record.

As mixing became the norm I worried how I was going to cope. When I was doing live events and clashing I was cueing up the dub plates and making the speeches all by myself, but it became apparent that I was going to need assistance because the whole pace became much faster. I began using Pee-Wee from New York and Seani B and RS Digital from London, who were all great mixers.

But I'm fortunate that my two sons are very musically aware, so I have been able to remix tracks in order to keep up in the game. Jamie is not only a radio DJ but one of the best mixers I know. Oliver is a successful music producer who goes by the name Cadenza. I didn't encourage them to go into music. I would not give them a leg up or write letters on their behalf, and told them that if they thought it was an easy life they were sadly mistaken. They had to do it entirely off their own bats.

Both Jamie and Oliver helped me in remixing 'The Mission' by Bob Marley's sons, Damian and Stephen. I found a dub of Dennis Brown's 'Africa' mixed by King Tubby and realized that the tempo would fit 'The Mission'. We got the vocal of Damian, and Jamie managed to make it sit in time with the 'Africa' mix. We later put another Damian Marley track, 'One Loaf of Bread', on top of King Tubby's mix of Dennis Brown's 'Tribulation'.

I also began to cut dub plates from the Dubstep world. I got to meet Arthur or Artwork (who along with Skream and Benga is part of the big Drum & Bass act Magnetic Man). I then made a dub plate of Magnetic Man's 'Fire', featuring Ms Dynamite on vocals. And then I cut 'Wile Out' by DJ Zinc, another Drum & Bass legend, again featuring Ms Dynamite.

Those recordings by Ms Dynamite are two of my most precious dub plates because she did them so well. The energy, commitment and sheer gusto she brought to her performances means there is a real vibrancy to those dubs.

I used the dub plate of 'Hard' by Breakage, featuring vocals from Footsie of Newham Generals, at a big Reggae sound clash – UK Cup Clash – at Stratford Rex in east London in 2010. The different genres could live side by side.

It wasn't just me who found it surprising that a man of six decades who looks like an accountant or a dentist was of interest to young clubbers. I was the subject of a news feature on the BBC Radio 4 *Today* programme, which is the most important news show in Britain and very serious. I had the most amazing response to it, with lots of old actor mates getting in touch and other people from my days with Armed Forces Radio. The piece, which ran directly after an item about Margaret Thatcher, asked the question: 'What is it about this sixty-year-old actor that all these young people want to come and hear him play records?'

Radio 4 came down to the Elephant & Castle in south London and recorded young people standing in the queue outside a club.

'Who are you here for?'

'Rodigan!'

My acceptance by the Dubstep and Drum & Bass crowds suddenly opened up another new world to me: music festivals.

I knew of them when I was growing up in the sixties but dancing in a field had never been my thing because I played Reggae gigs to a Reggae audience. Suddenly, all these years later, I found myself catching the festival bug.

My initiation was Bestival, which takes place on the Isle of Wight off the South Coast of England in September. I'd been booked to play in something called the Bollywood Tent.

I found the whole experience strange, a feeling enhanced by going across to an island on the ferry from the mainland. The festival had a reputation for being bathed in sunshine but it was pouring with rain, to a point where the event was almost washed out.

I was way out of my comfort zone and, despite all these years of playing, I was – yet again – full of nerves. It was like the Fabric feeling once more – I wasn't sure I was even supposed to be there. We found the Bollywood Tent and it was dressed in Indian drapes and hangings. We were standing there in our Wellington boots like drowned rats. Before I went on at 5 p.m. I joked to Jon, my manager, that it felt like a scene from *Shutter Island*, the Dennis Lehane book and Martin Scorsese film about an island for the criminally insane.

I needn't have worried because it was a great gig and a game changer for my career. The crowd were open to the music and Don Letts, who introduced the Punk generation to

Jamaican music and produced the film *Dancehall Queen*, played a Reggae set earlier in the festival. Rob da Bank, organizer of Bestival, saw the way I went down and booked me to return the next year. I've played Bestival many times since under our Ram Jam banner and in 2015 the festival made me the first recipient of its 'Resident for Life' award, meaning I can play there every year.

After my first Bestival I went to The Secret Garden Party, an incredible fantasy festival in the landscaped gardens of a Georgian farmhouse in the heart of the Cambridgeshire countryside. That world was opened up to me by Delroy Williams, who is the agent for Prince Buster and worked with Desmond Dekker as his manager in the seventies, helping to re-establish his career. Delroy worked for the festival and booked me to appear.

We arrived at Secret Garden at 2.59 p.m., one minute before I was due on stage, and I was faced with lots of chilled-out people spread out on the grass. Again I was filled with self-doubt and thought, 'What am I going to play?' I had to entertain an audience that was very laid-back and I wasn't sure if they were the least bit interested in me. But within about fifteen minutes the space in front of me had filled up and after about twenty minutes the whole place was rocking. I've gone back year after year. More recently I've been able to play a highly eclectic selection. I might go from Drum & Bass tracks like Shy FX's 'Original Nuttah' or 'Incredible' by General Levy through to DJ Q, who is a producer of Bassline, a fast-paced dance subgenre that grew out of Sheffield in northern England. DJ Q cut me a Bassline remix of 'Go Home to Your Nana' by the Reggae singer Cocoa Tea.

For the first time I went to Glastonbury at Worthy Farm in Somerset, the most famous festival of all. I'd seen it on television but didn't realize the special feeling you get there; one that people only understand once they've attended 'Glasto' and picked up the strange energy on the ley lines that cross that part of the English countryside. It was like going back to the sixties.

Jon Bailey had the idea of taking my career beyond the immediate Reggae scene to a wider audience that wanted to hear the music. The shift to playing all these festivals also couldn't have happened without Ricky McKay at Soundz4u, my booking agent for the past twenty years. I've known him since he was living in Germany and working in Neons, the discotheque near the British Army base, and he called me up to hire me. Since then he has been booking me for gigs all over the world. Prior to Ricky I was sorting out my own dates over the phone.

Not all the new festival gigs took place in fields. The Warehouse Project in Manchester was different entirely. It's based on the brilliant idea of turning a daytime underground car park in the middle of the city into a nightclub.

That opportunity came from playing at the Reggae night Rootikal at East Village in east London and being approached by Richard McGuinness, who said, 'I liked what you did there!' I didn't know he was involved in Creamfields, the global music festival that began in Merseyside. He booked me for Chibuku, a club in Liverpool, which was an amazing night and my first ever gig in the city. It was there I met the team from Warehouse Project.

That underground car park blew me away. I was taken below street level and at first it was just an empty space, but as we descended I heard a bassline growing louder and then saw a big stage and thousands of people.

On Monday morning the club would revert to a car park again. They do that from autumn to Christmas, putting thousands of people in an underground space where they're not going to disturb anyone. It's genius. That was another significant moment in the change in direction of my career.

We were having so much success outside the usual Reggae arena that Jon and I decided to start doing our own Ram Jam events. My catchphrase became 'Give Me Some Signal', which was an expression I never realized I used so much on stage. Apparently I do! The idea came from Charlotte Coker, my producer at Kiss, who was in her hotel during Bestival and heard some young guys in the corridor doing Rodigan impressions and shouting 'Give Me Some Signal!' We ended up putting it on posters and T-shirts.

A Ram Jam night was a sign to people that they were going to get a fusion of musical styles – there would be Reggae and Dub, of course, but also Drum & Bass and Dubstep. It would be an eclectic collection. What brought Ram Jam to a head was treating it like a party within a bigger festival, such as Lovebox in London or Parklife in Manchester, which is staged in an amazing grass amphitheatre. From there we were able to set up our stand-alone Ram Jam nights in some of the UK's biggest music venues. Toddla T – a DJ who came out of the Sheffield bass scene and has a radio show on the BBC – has been a great Ram Jam ally. I saw in him a younger version of myself with his passion for Dancehall and Reggae, so we invited him to join us.

I was getting bookings I'd never had before. The Southport Weekender is a famous seaside event for real Soul music connoisseurs and I'd never played it. Suddenly they wanted me. I got a great response playing Reggae.

Everything seemed to be opening up. Universities began to book me to play for the student crowd. World HQ is a club in the north-east of England that supports black music and is popular with students from all the universities and colleges in Newcastle. I couldn't believe the size of the crowd. Then I did the end-of-term ball at Manchester University. I've yet to play Oxford University, despite the fact that I used to go with my family to watch the students jumping into the River Cherwell each year.

In 2011 I had an approach from BBC Radio 2.

It's a sign of how much my world was changing that when the call came I was at the Snowbombing festival – a crazy party for skiers and snowboarders in the Austrian Alps. I was booked for the festival by Urban Nerds, who did a video interview with me on the mountainside. I was asked to name the 'Top three tunes that represent Rodigan'. I named 'Declaration of Rights' by The Abyssinians, 'Unchained' by Bob Andy and 'Dub Plates Playing in the Ghetto/Rock It Tonight' by Johnny Osbourne. I took the chance to say thank you to the Dubstep scene for 'the way in which they have embraced me and welcomed me into their fraternity'.

I was asked if it was difficult for me as a white man going into the Reggae world. I recounted the early days of my career when black audiences were shocked to discover my skin colour. But I also pointed out that Reggae addicts now come from all over the world. 'I'm not unique – there are millions of us.'

In Austria I took the call from Nicky Birch of the production company Somethin' Else, who said BBC Radio 2 were inviting pitches for specialist music programmes and she'd love to put one forward with me as a presenter.

'Forget it. I'm not interested,' was my response.

She asked why and I told her it was because we had tried a pitch to the previous controller of Radio 2, Lesley Douglas. It was rejected – Ms Douglas gave a Reggae show to the television presenter Mark Lamarr (who kindly invited me on as a guest) – and I didn't want to go through another song and dance if I was wasting my time.

Nicky was persistent and was convinced there was a realistic chance. I told her Kiss would never allow me to do it. She persuaded me to speak to Andy Roberts and, to my surprise, he was incredibly generous and said he would not stand in my way. I will always be grateful to him for that because it's very unusual in the industry to allow a presenter to work for two networks at the same time.

The new Radio 2 controller, Bob Shennan, decided to add a series of Reggae programmes to the schedule of the nation's biggest radio network, with me as the host. It allowed me to present Reggae to a very different and much broader audience to the one I had on Kiss.

I had started my career on the BBC, working at Radio London in 1978, but this was the first time I'd had a show on national BBC radio. I'd grown up with the Corporation and I don't think there's anything comparable to it in the world. As a teenager, my hero was BBC Radio 1's Mike Raven with his Sunday-night *Mike Raven Blues Show*. I idolized John Peel, who recorded a live session of Bob Marley and The Wailers in 1973, and other great BBC broadcasters such as Kenny Everett and Johnnie Walker. Now here I was in a position to speak on a national station to people who loved Reggae as much as I did.

I was so proud that first day when I nervously waited downstairs in the reception of the Radio 2 building, Weston House. I hadn't known where Radio 2 was based – I presumed it was in Broadcasting House, the main headquarters of the BBC, which is a short walk away.

I was in awe of Radio 2. It's the biggest station in the UK with an audience of around ten million listeners a week and has been home to so many broadcasting legends, such as David Jacobs, Bob Harris and Terry Wogan. Lorna Clarke, who I worked with as programme controller at Kiss FM, was a familiar face at Radio 2 and someone I had great respect for. I know she championed the idea of me having that Radio 2 show because she's Jamaican and loves the music.

Steve Wright, one of Radio 2's main presenters, promptly invited me on his show to talk about my new ten-part Thursday-night Reggae series. He has been a cornerstone of the BBC in the last thirty-five years and is a very funny broadcaster known for the comedy characters he has created. Steve is revered in the industry because he is a perfectionist. As usual, I was full of nerves joining someone of his status in the studio, but he did everything to make me feel welcome.

'Our old friend David Rodigan is here! Wahey! Let me just play this, David . . .'

And he put on the old 'Roddy! You a Dubwize S'm'ody!' jingle from my *Roots Rockers* show on Capital Radio.

'What can I tell you about David Rodigan?' he asked his listeners. 'He's a hero to Jamaican music lovers everywhere!'

He asked me to describe the differences between various types of Jamaican music and I was soon differentiating between the 'driving, crazy backbeat' of Ska and the laid-back sound of Rock Steady.

'It was a very hot summer in '66,' I told him. 'And this cool Rock Steady beat was much slower in pace, the bass rolled and it allowed the singers time to express themselves, and that whole period of Rock Steady in '66–'69 is referred to as the "Golden Period".'

Steve was obviously familiar with the music as he chipped in with questions.

'Who were the first *real* Reggae performers? Mighty Diamonds? . . . U Roy? . . . I-Roy?'

He asked me who – placing Bob Marley to one side – were my favourite Jamaican artists. It's a question I've been asked many times and I answered Steve like this: 'I would have to reach for Bunny Wailer. I think his *Blackheart Man* album is truly magnificent. I would also have to mention a group called The Abyssinians, who wrote and recorded some truly magnificent songs, and also Bob Andy of Bob and Marcia. Those are the names that would immediately come into my head when I'm talking about great Reggae stars.'

I explained my love for Reggae with a favourite expression: 'Once you have this fever there is no known antidote!' As I spoke about the forthcoming show I talked about the music I would be playing from the previous fifty years and the new sounds that were emerging. But I also found myself expressing an underlying frustration with some of the modern music coming out of Jamaica.

'Jamaica, musically, has not been as exciting and creative in my opinion in the last two or three years as it could have been, because it's starting to make a kind of Euro Pop. That sounds bizarre but if you listen to some of the new recordings from Jamaica they are frankly odd. They are not Dancehall, they are not Bashment, they are not Reggae, they are not One Drop, it's just Euro Pop meets Rap. It's young Jamaicans doing their thing, which is fine for them, but the rest of the world still wants Reggae.'

I told the audience about the Reggae stars around the world, from Germany to Hawaii. 'That's the thing about Reggae. It's like Jazz, it really is. It's a universal message, it's a universal language musically, and it's very, very exciting and still coming up with very interesting pieces.'

The colleague who really shocked me with her knowledge of Reggae music was the early-morning presenter Vanessa Feltz, who everyone in the UK knows as an extremely popular television and radio broadcaster. She combines a warm presenting style with the brains of a University of Cambridge graduate.

I was a guest on her show to promote my arrival on the station, and as soon as she saw me she dashed over and gave me a big hug and started enthusing about Reggae. I said I didn't know she was a fan and she responded by saying she'd seen videos of my sound clashes with Killamanjaro and others. I was stunned. She later turned up at a Chronixx concert in London to interview me for a BBC Radio arts piece and was seen dancing in the circle at the show – even though she had to be on air at 5 a.m.

Being on Radio 2 gave me access to the BBC vaults and classic live recordings from the likes of Culture and Gregory Isaacs. The show went down so well I won a third Radio Academy Gold award in 2012, the second time I'd won Specialist Music Broadcaster of the Year. We narrowly beat Ronnie Wood of the Rolling Stones with his wonderful show for Absolute Radio where he explores the musical roots of a special guest. The morning afterwards I took the award in to show it to Bob Shennan, the Radio 2 controller who had shown faith in me by putting the show on the biggest radio station in Britain.

Then, in the spring of 2012, I was stunned to be awarded The Most Excellent Order of the British Empire (the MBE) in a ceremony at Buckingham Palace.

When I learned of it I had to sit down. There was a standard format letter which asked if I would accept the award if I was offered it. I was warned not to tell anyone I had received the letter. I wanted to share my news with close friends but was worried that the committee who awarded the MBEs might have second thoughts, so I kept quiet.

It was a very special day with my family as we were driven down to Buckingham Palace. I went inside and the awardees were guided into a picture gallery with some magnificent works of art.

I was with people from all walks of life. One of the things that impressed me most were the awards given to people for genuine and courageous acts of charity in their communities. They are people whose names we often don't know but who have done so much within their world.

My MBE was for services to broadcasting over thirty-four years. I saw it as recognition for Jamaican music as much as for me personally. What does David Rodigan broadcast? Not Country & Western but the music the world knows as Reggae.

It was in the daily newspapers in Jamaica and immediately I had phone calls and texts. I was really pleased. I didn't expect such an awesome level of response from Jamaica. Two of the most popular radio presenters on the island, Richie B and my old friend and clash sparring partner Barry G, were both very quick on the phone to get me on their shows.

I received the MBE personally from Prince Charles.

'You love Jamaica,' he said to me.

'Yes, I do.'

'So do I,' he said. 'How did you discover this music?'

'I heard "My Boy Lollipop" by Millie,' I said. 'It's a great song and I love Ska music.'

'Do you go to Jamaica a lot?'

'Yes.'

'So do I,' he said. 'It's marvellous. What time is your show on again?'

'Sunday nights at 11 o'clock.'

The Prince extended his hand. That's the sign to shut up and stop talking as he moves down the line.

I'd had such a great run; the Dubstep nights, the festivals, the Radio Academy Awards, the Radio Academy Hall of Fame and the MBE. And then, quite suddenly, my world crashed around me.

I found myself without a job.

Looking back now, it had been coming. Kiss had been rebranded from the original Kiss 100 by Emap in 1999, around the time I ran into trouble for playing the Beenie Man track that wasn't on the playlist. The station moved from the original building in Holloway Road to a new location in the West End of London and some listeners felt it was losing touch with its roots.

When Kiss started we had three Reggae shows, presented by Nick Manasseh, Joey Jay and myself.

By the year 2000 things were changing fast. If you wanted to hear a genre-based specialist show playing Drum & Bass, Techno, House or Reggae you had to stay up late. My show on a Sunday night was moved from 10 p.m.–midnight to 11 p.m.–1 a.m. Then they cut it back to one hour, as they did with a lot of other specialist shows. I was deeply upset but because it was still starting this side of midnight I carried on and tried to make it the best sixty minutes I could.

The German-headquartered Bauer media company bought Kiss from Emap in 2007 and the corporate approach became even more obvious.

Kiss became increasingly obsessed with competing against Capital Radio. I started to hear records that I couldn't believe were being played on the station I'd joined fresh from its pirate days in 1990.

I was told there was concern at Capital that Kiss was allowed to play these tunes. Kiss was licensed to broadcast dance music – not to interfere in the Capital playlist. I thought it was counter-productive. Kiss was exploiting a grey area of 'dance music' by playing Pop tunes by the likes of Olly Murs from ITV's *The X Factor*. Why were we playing records by reality TV contestants? That was not why the station was created or given a licence.

The final straw came in 2012 when I was told – not asked – that my show would not start until midnight.

As far as I was concerned that was a step too far. It was insulting to expect people who care passionately about a genre of music to wait until the small hours of Monday to hear it when they might have work in the morning.

This was Reggae – the music of people who so wanted Kiss to exist that they supported it by going to Kiss events, fund-raising and signing petitions for it to get a licence. That licence was owned by the Bauer family but Kiss has a history rooted in ethnic urban music: Soul, Reggae, R&B, Rap. To say those genres are no longer important and that if you want to listen to them you have to be an insomniac is unacceptable. I can feel my blood rising when I think about it.

My objections fell on stony ground. 'You're living in the past, David,' Andy Roberts, the Kiss programme controller told me. 'You have to understand that listening habits have changed and we no longer depend on hearing something at a specific time.'

Of course I knew about the growth of listen-again features and the changing importance of the old-style linear radio schedule. Nonetheless, I believed it was demeaning to say Reggae was not worthy of a sociable hour.

I wasn't alone in that view. I was invited to the BBC's historic radio studios in London's Maida Vale for a series called *Mastertapes*, where the BBC Radio 4 presenter John Wilson focuses on a single album. In this case it was Aswad's *New Chapter* album and the west London band's leader Brinsley Forde was his guest. In the break, one member of the audience recognized me.

'Why have they put your show on after midnight now? That's really marginalizing the music. That's not on,' he said.

'I agree. Thank you.'

The stranger's words rang in my head. They were typical of the public's reaction to the show's new start time. But the Kiss management kept telling me, 'All the other specialist shows begin after midnight, what's your problem?'

The day I resigned was a Thursday. I had come in that morning to pre-record my show and saw the singer Craig David leaving the Kiss building with a video team filming him. He got into a car and drove off.

I don't have anything personal against Craig and he is a very successful recording artist. But it was his show that was pushing mine into the midnight hour and his format was playing hits on a premix tape from his rooftop apartment in Florida.

I felt hurt. I went into a café over the road to think. As I sat there drinking coffee I pondered on how Craig's show was so important to the future direction of Kiss that the station had a video-team filming him.

The video crew came in to the café and I asked them what they were filming. It transpired it wasn't Kiss making the video – it was Craig David's own people. But by then I'd made up my mind that it was the end for me at Kiss. Craig had actually done me a favour.

I wrote my resignation statement on my phone and sent it to my manager. Then I walked into the Kiss building and upstairs to the music department floor, looking for the bosses. Andy Roberts was on holiday so I spoke to Simon Long, deputy programme director.

'Here's my pass. I'm sorry it's over, I can't do this any more.'

I felt the need to make a little speech, explaining how I felt.

'I need to politely remind you,' I continued, 'that the reason we are here is that twenty-two years ago a group of individuals decided they wanted London to hear a type of music so much that they broadcast it from the rooftops of blocks of flats and their impact was so powerful that the government had to give in and grant them a licence. That was Kiss FM. That's the station that was created but that's not the station we now have.'

I don't want to sound disrespectful to fellow broadcasters who go on air after midnight: we need night-time radio. I speak as someone who remembers when the BBC signed off at midnight with the national anthem and who listened to Radio Luxembourg in my bed under the sheets with a torch. The start of twenty-four-hour radio was a wonderful moment. But that doesn't alter the fact that the audience after midnight is one of night workers and insomniacs.

'That show should be on at a sociably acceptable time,' I repeated. 'And if it's not, I protest by resigning and walking out of this building.'

I don't think my actions were pretentious or arrogant. Although I was still making special shows for Radio 2 I hadn't lined up any other regular jobs to replace Kiss. So I was effectively putting myself out of work because I believed that a genre that had been part of the music infrastructure in Britain for more than fifty years was being insulted and ignored. I asked the Kiss bosses why they thought there was a proliferation of pirate stations playing Reggae music.

'Are you telling me people don't enjoy it?'

Jon, my manager, was concerned. A few weeks earlier, when I first heard they were going to push back the show again, my reaction had been that I should go. He had told me, 'Don't walk until you have somewhere to walk to.' Friends told me my audience would use listen-again. They reminded me I was still on the radio and sharing the music with people who love it, and that by resigning I was only depriving them of the show. It was a valid argument but in the end I couldn't stay.

On 22 November 2012 I issued a statement:

> I write this to inform you that today I have resigned from my position as a broadcaster on Kiss FM. I've been with the station for twenty-two years, shared some wonderful times with many fantastic artists and members of staff and it's with great sadness that I've come to this decision. Due to their continued marginalization of reggae music into the twilight zone of radio scheduling, it has left me no option but to make a stand for my passion and the music I love so dearly.

As Bob Marley famously said, 'the stone that the builder refused will be the head corner stone'. Reggae was originally played on the streets, not on radio, and Kiss' refusal to schedule the only reggae show on their network to a socially accessible time has resulted in this decision. Reggae is worthy of more respect and so are the fans and lovers of this music.

David Rodigan

In response, Kiss issued its own statement.

We are very sad and disappointed to confirm that David Rodigan has left Kiss after 22 years. We have the utmost love and respect for David both personally and professionally – he leaves with our sincere appreciation and gratitude for all that he has achieved with Kiss. Kiss remains passionate about broadcasting a brilliant cross-section of music genres, including reggae, to our audiences across multiple platforms and devices.

The *Independent* broke the story and the news was picked up by a number of other newspapers and websites. I had lots of tweets of support.

When I quit I had no regular job. But I felt liberated by my action: I thought I had made a stand for the music after it had been disrespected. The first response in the industry was from a younger London urban music station, Rinse FM, which told me I had a job there as soon as I wanted it. Thank you to everyone at Rinse FM for that! Another offer came from Irie Jam Radio in New York.

There was an amazing response in Jamaica. The feeling was: 'Well done for taking a stand!'

There has been this long, long battle in getting radio stations past this apparent problem of play-listing more than one Reggae record. And I'm sad to say there has not been a Reggae show on Capital Radio since I left in 1990. They chose to abandon a tradition that began with Tommy Vance's *TV on the Radio* show in 1975.

Kiss has not given this music its own programme since I left in November 2012. On Choice, all the Reggae presenters were taken off air when the station's owners Global launched a new network, Capital Xtra, which at the time of writing has no Reggae shows. This music is fighting an ongoing battle which stretches back a long time. The irony is that when the original pirate music stations existed in the sixties, Jamaican music was played openly and freely. Ska was Pop music.

20

New Roots

Throughout my life, Jamaican music has shown a remarkable endurance, constantly reinventing itself and finding new life and energy.

Just as with my career in radio – which has been inextricably linked to Reggae's own fortunes – there have been moments when it has struggled to find the appreciation I feel it merits. But it has always found a way back.

And so it has transpired that a new generation of young Jamaican artists has reinvigorated the scene. Bob Marley's own children, Damian especially, have played a key role in ushering in this New Roots era.

Performers including Chronixx and Protoje have shown their appreciation of true musicianship and original song writing, and encouraged a phalanx of young multi-instrumentalists who respect the organic origins of Reggae.

This resurgence has been a blessing for me as I have taken my broadcasting career to a place that I only dreamt of, as a boy growing up listening to crackling radio stations from my bedroom in the countryside.

The irony of my resignation from Kiss is that it came at a moment when I was the reigning world champion of Reggae sound clash.

The night I won the trophy featured one of the biggest and best line-ups in the history of clash culture. My friends, the New York promoters Irish and Chin, were celebrating fifteen years in the business and were determined to put on their best show yet in this great musical sport.

It meant a return to the cauldron atmosphere of Club Amazura in Queens, New York, the venue for the first of these World Clash contests in 1998 and where I previously appeared in an Elvis outfit in that friendly clash with Ninjaman.

This was no amicable battle. 'Are You Ready for the War?' was the cry by the Master of Ceremonies to the audience as the venue began to fill up.

There were seven sound systems competing. Two of the others, Tony Matterhorn and Fire Links, were solo operators like me. Tony 'Mentally Ill' Matterhorn, the bad boy of the New York clash scene, learned his trade on the King Addies sound system from Brooklyn before going it alone. Fire Links was schooled by Johnny from Jamaican system Bodyguard, who I'd had some of my earliest clashes with in the Clarendon countryside over twenty years before.

Then there were two big Jamaican systems, Bass Odyssey and Black Kat, and two from the US – Earth Ruler from New York and Poison Dart from Tampa. The Japanese sound Mighty Crown, known as the 'Far East Rulers', were in the house but not competing because it was so soon after the 2011 Japanese earthquake.

I'd had my reservations about performing. I'd told Irish and Chin that I was still feeling frustrated by the Pop tunes that were coming out of Jamaica, which, in my view, didn't always have the same quality as the music that had gone before.

'I can't relate to this new Pop. I'm not wasting my money on cutting dubs by artists that have no substance,' I told them. 'I need tunes that are going to stand up over time and there aren't enough of them.'

But they persuaded me to do one last big New York clash.

When I came on stage they introduced me as the 'Gentle Giant, all the way from London, UK, Mister David Rodigan.'

'Good evening, New York,' I said, and gave the crowd my 1991 impression of the great Dancehall artist Rodney 'Bounty Killer' Price and his catchphrases: 'Lawd-av Merrcyy! Dem Get Big and t'irsty!'

Before the clash started, Irish and Chin blindsided me with a special award for 'your continued contribution towards the global positioning of Jamaica's music and Jamaica's culture'.

I took the mic. 'Ladies and Gentlemen, this is indeed an honour. Thank you, New York, thank you to [New York radio station] Irie Jam, thank you to all the people who love this music as I love it. If you love Reggae give me some signal, New York!'

I had Pee-Wee doing my mixing and I was the first sound to play in the first round of the clash. I kicked off with Beres Hammond and then asked the crowd, 'Are you ready for the biggest tune in New York?' before dropping Christopher Martin's 'Cheater's Prayer', with customized lyrics: 'Rodigan's gonna murder yuh soundbwoy, and the whole of Amazura can see, that the rest of the selectas a nobody!'

The rules stipulated that no sound would be eliminated from the first round of the clash – but the second round called for something more serious, because someone was going to be sent 'back to JFK', as the host MC bluntly pointed out. I picked up the mic once more.

'Let me start with something completely different. Down the coast is the city of Baltimore, where they filmed one of the greatest television dramas that the world has ever known, madder than *The Sopranos* . . . Anyone inside the house who's ever seen *The Wire* give me some signal!'

Pee-Wee pressed play on one of my trademark Rodigan hitman intros, but this time I had written a script around the character Omar, the much-loved star of *The Wire*, the cult American crime drama that I was confident would be well known to the crowd.

'Some of my Jamaican DJ friends are goin' to get hit tonight, ya feel me?' complained the Omar voice in my dub, making a cry for help to Brother Mouzone, the bow-tie-wearing hired assassin from *The Wire*. Omar warned that the hit was planned for Club Amazura. But when Mouzone heard that it was Rodigan on the Jamaicans' trail he sadly had to conclude that he couldn't get involved: 'I do know him and I have to tell you there is absolutely nothing I can do to help your Jamaican brothers Omar, except to say that they are dead men walking!'

I then unleashed dub plates by Shinehead (a special of his hit 'Jamaican in New York' cut as 'An Englishman in New York'), followed by Junior Reid, Cocoa Tea and a dub cut by the legendary Ninjaman, freshly released from prison and containing disrespectful references to what he called the 'idiot sounds' in the contest, such as Poison Dart and Earth Ruler. Trash-talking your opponents is all part of sound clash culture.

The received wisdom before the event had been that Rodigan would only bring his old box of trusted dub plates. Wrong! I was taking the event very seriously and had cut a whole bag of new special plates by younger Jamaican artists such as Mavado, Popcaan and Khago.

At the end of each round the MC for the night, Dub Master, asked the crowd to put their hands up for the sound they wanted to go out. Poison Dart and Black Kat went first. Earth Ruler followed. The remaining four contestants – Bass Odyssey, Fire Links, Tony Matterhorn and myself – played the next round of just five minutes each, with two more to be eliminated at the end. 'It's sticky! It's serious!' shouted Dub Master.

I was first back on, playing Alton Ellis and his son Christopher on a classic Treasure Isle rhythm. I only had a short time and dropped in one of my biggest dubs – 'Your Sound is Overdue' by Gregory Isaacs, followed by a Shinehead dub dedicated to the veterans of the Reggae scene in New York, and finally 'Conquer We' by Johnnie Osbourne, mixed for me in 1983 by King Tubby himself.

Fire Links was on next. Fighting for his life, he pulled out his big tune as his final selection – a rare dub plate from Rita Marley herself. Bass Odyssey drew for some of its Bounty Killer dub plates, always popular in New York.

'It seems very clear to me and to oonuh [you] too,' said Dub Master. 'Fire Links goes home.' The Rita dub wasn't enough. Matterhorn too was voted out. It meant I had to play tune-for-tune for the trophy with Bass Odyssey, for over twenty years one of Jamaica's greatest sound systems.

We were to fight it out over ten rounds. I was again first to play. I thanked the crowd for a 'wonderful night' and symbolically placed a cap on my head. 'In Jamaica they say "The older the moon, the brighter it shines."' I gave respect to Damian and Worm, the two young selectors for Bass Odyssey who had taken over from my friend and old adversary Kevin 'Squingy' Bennett, who died the year before after building the sound's great reputation.

'I have a message from the fishing village of Rocky Point in Clarendon,' I said.

Most of the crowd would have recognized that as the home of the singer Cocoa Tea and understood it as the cue for one of my big dub plates and its opening lyric: 'Now this one is dedicated to all just come selectors who want to try and test David Rodigan. Sound bwoy, won't you go home, go home to your nana!'

But Odyssey struck back with a classic dub from Beres Hammond: 'Nothing you can do to stop your sound from dying . . .'

The crowd gave them the vote, even though many patrons realized the tune was 'played back' (it had been heard earlier in the evening), a cardinal error in the rules of sound clash which should mean disqualification.

I pointed this out but thought it best to just carry on, referencing another Jamaican country singer, the late Garnett Silk, and cueing up his 'Keep Them Talking'. Odyssey, as Jamaicans, objected to my frequent geographical references to their country and, reminding the crowd that they were natives of the island, played their own Garnett dub. Two–nil to Bass Odyssey.

'It's getting sticky for me,' I admitted on the mic. I reached for a very special dub, telling the crowd it was one 'that no sound in the world can play'. The voice of Phyllis Dillon, the Queen of Rock Steady, filled the room. But Odyssey took the next round too with a Ken Boothe special.

Fighting for my life, I played Super Cat's 'Don Dadda', one of my most trusted weapons. On a second vote, it narrowly beat Bass Odyssey's cut of Junior Reid's 'One Blood'. I was back in the contest, but still down by 3–1.

Next up I went straight for 'Golden Hen' by the late great singer Tenor Saw, which I reminded the crowd I recorded for a clash right there in New York in 1985 'in December when the snow was falling'. It was guaranteed to deliver me a huge forward from the audience. Bass Odyssey knew that dub was coming at some stage. Tenor Saw died in 1988, before their sound was even formed, so there was little they could do to counteract it. 'Big bloodclaat tune, no other sound can get that again. We nah have it,' Bass Odyssey admitted, and tried to come back with Toots and the Maytals' '54-46, That's My Number'. It wasn't enough, because many sounds have a dub of that song. So: 3–2.

I went for another one I knew they couldn't match – from 'the first Jamaican superstar' Prince Buster: 'Hard Man Fi Dead'. Odyssey replied with Big Youth's 'Hit the Road Jack': 3–3 and all to play for.

'Pee-Wee!' I shouted, and my mixer let go Half Pint and 'Substitute'. Bass Odyssey responded with Dennis Brown's 'Wolfs and Leopards'. I was in front for the first time at 4–3.

Next I went for Wayne Wade's 'Love You Too Much', which was unfortunately no match for their dub from Beres Hammond and Marcia Griffiths. Back to 4–4.

So now I went for Marcia Griffiths, this time in combination with Bob Andy, one of my all-time favourite singers. Bass Odyssey beat that with Freddie McGregor: 5–4 down. At which point, I couldn't afford to lose another round.

I turned to King Tubby for a dub plate mix of Barrington Levy's 'What Kind of World', which saved me and tied the contest.

'So the scores now, 5 to 5,' said Dub Master. This was it. Next round decides it.

I lifted the mic and made a speech about that first night I'd spent on my first visit to Jamaica in January 1979. I told the crowd how the mosquitoes in Edgewater 'had me for dinner, lunch and breakfast'. But I reminded them it hadn't stopped me from chasing down a dub plate special of the number-one tune of that month: 'No Fuss' by Barrington Levy. On went the dub.

Klaxons sounded, cheering erupted. Bass Odyssey went back for more Garnett Silk. But their dub 'Keep Them Talking' had been played already.

'New York,' shouted Dub Master. 'It went down to 5–5. With the deciding tune, David Rodigan wins 6 to 5! He's the World Clash champion of 2012, the legendary Sir David Rodigan!'

I appreciated the knighthood. 'Ladies and gentlemen, please give me some signal for Pee-Wee,' I said. 'It's been a wonderful night. Thank you to all the competitors, thank you to you for coming, for supporting the music and keeping it alive!' I thanked Irish and Chin and last of all Henry Lewis, my right-hand man in Jamaica. 'Without you I couldn't have done it, Henry!'

It was one of the pinnacles of my career.

Not long afterwards I was staring at that massive Champions League-scale World Clash cup sitting on my trophy table in my music room at home in London – and wondering if I would ever work again in radio.

On quitting Kiss I was conscious I might not get another job offer. My hope of continuing to broadcast was that the BBC would renew the Radio 2 contract.

But I prepared for the worst. I told myself that I had served the music proudly, that nothing lasts forever and that if this was the moment when it all came to a close, so be it.

The music would always come first. Before it was on the radio it was in clubs, at parties and on sound systems because that was the only way we could hear it. If I had to go back to playing in clubs on tour, which I had been doing for thirty years, I was ready for that.

I never believed that BBC 1Xtra would be contacting me. Jon, my manager, was convinced they would. My thoughts were that if ever there was a time for me to have joined 1Xtra it would have been eleven or twelve years earlier when they started. I had remained loyal to Kiss and 1Xtra already had a Reggae show presented by Robbo Ranx.

But at 10 p.m. on the day I resigned from Kiss, BBC 1Xtra got in touch. Jon was right. I'd not long had my iPad and I heard a noise and wondered what it was. I looked at the screen and there was an email from Rhys Hughes, head of programmes for Radio 1 and 1Xtra. He wanted to talk.

I nearly fell off the sofa. Radio has been my life so, having put myself out of a job, I was overjoyed to receive that email. A meeting was set up a few days later with Jon, me and Rhys in the old Radio 1 building, Yalding House. It was a foggy and chilly winter morning and the station was preparing for its Christmas party. Radio 1 was about to move to a brand new £1 billion London headquarters nearby at New Broadcasting House and Yalding House was almost empty, except for a few desks.

We sat down and Rhys said, 'We'd love you to join 1Xtra.' I wanted to jump at the offer but one of the first things I asked him was about the demographic. The station is required by the BBC's Royal Charter to target fifteen- to twenty-nine-year-olds – and I was sixty-one years old. Rhys wasn't worried. 'You know about the music, that's what we care about at the BBC.'

A subsequent meeting was set up after the Christmas holidays with Rhys and Ben Cooper, the head of BBC Radio 1 and 1Xtra, in the boardroom of Radio 1's spectacular new premises on the eighth and top floor of New Broadcasting House. I looked out of the window at the stunning view over the spire and columns of All Souls church at the head of Regent Street. It was on the steps of this church that all the original Radio 1 presenters had gathered for an iconic photograph to mark the station's launch in 1967, the most important year of all in my teenage journey of musical discovery. I went into the meeting, we came to an agreement and I floated home deliriously happy.

I had only just been shown around 1Xtra for the first time when I met Zane Lowe, then one of the most important DJs at Radio 1, at Soho House, the London private members' club. A few weeks afterwards he invited me on his show as a guest and we had a ball playing music that mattered to both of us.

I recognized in Zane something that's always been important to me in broadcasting, which is reverence for the music. I've tried to connect with the young 1Xtra audience by showing that enthusiasm for what I'm playing. I try not to take myself too seriously and when I find myself being a little pious or nerdy about a record I try to rib myself on air by talking to myself in the third person: 'Too much information, Rodders!'

I started at 1Xtra in February 2013. The show takes a lot of preparation in downloading, pre-production, scripting and cross-referencing for special features as well as the actual recording. But it has been well received and after my first year at Radio 1Xtra, the Radio Academy gave me their Silver Award for Best Specialist Music Programme. I am seeing a new young audience at my live shows, drawn to Reggae through the 1Xtra show.

But the acclaim hasn't quite been universal. One or two individuals appear to resent my recent good fortunes. I have been the subject of spite in pamphlets and online radio broadcasts. One person in particular, though he is always friendly to me in person, likes to denounce me as a 'culture vulture', even after I have dedicated almost forty years of my life to promoting Reggae.

Being on the BBC has opened more doors. I'd only been at 1Xtra a few months when I found myself playing the extraordinary Shambala festival in Northamptonshire in the English countryside. It is such a green event that they won't allow any sponsors or even water bottles because they're unsustainable. Instead, you get issued with metal tankards, which you fill up from standpipes as you walk around. The tent I played in was beautifully decorated and the way people dressed reminded me of the Mary Quant era in the 1960s.

I've always loved the city of Liverpool and I played at the Shipping Forecast, a great music venue in the heart of the old port, to an audience where no one was over twenty-five. Liverpool is not really recognized as a Reggae place because the Jamaican community is small, but by the time the sun was setting over the River Mersey there was a long queue around the block and I found myself playing Rock Steady and old-school Reggae to a heaving crowd of students. When I came out after a two-hour set I was dripping in sweat.

That was one of the best nights of my career. Another was the Red Bull Culture Clash of 2014 before a crowd of around 20,000 at Earl's Court in London. Screened live to a vast audience online, Culture Clash takes place every two years, with four music crews competing inside a huge exhibition space.

Red Bull had asked me to participate on several occasions but I'd politely declined because I didn't feel sufficiently well versed in other forms of music. Culture Clash takes in other bass-heavy music genres from Hip Hop to Grime and Drum & Bass. I thought a Reggae specialist would be at a disadvantage because Red Bull promote the clash to a very diverse young audience and the diehard Reggae fans will always be in a small minority.

I was approached by the Drum & Bass artists Chase & Status to play alongside them, and again I declined, but then changed my mind. I realized it was an opportunity for me, as part of a team, to reflect what I thought was important about Reggae and to give the historical context of what a clash is. After all, clashing comes out of Reggae culture. After my experiences on the festival circuit and in Dubstep clubs I felt more comfortable in a diverse musical environment. As Chase & Status, Rodigan and Jungle pioneer Shy FX, we formed something entirely new, which we called Rebel Sound.

We knew we were in for a tough battle because the reigning champions, the Grime collective Boy Better Know (BBK), and the red-hot Hip Hop crew A$AP from Harlem, New York, were guaranteed huge followings in the audience. I knew most of the Reggae crowd would gravitate towards the other contestant, the great Stone Love sound system from Jamaica. Facing all those, Rebel Sound was an unknown quantity, making our debut public appearance. But collectively we were a formidable force.

We rehearsed amid the upmost secrecy. At the first meeting I turned up with a clipboard which became a running joke. On day one I stated the dub plate contributions that I could make. I insisted we should be quite precise in what each team player was going to achieve by way of dubs. I articulated very firmly how this should be approached as a mathematical equation – we needed so many songs and they needed to last so long. On the clipboard I had written in my own graffiti 'Keep it Simple' and whenever things started to get heated I called out 'Gentlemen!' and held up my board.

I made special dubs with Burro Banton, Beenie Man, Barrington Levy, Damian Marley and many more. Some of them weren't even used. These were not dubs for Rodigan, they were all cut for Rebel Sound, naming our team players in the intros. Some were customized for that night, calling out the names of our competitors. That didn't stop Saul from Chase & Status cutting even more Reggae dubs on top of what I'd cut, reflecting his own obsession with sound clash culture.

The Culture Clash was a masterclass in promotion from Red Bull – you couldn't walk through London without seeing a Culture Clash billboard or an advert on a taxi, bus or phone booth. On the night, there was a very young and energized audience and you could watch the crowd movement as they entered the enormous arena and headed towards the sounds they wanted to support.

As we were doing our soundcheck, one of the A$AP crew jumped out at me and said he'd seen me in a clash in Miami. 'Tonight we're going to give it to you,' he said. 'Great,' I thought. 'They know the culture; game on.'

On the night, Rebel Sound was sharp, focused and delivered exactly what we intended. We had a game plan. Chase & Status put the extra effort in and came up with their own special effects, sound rig and staging which looked quite different to that of the other contestants'.

There was plenty of controversy, notably when we brought out Grime artist Tempa T, who Chase & Status had previously worked with but who we'd persuaded to be in our camp rather than BBK's. He burst onto the stage with lyrics aimed straight at BBK, who, as the Grime sound, were furious. It was controversial but that's what made it exciting.

We also played a dub of Rihanna's 'We Found Love', which was produced by Chase & Status when I was in Jamaica. As far as I'm concerned under the rules of sound clash that was a legitimate dub, but within the camp there was friction as to whether it should be played. Some thought it was too Pop for a sound clash and didn't fit in; others felt it did. On the night it had a big impact.

A$AP thought that because they were the hottest thing in Hip Hop all they had to do was turn up and do what they do in their stage act. I wasn't having that. The culture of clashing is entrenched in Jamaican musical history and the origins have to be defended. I lashed out on the microphone, because that's what you do in clashes. 'You need to get your arses out of Harlem and cut some dub plates in Flatbush (Brooklyn) and mix with some Jamaicans, because you didn't think about this at all.' I told them they were a 'living joke' because they hadn't prepared and I didn't hear one significant dub plate – they hadn't bothered to cut them. 'You need to get your cheque and go home.'

I think A$AP were surprised. When the clash was over there were a lot of miserable faces in their dressing room. They were classic examples of pride before a fall.

BBK were our toughest opponents. They represent a whole movement of music which is unique to the UK. It's given the heading Grime but it is in essence connected to when Smiley Culture, Tippa Irie and Philip Levi were rapping on Reggae rhythms in Jamaican and Cockney accents thirty years before. Today they are not doing it on Jamaican rhythms and they're not talking Jamaican. It's no longer a Jamaican or Trinidadian thing, it's a London thing. BBK is a very successful organization and clearly there are highly intelligent and motivated people within that team.

They tried to embarrass me with a dub with an actor impersonating my voice and claiming to be me playing a Pop Reggae record by Peter Andre. There was the seed of a good idea there in trying to show that I once played the Kiss daytime playlist. But the dub wasn't well executed. The first thing they got wrong was that they said it was a recording of an old show and used my current jingle from Radio 1Xtra. More significantly, I have never played that Peter Andre record.

What did irritate me was when they publicly criticized the way I introduced my dubs. 'Rodigan, bro, you're in England – stop talking about Jamaica, bro.'

I had to respond.

'BBK make a speech [saying,] "I shouldn't talk about Jamaica". Are you mad? This thing started in Jamaica!' I said. 'Don't tell me not to talk about the island that I love, the land of wood and water.'

BBK started addressing Rebel Sound individually and disrespectfully – which is part and parcel of sound clash. Shy and Saul were beginning to respond to the abuse and I knew it didn't look good to the audience. I addressed our crew.

'Gentlemen, at this point what we need to do is very slowly turn our backs and walk off and start conversing down behind the stage as though we're not remotely interested. Now, please, off!'

I'd learned that trick. I got caught out in my early years of clashing by rising to the bait and retaliating against Mighty Crown and Ricky Trooper. They throw insults out there and reel you in and they have got you angry and off-key. The audience see that you're hurting. This time they could see us chatting beneath the stage while BBK vainly tried to provoke us. That pisses off your opponents.

Everyone said we won every round of Culture Clash and I believe we did. But at least with BBK officially winning one of the rounds it made it more of a contest. To win an event of that scale was exhilarating.

In each of my first two years at 1Xtra I went back to Jamaica to make a series of radio broadcasts with Robbo Ranx and Toddla T. The first year we went to the Tuff Gong International studios in Kingston and the trip filled me with hope for the future of Jamaican music and the talent of its young artists.

I met Chronixx for the first time, one of the great hopes of conscious Reggae. He was an hour late but when he walked into the studio he came straight up to me.

'Father Rodigan, I'm so sorry, I don't want to disrespect you or the BBC but I got caught in a video shoot in down-town Kingston and I was trying to get out.'

Within minutes he was doing his first song and I was seriously impressed with his abilities. We were also blessed with the presence of Pentateuch, another young Jamaican band I've been championing. What really struck me was when they told me that the bass player wasn't able to come because he is a school-teacher and refuses to leave the classroom when he is scheduled to be teaching. The band said they endorsed his stance and would be doing a semi-acoustic set without their schoolteacher bass player. And it was amazing. They ran through some of their best tunes: 'Kingston', 'Pressure' and 'Black Face'. When they were performing you could have heard a pin drop.

I can also never forget the professionalism of Damian Marley and his fellow deejay Cham as they performed their hit 'Fighter'. They did so many takes. We kept telling them 'You've got it' but each time they insisted, 'No! That wasn't right. Again, we have to do it again.' There must have been nine takes of 'Fighter' and then Cham went into his hit 'Ghetto Story'. There was the whole band behind them and the drummer stripped to the waist with sweat gushing off him. That night I was walking back to my room in the hotel and felt giddy and light-headed. Then I realized what it was. I'd been passively inhaling ganja all day at Tuff Gong. That was a great trip to the land of wood and water.

The next year, 2015, we went to Big Yard Studios in order to give the audience an idea of freestyle dub plate voicing in an open yard. We commissioned Phillip 'Winta' James, the keyboard player for Damian Marley, to build us a rhythm, which he called Sidewalk. Young artists such as Jesse Royal, Kabaka Pyramid, Iba Mahr and others came down to do their own cuts and we made that into a free download.

Radio 1Xtra reunited me with Lee Perry, who came to the studio for an interview. He's almost ageless and looked exactly as he had more than thirty years earlier when I'd found him gardening outside the Black Ark Studio, when he was calling himself Pipecock Jackson. At the age of seventy-seven he was lean, sharp and agile.

Lee Perry is the Salvador Dalí of Reggae. He walked into the BBC with a wheelie trolley filled with his paraphernalia, like a music hall act coming on stage with a collection of theatrical props. As usual he was dressed in the most colourful and bizarre manner and his hair had a red wash in it. Most of all, you notice his sparkling eyes.

I'd interviewed him three times before and knew that asking Lee 'The Upsetter' Perry a direct question was almost a pointless exercise because he was going to answer in whatever way he chose.

The man is an enigma. What he's very good at doing is juxtaposing words. He has an ability to juggle language and create something different and perhaps more meaningful. During earlier interviews with me, I'd listened to some of the words he put alongside each other and scratched my head, wondering if there wasn't something utterly profound in what he'd said. He's a wordsmith.

He's also an artist. He likes to paint things. In the BBC studio I showed him the sleeve of my copy of his album *Roast Fish Collie Weed & Corn Bread*, which he had drawn all over when visiting my flat in Barnes all those years earlier. There on the LP was his signature 'Pipecock Jackson'. I'd also dug out an early interview I had done with him in 1980 in *Black Echoes*. He enjoyed that.

I said, 'I'd love to play some records of yours that I think are wonderful and I'd like you to react to them.'

I started with the Scratch-produced 'Check Him Out' by vocal group The Bleechers. The song is otherwise known as 'The Upsetter Shop' and it's almost an advertising jingle for Perry's original premises in Kingston. The lyrics tell listeners, 'You better check him out' at 'Number 36 Charles Street'.

I could see Scratch smiling and said, 'Let's imagine we are in a dance and I'm playing and you're on the mic.' The BBC

Radio camera crew – the 'visualization team' for the BBC website – came in and, as I expected, Lee played up to the camera. He's an entertainer and what he wears is his costume.

I was playing rhythm tracks, instrumentals and dubs but not really saying anything while Lee 'Scratch' Perry was MCing, toasting lyrics over the music. Some of what he was saying was bizarre and he made a lot of comments about famous individuals, some of which were, to say the least, controversial, if not libellous. He had a pop at Duke Reid because the Treasure Isle producer had once said Lee couldn't sing.

These vocal gymnastics went on for sixty-minutes almost non-stop as he was rolling the mic around his lips. Some of it didn't make a great deal of sense and some did. I tried a couple of questions but he didn't respond. So I ended up throwing him words, people or places as prompts and he would bounce back a lyrical response.

That night after the 1Xtra interview, Lee played at the north London venue The Garage, as part of a show for the clothing brand Fred Perry. I was in the building and the next thing I knew he was calling me on stage.

'Where's David Rodigan?'

He started singing happy birthday to me, even though – of course – it wasn't my birthday. Eventually I got to the side of the stage in the wings, and near the end of his set he saw me and called me on.

We shook hands and it was a lovely moment. It dawned on me then that one of the reasons he has such an appeal is that it's as if he's here on earth as a space traveller. There's something boyish and innocent about him when he's on stage and his show is bizarre, an eclectic mix of music. Some people in the audience were really into him and some were quite bemused.

But they were in the presence of a Reggae legend who created some of the most amazing rhythms and one of the first Dub albums, *Blackboard Jungle*. In his stage show he sings 'Jah Live', and rightly because he co-wrote and co-produced it with Bob Marley. But he doesn't produce records any more and lives on the banks of Lake Zurich with his wife Mireille.

Most memorably of all, I've had the chance to sit down and reason with Damian 'Junior Gong' Marley, the keeper of his father's flame. I think Damian combines great song-writing and powerful on-stage delivery with a humility and stillness in his performance which commands attention.

I got to know him during a couple of interviews when I was still at Kiss FM, the first after the release of his album *Welcome to Jamrock* and again after his project with the rapper Nas, *Distant Relatives*.

We performed together at a concert in the Swiss Alps, where I came on to play records at the end of his set. Halfway through I looked into the wings and saw his band members watching me playing the records. I noticed Damian was among them and called him to join me on the rostrum.

I said, 'Would you mind pressing play on this CD player because there is a song I want you to hear?'

I jumped down from the record decks and talked directly to him about his father and the passion I know Damian has for the vocal talents of the late Dennis Brown. Then I got him to play a dub of himself recorded over Dennis's *Tribulation* rhythm with Dennis's original vocal also on the track. I had mixed it with my sons Jamie and Oliver. Damian beamed a big smile back to me. I felt honoured that he should have chosen not to go back to his hotel but to stay and watch me play records.

That led to Damian performing for our Ram Jam event for the Red Bull Music Academy at London's Notting Hill Carnival in 2013. On stage, Damian blew the place away as he always does. Part of our contractual agreement was to attend an after-party in the Macbeth pub, a grungy spot in the trendy east London district of Shoreditch.

When I arrived at 10 p.m. I was shown to an upstairs area and Damian was already there with the singer Wayne Marshall, Damian's keyboard player Winta and Dan Dalton Jr, Damian's manager.

That night I had my first long in-depth conversation with Damian away from the radio studio and the microphones. He was leaning over the counter of the bar as we waited to go downstairs to do a meet-and-greet at the after-party. He turned to me with a serious look on his face.

'Why aren't you telling the history of this music? Why haven't you done a documentary?'

He was very demonstrative.

So I told him I was writing this book.

'You need to tell the story,' he insisted, 'because you've been immersed in the music for all these years. I'm insisting you do this. You're an elder. You knew and interviewed my father and you need to tell it as you have witnessed it.'

I was being given a telling-off. I looked at him and thought of his remarkable father, turning to wave at me through the back window of a car after our chance meeting in a shop doorway forty summers before.

Acknowledgements

The authors would like to thank the Rodigan family, Jenny and Joel Burrell, Jon Bailey and Jonathan Lloyd for their support in this project, and Steve Barrow, Noel Hawks and John Masouri for their help with the manuscript.